Infants & Toddlers

CURRICULUM AND TEACHING

Infants & Toddlers

CURRICULUM AND TEACHING

Second Edition

LaVisa Cam Wilson

College of Education
Auburn University

 DELMAR PUBLISHERS INC.®

NOTICE TO THE READER

Cover photos by Jerry Howard/POSITIVE IMAGES
Cover design by EX LIBRIS, Inc.

Delmar Staff
Associate Editor: Jay Whitney
Managing Editor: Gerry East
Project Editor: Christopher Chien
Production Coordinator: Larry Main
Design Coordinator: Susan Mathews

Printed in the United States of America
Published simultaneously in Canada
by Nelson Canada,
a Division of the Thomson Corporation

10 9 8 7 6 5 4 3

Library of Congress Cataloging-in-Publication Data

Wilson, LaVisa Cam.
    Infants & toddlers: curriculum and teaching / LaVisa Cam Wilson.
    — 2nd ed.
        p.   cm.
    Includes bibliographies and index.
        ISBN 0-8273-3967-4 (pbk.). — ISBN 0-8273-3968-2 (instructors guide)
        1. Child care—United States.   2. Infants—United States.   3. Toddlers—United States.
    4. Child development—United States.   5. Day care centers—United States.   6. Family day
    care—United States.   I. Title.   II. Title: Infants and toddlers. HQ778.7.U6W55   1990
    362.7'1'071—dc20   89-11804
                                                                                            CIP

CONTENTS

PREFACE

This book is intended for people who provide care for infants and toddlers. It includes information to help caregivers select and use curriculum appropriately individualized for each child in their care.

Students in child care training programs will find the book filled with examples of children and caregivers to introduce and reinforce concepts. In addition, activities are provided to help students develop caregiving knowledge and skills.

Family day care providers and day care center caregivers and administrators will find the book packed with information which can be put to immediate use in their program. Parents will also be interested in the information on child development and in the materials and activities suggested for use with infants and toddlers.

Children, parents, and caregivers are viewed developmentally, a view that provides the basis for selecting and implementing curriculum. Special attention is given to the sequence of development in children while recognizing differences in their rates of development. A holistic emphasis focuses on curriculum which provides for the physical, emotional, social, and cognitive development of the child. Language development is also an important part of the development of the infant and toddler.

Special features of the book are

1. a curriculum development cycle.
2. caregiver roles for working with infants and toddlers.
3. information for designing an environment for infants and toddlers.
4. seven chapters in Part III which relate to specific age levels by
   a. identifying materials appropriate for each developmental level.
   b. providing directions to make over sixty homemade materials appropriate for infants and toddlers.
   c. including sections of a Developmental Profile for infants and toddlers which can be used for curriculum planning and for sharing with parents. The complete Developmental Profile is included in Appendix A.
   d. identifying specific caregiver strategies to match the child's developmental needs.

The Competency Standards for infant/toddler caregivers have been developed as a part of the Child Development Associate program focusing on improved caregiver skills. The nationally recognized CDA credential is awarded to caregivers who successfully complete the assessment.

The CDA competencies include the following six goals and thirteen functional areas:

I. To establish and maintain a safe, healthy learning environment
    1. Safe
    2. Healthy
    3. Learning Environment

II. To advance physical and intellectual competence
    4. Physical
    5. Cognitive
    6. Communication
    7. Creative

III. To support social and emotional development and provide positive guidance
    8. Self
    9. Social
    10. Guidance

IV. To establish positive and productive relationships with parents
    11. Families

V. To ensure a well-run, purposeful program responsive to participant needs
    12. Program management

VI. To maintain a commitment to professionalism
    13. Professionalism

Parts I and II of this text provide opportunities for caregivers to increase their knowledge and skills. Symbols are used in the left margins of pages to indicate the relation of specific CDA functional areas to the text. The following outline shows the CDA functional areas addressed in Parts I and II.

Part I
    1. History and Trends
        1-9. Curriculum
        11. Families
        13. Professionalism
    2. Settings for Child Care
        3. Learning Environment
        12. Program Management
        13. Professionalism

7. The Indoor and Outdoor Environment
  1. Safe
  2. Healthy
  3. Learning Environment
  4. Physical
  7. Creative
  10. Guidance
  12. Program Management

The chapters in Part III show the CDA functional areas integrated into the actual caregiver decisions and behaviors with age-specific infants and toddlers.

The Child Development Associate Competency Standards for Infant/ Toddler Caregivers are included in Appendix B. These standards and examples of caregiver behavior will be of help to CDA candidates for the Infant/ Toddler CDA Credential.

Curriculum development for infants and toddlers is a dynamic, constant, decision-making process. This book provides information and assistance in this very important part of a day care program.

ACKNOWLEDGMENTS

I wish to thank the reviewers of this second edition for their suggestions and recommendations:

Gail Healy
Consumnes River College
Placerville, California

Mary Beth Mann
Southwest Missouri State University
Springfield, Missouri

Donna Mese
Cambrian College
Sudbury, Ontario, Canada

Jan Shera
Western Oklahoma State College
Altus, Oklahoma

Special thanks are given to my husband, Russell, and our son Cameron, who provided many kinds of support to this writing project. Thanks also to our son Jeffrey who provided graphics. I thank Cameron's family day care providers, Lynn and Randy Yearwood, who allowed my early childhood education students and me to observe their family day care home for ethnographic research; this provided additional insights of children and curriculum. The staff, parents, and children at our new center, The Learning Connection, have helped by implementing some of the ideas and materials included in this book. I am especially grateful to the children and staffs of the Auburn Day Care Center and The Learning Connection for allowing me to photograph some of their interactions.

ABOUT THE AUTHOR

LaVisa Cam Wilson has taught children in an infant day care center where she also served as a liaison between the center and family day care homes. She also taught kindergarten and first grade. She has been in teacher education for eighteen years, working with undergraduate and graduate students and with day care, Head Start, preschool, and primary teachers in in-service programs. She is a professor of Early Childhood Education in the Department of Curriculum and Teaching at Auburn University and serves as a Child Development Associate training project director.

Dr. Wilson served on the Board of the Day Care Council of America for ten years and was editor of its journals for three years. She is serving on the Board of Directors of the National Child Care Association. Dr. Wilson has been elected as Vice President Representing Infancy of the Association for Childhood Education, International, and is the editor of its publication, *Focus on Infancy*. She also served on ACEI's Early Childhood and Publications committees and the Early Childhood and Reading Development Committee of the International Reading Association. Dr. Wilson wrote the text and filmstrip set, *Caregiver Training for Child Care*. She has established a non-profit education and research corporation that operates an exemplary child care program for children from 6 weeks to 14 years of age.

Part I

Infant and Toddler Care

Changes in society have greatly increased the number of infants and toddlers being cared for outside their own homes. The many day care homes and day care centers which provide care for infants and toddlers offer unique experiences for the child and unique responsibilities for the caregiver.

Parents and staff both contribute to the quality of a child care program. Effective communication among parents and staff is essential to support the parent and child. Good staff communication and support systems increase the caregiver's competence.

1
History and Trends in Infant and Toddler Care

OBJECTIVES

After completing this chapter, the caregiver shall

Explain changes in the need for child care.

Differentiate among cultural views of child care.

Identify the area of infant and toddler curriculum.

HISTORICAL PERSPECTIVES

View of Infancy

For generations people thought infants in the first months of life could not involve themselves in their world. They believed that physically infants could not focus and make sense of what came in their eyes and ears, thus making their world a blur. They thought that infants were passive, controlled by those people who attended to their needs.

Cultural Needs and Expectations

In the early twentieth century, fewer mothers of infants were in the work force than are today. Mothers who worked in situations where they could not take along their babies usually counted on older children, female relatives, or neighbors to care for their infants.

One factor limiting the number of working mothers of infants at that time was the idea that only the mother could provide proper care for the infant. A sibling or another relative might suffice, but an outsider would not be able to meet the infant's needs (see Figure 1–1). The mother-infant attachment was crucial and might be weakened if the infant became involved with someone else. Only the mother knew her infant well enough to meet the infant's emotional needs.

Another factor affecting the number of working mothers was the prevalent cultural view that the woman's place was in the home. The husband was to provide for the family's financial needs; the wife was to provide all domestic responsibilities: cooking, sewing, housework, and child care. Women who,

Figure 1–1 Grandmothers share in caring for the infant.

from either need or desire, went to work outside the home were often considered out of place.

Early Research on Care Outside the Home

Institutionalized infants provided the most easily accessible group of children outside the home to study. Research focused on the effects of infant care by people other than the mother as it occurred with infants and young children in hospitals and long-term care facilities. The mother-child attachment did seem to be weakened with infants in those situations (Bowlby 1951; Goldfarb 1943; Spitz 1945).

Early observations of child care centers identified several characteristics:

- Care of infants usually took place in unlicensed homes and centers since state regulations often did not permit infants in centers and often did not have the mechanism to regulate day care homes.
- Each caretaker took care of many children.
- Much care was custodial, that is, the caretaker looked after the infant's physical needs but otherwise had little interaction with the infant.

CURRENT PERSPECTIVES

Views of Infancy

Research, observations, and intuitive feelings have helped to change our views of infants and toddlers. These changes have in turn affected the curriculum of child care facilities.

We now know that infants can see and hear acutely from birth. By the eighth month the infant can see at a range similar to adults. Even before birth infants respond to sounds. With age and experience they learn to discriminate sounds and eventually to produce some of them.

Infants participate actively in their world, both initiating engagement with others and responding to their invitations, both controlling others and being controlled by others. Infants and adults establish dynamic relationships, giving and taking, adjusting to how each other behaves. What adults do can modify how infants behave.

Cultural Needs and Expectations

In 1988 more than 70 percent of women ages 25 to 34 were in the labor force; in 1950, that figure was only 35 percent. By the year 2000, 61.5 percent of women will be at work. Three fifths of the new entrants into the labor force between 1986 and 2000 will be women. In 1950, only 12 percent of women with children under the age of 6 worked; today, that figure is

57 percent. Almost two thirds of all mothers with children younger than 14 are in the work force. Fewer than 10 percent of families have a father at work and a mother at home taking care of the children. This is a sharp change from just ten years ago, when 18 percent of families had that arrangement. (U.S. Department of Labor 1988, 7–8).

The sources of child care are changing. More children are being cared for outside their home by non-relatives than previously (Hofferth 1982). Though family day care homes care for more children than centers (40%–15%), child care center enrollment is increasing faster (Hofferth & Phillips 1987). Greater mobility has often meant that relatives who might have provided child care no longer live nearby, and the cost of in-home care has risen so that many families can no longer afford this form of child care.

Surveys in the past of mothers working full-time have shown their persistent concern about child care arrangements and quality child care. Even with increases in the number of child care facilities and improvements in their accessibility, "problems with making satisfactory child care arrangements still exist" (National Council of Jewish Women 1987).

Where in the past people used to stress the importance of mother-infant interaction, more recent research has included father-infant relationships.

> Fathers have been viewed in our culture in economic/provider roles while mothers have been considered to be in caretaking and nurturing roles. Because of changing definitions of fathering and masculinity, changing family life styles and a more egalitarian society, fathers are allowed greater roles in pregnancy, labor, childbirth, and nurturing roles. Evidence reveals that nurturing responsibilities are learned rather than innate and fathers are capable of caretaking responsibilities. The research does not imply that fathers are superior to mothers. Fathers experience the same problems, difficulties, and frustrations as mothers. However, with the acceptance of these problems, fathers are now able to enjoy many satisfying, fulfilling moments that have been previously denied. . . .Society needs to accept fathers as capable of warmth, kindness, compassion, and nurturing responsibilities (Manning and Swick 1982, 37) (see Figure 1–2).

Many professions are involved in child care. Social workers have been concerned with professional child care as it relates to the needs of the children, the parents, and the community. Health specialists look upon professional child care positively, especially because it can ensure that young children have necessary check-ups and immunizations. They also are providing leadership in planning for health practices which maintain health and minimize illness in child care settings. Psychologists, child development specialists, and educators contribute to increased knowledge of development, learning, and teaching.

Research on Care Outside the Home

The increasing number of mothers in the work force created demands for infant child care. Many parents feared, however, that putting their child in child care centers might hurt the child.

Figure 1–2 Fathers are participating more and more in caregiving responsibilities.

Research on infants and toddlers in child care settings is just beginning. Researchers indicate that infants in child care show less or more attachment to their mothers, or less or more intelligence, or less or more aggressiveness than those reared at home. Today's research reports have made parents and caregivers anxious by drawing broad conclusions from very limited and sometimes faulty research. Though the findings are contradictory and confusing, continued research is needed to address many questions (Phillips 1987). What is quality infant and toddler child care? What factors contribute to quality? Do several factors interact, or can one factor influence much more powerfully? Is quality replicable throughout the infant and toddler child care community?

Infant and Toddler Curriculum

We are just beginning to develop adequate curricula for infants and toddlers. Up to now most day care research has focused on child development, or facilities, or administration issues. Most caregivers selected their own curriculum. If they knew a good deal about child development and how caregivers could nurture and stimulate children, then they planned their curriculum and evaluated it. If they had limited knowledge of child development and the strategies which foster development, they had to rely on intuitive decisions and actions.

Curriculum encompasses all the experiences in the child care day. Program goals will affect what the curriculum is for a particular child in a particular situation.

At the present time, infant and toddler curriculum has borrowed from child care, child development, learning theory, instructional theory, and curriculum design. Research may focus on characteristics of infant and toddler curriculum which can be identified as affecting all developing children positively. But since the curriculum is developed for each child as an individual, its effectiveness must be identified and assessed individually.

HEALTH AND SAFETY ISSUES

Environment

A healthy child care environment is a necessity. Local and state regulations provide guidelines to follow to reduce health risks for children, parents, and staff. Regulations set standards for sanitation of buildings, equipment, toys, and food services and establish immunization schedules. Health regulations along with health practice information from the American Academy of Pediatrics are implemented in center/home policies and procedures for the exclusion of sick children, diapering, handwashing, and so on.

Disease

Disease in child care is getting increased attention. The Centers for Disease Control issue regular reports on diseases affecting children in child care. The newest disease to affect child care is AIDS (Acquired Immune Deficiency Syndrome). Estimates of the number of children who will have AIDS by 1991 range from 3,000 (Koop 1987) to 20,000 (Oleske 1987). Infants and toddlers with AIDS are usually very sick babies, few of whom would be in child care centers/homes. Children with AIDS or carriers of AIDS are covered under the Civil Rights Anti-discrimination Act and cannot be refused care. Therefore, the child care and health care communities are seeking ways to make such care safe also for the people who have contact with the child with AIDS.

Continued data collection and increased use of disease-control methods are needed to reduce the occurrence of disease in infant and toddler care. The Centers for Disease Control provide a kit of specific ideas for child day care directors. *What YOU Can Do to Stop Disease in the Child Day Care Centers* (1984) contains handbook sections for the director, caregivers, and parents as well as posters to use in the center. This information is also applicable to family day care homes. State departments of health distribute the kits in their areas.

Safety

Accidents claim the lives of more children than all childhood diseases combined. Caregivers must have both knowledge of and skill with safety procedures in working with infants and toddlers.

Auto safety is receiving higher priority as states mandate seat belts and car seats for infants and toddlers. Child care providers who transport infants and toddlers must know how to use the infant car seat restraints properly.

BALANCING THE NEEDS OF PARENTS AND THE NEEDS OF CHILDREN

CDA
IV . 11

In child care both children and parents have needs, and these needs are different although both sets are real, vital, and of major concern. As a caregiver you will be making decisions about meeting some of those needs (see Figure 1–4).

Figure 1–3 Children in high-quality child care programs maintain the mother-child attachment.

Figure 1–4 The child care program seeks to meet the needs of parents and children.

Parents often need to learn how to be a parent. How much information and time should the caregiver provide in this area? Parents want their children to learn the parents' cultural expectations and values. How does the caregiver fulfill this desire? Parents need care for infants. What kinds of care can caregivers provide? Parents require high-quality infant care. How can caregivers of infants and toddlers become competent?

Infants and toddlers have developmental needs. How knowledgeable is the caregiver about each infant's development and how does the caregiver facilitate that development? Infants and toddlers have physical, emotional, social, and learning or cognitive needs. Providing physical care is not enough. Nurturing emotionally is not enough. How can the caregiver provide holistic care, care which covers the entire range of infant needs?

Caregivers have responsibilities to both the child and the parent. They play an important role in the lives of each. Caregivers cannot ignore parents, using the rationale that the parents hired them to care for the child. They cannot provide merely custodial care, rationalizing that they are keeping the child safe. What are the caregivers' responsibilities to the parent and to the infant or toddler? How can they meet those responsibilities?

REFERENCES

Bowlby, J. 1951. *Maternal Care and Mental Health.* Geneva: World Health Organization.

Centers for Disease Control. 1984. *What YOU Can Do to Stop Disease in the Child Day Care Centers.* Atlanta, Georgia: Author.

Goldfarb, W. 1943. The effects of early institutional care on adolescent personality. *Journal of Experimental Education.* 12:106–129.

Hofferth, S. 1982. Day care demand for tomorrow: A look at the trends. *Day Care Journal.* 1(2), 8–12, Fall.

Hofferth, S. L. and Phillips, D. A. 1987. Child care in the United States, 1970 to 1995. *Journal of Marriage and the Family.* 49(3), 559–71.

Koop, C. E. 1987. *Report of the Surgeon General's Workshop on Children with HIV Infection and Their Families.* DHHS Publication no. HRS-D-MC 87-1.

Manning, N. L. and Swick, K. J. 1982. Changing father roles. *Day Care Journal.* 1(1), 35–38, Summer.

National Council of Jewish Women. 1987. *A Survey of Working Conditions Affecting Families in the U.S.* New York: NCJW Center for the Child.

Oleske, J. 1987. Natural history of HIV infection II. In *Report of the Surgeon General's Workshop on Children with HIV Infection and Their Families.* DHHS Publication no. HRS-D-MC 87-1.

Phillips, D. A. 1987. *Quality in Child Care: What Does Research Tell Us?* Washington, D.C.: National Association for the Education of Young Children.

Spitz, R. 1945. Hospitalism: An inquiry into the genesis of psychiatric conditions in early childhood. *Psychoanalytic Study of the Child.* 1:53–74.

U.S. Department of Labor. 1980. *Employment in Perspective Working Women.* Report 531. Washington, D.C.: Author, Bureau of Labor Statistics.

U.S. Department of Labor. 1988. *Child Care—A Workforce Issue.* Executive Summary Report of the Secretary's Task Force. Washington, D.C.: Author.

STUDENT ACTIVITIES

1. Interview one woman who had preschool children and was working full-time before 1950. Interview one woman who has preschool children and is working full-time now. Compare their responses to these questions:
   a. Who was/is providing child care for your preschool children? What kind of facility was/is being used (home/center)?
   b. Why were/are you working?
   c. What did/does your mother say about your working and putting your children in child care?
2. Discuss the different effects reported in research findings about institutionalized children and children in high-quality child care programs today.
3. Observe for 15 minutes an infant or toddler in a child care setting. List the child's experiences by categories (physical, emotional, social, cognitive).

REVIEW

1. List three reasons for the increased need today for infant and toddler child care.
2. What is meant by "balancing the needs of parents and children" in child care?

2

Settings for Child Care

OBJECTIVES

After completing this chapter, the caregiver shall

Identify characteristics of the family day care home.

Identify characteristics of the day care center.

Distinguish among the regulations of child care.

Categorize child care program emphases.

Compare caregiver support systems.

CHAPTER OUTLINE

I.   Home-Based Care
A. Staffing
B. Unique characteristics
C. Regulations
II. Center-Based Care
A. Staffing
B. Unique characteristics
C. Regulations
III. Program Emphases
A. Holistic

B. Developmental
C. Quality
IV. Program Funding
A. Public tax support
B. Private support
V.   Support Groups
A. Day care systems
B. Day care networks
C. Associations

CHILD DEVELOPMENT ASSOCIATE FUNCTIONAL AREAS

I.   3 Learning Environment
V.   12 Program Management
VI. 13 Professionalism

Care outside the child's home may be provided in a family day care home or a day care center. There are some similarities and differences, some advantages and disadvantages, in each place of care. Family day care homes and day care centers may be either licensed or unlicensed.

Regulation . . . refers to any uniformly applied system of quality control across programs. It consists of three parts: Establishment of standards; application of standards to programs; use of sanctions to assure that programs meet the standards (Morgan 1984, 165).

In many states and localities a governmental agency regulates child care outside the home in order to control the quality of care to some degree.

Cris Ros-Dukler, assistant commissioner of licensing for the Texas Department of Human Services, stated,

> The compelling interest of the state is to insure the safety of children by developing and enforcing minimum standards when children are being cared for in out-of-home settings. . . . Whether that out-of-home care is in a religious environment or a for-profit or a non-profit setting or a public facility, all children deserve equal protection. And that's what our regulations are supposed to do—to reduce the risk for these children when they are being cared for in out-of-home settings (Pearson 1987, 15).

HOME-BASED CARE

Staffing

The family day care mother provides care in her own home for children other than her own. The caregiver in a family day care home is usually a woman in the household; she may be single or married, a non-parent or parent.

The number of children one caregiver can care for varies; it usually depends on the ages of the children. Many states restrict the number of infants the caregiver can include. A family day care provider with her own 3- and 5-year-old might also care for four other children (see Figure 2–1).

A group day care home provides care for a greater number of children, often from six to ten or twelve. In some states one caregiver may be responsible for this group of children; other states require an additional caregiver for this number.

Unique Characteristics

A family day care home provides an environment for children which is home-like. Familiarity with the surroundings helps the child adjust to a new setting. The physical arrangements may resemble the child's own home. There is usually a kitchen where food is prepared; a bed, mattress, or cot on which to sleep; toilet facilities of some kind; and play areas in a room or rooms. The family day care home usually allows the child to move and play within several rooms.

The small number of children in a family day care home means the children and caregiver have time to develop close relationships. The stability and depth of this relationship contribute to the child's feelings of trust and security.

The family day care home often includes children of several ages. Two-year-old Sasha puts her arm around 6-month-old Jeremy and gives him a hug. Matthew, who is 3½, sits on the floor with 1½-year-old Michelle, putting shoes on her and fastening the Velcro tapes. Year-old toddler Suzanne fol-

Figure 2–1 Several children may receive care in the familiar setting of a family day care home.

lows Miss Jan into the kitchen, watches 4-year-old Larry get a drink of water, and then follows Larry into the den to pick up blocks. Multi-aged groups of children have opportunities to learn from and with each other. Older and younger children provide physical, emotional, social, and cognitive support and challenge to each other.

The program in a family day care home consists of the daily living together as a "family." The cooking and pick-up-the-room times contribute to the child's development, along with the stories, the art on the kitchen table or driveway, the tapping-pan-lid noises, the snuggles and hugs, the sitting alone under the table to watch, and the on-again/off-again interaction with other children and the provider.

The family day care home usually has a flexible schedule. The daily schedule may have a few fixed times, for example, lunch for children who are awake. However, it may permit great flexibility in times for eating snacks, sleeping, and playing. This flexibility minimizes the pressure on children to meet other people's schedules. The home often adjusts its schedule to the child rather than requiring the child to adjust to a schedule. For example, one child can be allowed to stay in the bedroom and sleep while other children can play in other rooms of the home without disturbing the sleeping child.

Family day care providers have autonomy. They decide what they will do, when they will do it, and how they will do it. No other adult is around to supervise or direct their actions.

One disadvantage for family day care providers is their heavy load of responsibilities. Caring for up to six children from eight to ten hours a day, five days a week, all alone, produces a heavy physical and emotional strain. To get time off during the day for relaxation or to attend meetings requires locating and hiring a substitute, activities demanding additional time and money.

Another disadvantage is the isolation from other caregivers. Working alone in their homes, family day care providers miss the informal sharing with other caregivers of ideas, frustrations, and concerns. Many communities do not have organizations which meet the emotional and educational needs of family day care providers, thus leaving them on their own to locate the support they need or to go without it.

Regulations

For many years a state or county agency, often the welfare, health, or social services agency, has regulated family day care homes.

> The regulation of family day care involves 1) the rights of children to be protected, 2) the rights of child care providers to carry on a legitimate home business without infringement of their rights, 3) the extent to which state laws can adequately regulate ALL the homes where children are in care, 4) the ability of the states to enforce their current laws, 5) the interpretation of standards to the public, parents, and potential family day care providers, and 6) the future needs of consumers of family day care who may not be able to find child care if regulations drive providers out of business (Adams 1982, 13).

Three types of regulation of family day care homes are licensing, registration, and certification. To be licensed, the family day care home must meet the standards established by the local governmental agency. These may include the number of children to be served, physical space, equipment, and health and safety factors. In some localities zoning requirements must be met.

Many people care for children other than their own in their homes but remain unlicensed. It has been estimated that more than 90 percent of all family day care homes are unlicensed (Corsini, Wisensale, and Caruso 1988). A proposed alternative to licensing is registration of a family day care home.

Only a few states use certification of family day care homes. "Certification (sometimes called approval) is a form of regulation for purchase of care. Certification standards are, in almost every state, some modification of FIDCR (Federal Interagency Day Care Requirements) standards" (Adams 1982, 10).

CENTER-BASED CARE

Staffing

A day care center provides care away from home for more than six children for some part of the day or night. Day care centers differ from family day care homes in several ways.

The day care center staff consists of a director and caregivers. It may also include a cook, custodians, bus drivers, an education specialist, social services workers, a health specialist, and others, depending on the size, goals, and financial support of the day care center.

The number of caregivers needed is determined by the ages of children served. Adult-child ratios vary slightly among the states. Typical requirements are one adult for each of the following numbers of children in a group:

AGE OF CHILDREN	NUMBER IN GROUP
3 weeks to 2½ years	6
2½ years to 4 years	10
4 to 6 years	20

The day care center facility may be a house or building converted to center use; education rooms in a church, community center, or school; or a building especially designed as a day care center. Each room often houses one age group of children. That room provides for sleeping, eating, and playing in specially arranged areas. The play areas may have blocks in one section, a home living section, a dressup section, and so on. Where a group of children use one room, most states require a minimum of 30–35 square feet of play space per child. Children remain in that room for most of the day, with other indoor play space available in some centers and outdoor play space available for most (see Figure 2–2).

Unique Characteristics

Mrs. Grayson parks her car and walks into the day care center with 2-year-old Ronnie and 4½-year-old Jenny. She stops at Ronnie's room and tells Mrs. Jenkins that Ronnie has had a restless night, getting up four times and fussing about going back to bed. She follows Jenny into her room to say hi to Mrs. Peters and wave goodbye to Jenny. At the end of the day she will be back to pick up Ronnie and Jenny as well as Billie, her 8-year-old, who will be picked up from school by the day care center van.

Children in day care centers are usually grouped with those of similar age. The licensing requirements for adult-child ratios make broader multi-aged grouping costly since the group must use the ratio for the youngest child in the group.

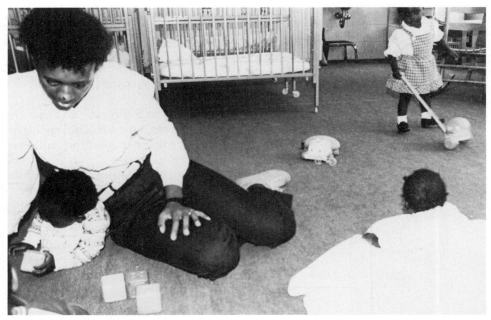

Figure 2–2 In a day care center, a group of children usually remain in one room for playing, eating, and sleeping.

Many toys and much equipment are needed for the number and age range of children in a center. Day care centers often can purchase expensive, sturdy play equipment and a variety of toys because the number of children using them make such purchases cost effective. The equipment may be used by several groups of children, and the toys may be passed back and forth among rooms to provide variety and stimulation without undue cost.

The director and caregivers plan the program in a day care center, sometimes with input from parents. The program should put the center's philosophy and goals into practice. It covers all aspects of the child's care, of the caregiver's roles, of parental involvement, schedule, routines, room arrangement, curriculum, assessments, and evaluations. The caregivers determine the quality of the program in their rooms.

A day care center has two or more caregivers. Having another caregiver can stimulate new ideas, help release tensions and frustrations, and provide support so that caregivers can take risks in relationships and other caregiving roles. However, working with another adult, whether in the same room or in the same building, also requires skills in getting along with others, sharing, compromising, and cooperating. Most adults need to work constantly on maintaining and improving their working relationships with adults. Many centers provide education and assistance through in-service education and participation in workshops and conferences.

CDA
Ⅴ . 12

Day care centers tend to have less flexible daily schedules than family day care homes. They have tended to borrow a daily schedule from schools, with fifteen to thirty minute time blocks which chop up a young child's day. However, this kind of schedule is not appropriate for infants and toddlers who need very simple schedules of large time blocks which fit their physical needs and their own interests.

Regulations

A state agency is usually responsible for day care center licensing. Each state has developed standards for day care center administration, staff, facilities, and program as a part of government's responsibility to protect its citizens. Local governmental agencies are involved with health requirements, fire codes, and zoning ordinances. Licensing identifies a set of minimum standards which a center has met; it does not guarantee quality of care.

PROGRAM EMPHASES

Holistic

Infant and toddler care must be holistic; it must consider the whole child. Physical, emotional, social, and cognitive development are all vitally important during these early years, so balance is needed to help the child properly develop (see Figure 2–3). Overemphasis of one area or limited involvement in another may create unnecessary stress or it may delay development for the child.

An infant needs to experience nurturance, love, consistency, touch, movement, exploration, interactions with others, comfort, challenge, and stimulation. These help develop the child's feelings of security and trust, self-worth and self-identity, curiosity, creativity, and active involvement with people and the world.

Developmental

The program emphasis in both family day care homes and day care centers is developmental. Each child, parent, and caregiver involved in child care is developing.

Children develop naturally. They do not need, nor is it helpful for anyone to push, prod, or pressure them to develop. Adults can enhance, encourage, and nurture children's development in a variety of ways by taking cues from the children to provide the appropriate "match" of materials and experiences to fit the children's observed needs, interests, and behaviors.

Each parent is developing both as a person and as a parent. How the caregiver behaves with the parent can help or hinder the parent's development.

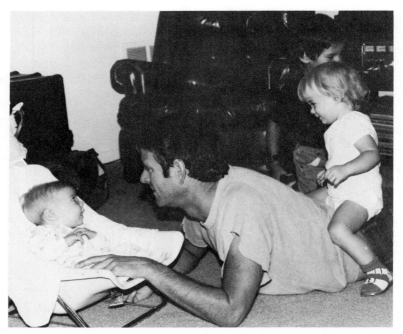

Figure 2–3 Child care programs must be holistic, meeting the child's physical, emotional, social, and cognitive needs.

Each caregiver is developing as both a person and a caregiver. Caregivers who view themselves as learners continually discover things about themselves; they come to know more about others; and they increase both their skills as caregivers and the roles they assume as caregivers.

Quality

High-quality care is required for each child. National accreditation is being used to identify homes and centers that attain standards of quality.

The National Association for Family Day Care began its Accreditation Program in 1988 to offer professional recognition and distinction to those family day care providers whose services represent high-quality child care. The accreditation process involves the provider in an in-depth self-assessment that focuses on physical provisions in the home, child care procedures and policies, and adult-child interactions. Dimensions of the family day care home that are assessed include indoor safety, health, nutrition, play environment, interaction, and professional responsibility. The provider's self-assessment is validated by a parent and a NAFDC representative (NAFDC 1988).

The National Association for the Education of Young Children established the National Academy of Early Childhood Programs to administer an accreditation system for child care centers. The academy defines a high-quality early childhood program as one that meets the needs of and promotes the physical, social, emotional, and cognitive development of the children and adults—parents, staff, and administrators—who are involved in the program. Each day of a child's life is viewed as leading toward the growth and development of a healthy, intelligent, and contributing member of society.

The criteria address all aspects of an early childhood program:

- interactions among staff and children
- curriculum
- staff and parent interactions
- administration
- staff qualifications and development
- staffing patterns
- physical environment
- health and safety
- nutrition and food service
- program evaluation (NAEYC 1987).

PROGRAM FUNDING

There are a variety of sources of financial support for child care programs. Some programs utilize only one source—for instance, parent tuition. Other programs may receive funds from several sources—that is, Title XX, United Way, and parent fees.

Public Tax Support

Two federal programs limited to children of low-income families are Head Start and Title XX Social Services subsidized child care. Part-time and full-time care may be available for those meeting income eligibility guidelines.

Some city, state, and federal governmental units and agencies provide child care services for their employees. These are tax subsidized through use of public buildings, utilities, employees, and so on.

Public schools are opening classrooms for full-day infant and toddler child care. The space and sometimes the utilities, personnel, and equipment may be paid with tax support.

State vocational and technical schools, community colleges, and universities may use tax monies to support child care as a part of their instructional program or as a service to their students and/or faculty and staff.

Private Support

The majority of child care in America is provided in private licensed and unlicensed family day care homes and day care centers, and it is paid for by parents through tuition and fees.

A few corporations are now providing child care alternatives (National Council of Jewish Women 1988; U.S. Department of Labor 1988). These include on-site child care centers, "child care reimbursement, information and referral services, family day care homes, educational programs for parents, and corporate contributions to community child care programs" (Burud et al. 1984, 5). The 415 companies in the 1982 survey conducted by the National Employer Supported Child Care Project reported many benefits. Examples were

- *Turnover:* 65 percent reported that child care had a positive effect on employee turnover.
- *Recruitment:* 85 percent reported that child care had a positive effect on recruitment.
- *Morale:* 90 percent reported that child care had a positive impact on morale.
- *Public image:* 85 percent reported that child care had a positive effect on public relations.
- *Productivity:* 49 percent reported that child care had a positive impact on productivity.
- *Absenteeism:* 53 percent reported that child care had a positive effect on absenteeism (Burud et al. 1984, 22–26).

Churches are "a major provider of child care in this nation" (Lindner, Mattis, and Rogers 1983, 101).

As the steward of substantial resources, including real estate, capital, administrative services and health and insurance benefits, the churches are in an ideal position to make child care delivery available to families. Churches taken in the aggregate are the largest single provider of child care in the United States today. Space, location, and tax exempt status contribute to the desirability of church properties for child care programs. Of course, churches will want to consider carefully the ethical implications of their fee policies for the use of space for this ministry of child care (National Council of Churches 1984).

United Way funds are used in many communities to provide child care services or to subsidize existing community programs.

SUPPORT GROUPS

Day Care Systems

Some public and private agencies set up day care systems. When several day care centers are administered from a central office, they often gain access to greater financial support; additional education, social, and health services; toys and equipment; caregiver training; and parent education.

A single day care center or a day care center system may make arrangements with neighboring family day care homes to serve as satellites to the center. This can benefit both home and center. The family day care provider can use center staff, toys, and materials. Since these family day care homes often care for infants and toddlers, their children often transfer to the center program when they are about 3 years old. The day care center is thus able to serve families with children both below and above 3 years of age without having to provide the more costly infant service in their center.

Day Care Networks

Many communities are establishing child care information and referral networks to serve parents, providers, and community agencies. They have several features in common:

- *Matchmaking:* a commitment to parental choice in child care and respect for all parents' ability to choose the child care setting most appropriate for their own child.
- *Universality of services:* a willingness and capacity to address [the child care information and referral] needs of all parents regardless of income and family circumstance.
- *Inclusive referral system:* a capacity to work nonjudgmentally with all sectors of the provider community, including home and center-based, public and private, profit and not-for-profit groups.
- *Community-level networking:* a cooperative relationship with community agencies and institutions that serve children and families.
- *Knowledge of child care policy and programs:* a thorough familiarity with child care regulations and public policy issues (Siegel and Lawrence 1984, 233).

Some agencies have established their own information and referral networks. One hospital, in an attempt to meet the diverse needs of its staff, developed a family day care network, "a personalized child care information service—a matching of employee child care needs with the availability of spaces in family day care homes" (Torres 1981, 45).

Three basic types of child care information and referral services are (1) information and referral; (2) technical assistance: training; and (3) advocacy: community education (Siegel and Lawrence 1984). Of these, technical assistance or training is directed most specifically to caregivers. Workshops, seminars, and telephone networks can provide caregivers with information and training regarding the program and give directors help concerning administrative functions.

Family day care providers have been especially active in some areas establishing their own networks. Meeting together, they have dealt with problems specific to their situation of caring for children in their own homes.

Associations

Family day care associations are being formed at the local, state, and national levels.

> At one end of the spectrum is the loosely organized group which meets mainly on a social level. . . . There is no set program, but providers use the time to air their grievances with the system in general and to discuss particular problems in their own day care businesses. . . . [The next level, meetings with the licensing agent] quickly becomes a way to get ideas filtered back into the bureaucratic system. [The next level involves a few dedicated caregivers plus an enthusiastic sponsor.] Meetings are held to discuss purposes, needs, expectations and even long-range plans. [County associations meet together to form state associations. Some state associations have met to form a national organization.] (Click 1981, 39–41).

One national family day care organization was formed recently:

National Association for Family Day Care
815 Fifteenth Street, N.W., Suite 928
Washington, D.C. 20005
phone: 202-347-3356

Day care concerns are included in several organizations that provide information for caregivers through publications and conferences:

National Child Care Association
P.O. Box 161206
Austin, Texas 78716–1206
phone: 1-800-543-7161
It is composed of grassroots, small business entrepreneurs who seek for all children responsibly regulated, quality child care services provided by public, private, and secretarian programs.

Association for Childhood Education International (ACEI)
11141 Georgia Avenue, Suite 200
Wheaton, Maryland 20902
ACEI phone: 301-942-2443 and 1-800-423-3563
Its journal, *Childhood Education*, and newsletter, *Focus on Infancy*, include articles and reviews relating to infancy and early childhood. Its annual conference includes sessions on infancy and caregiving. There are some state and local ACEI affiliates.

National Association for the Education of Young Children (NAEYC)
1834 Connecticut Avenue, N.W.
Washington, D.C. 20009
NAEYC phone: 202-232-8777 and 1-800-424-2460
It publishes a journal, *Young Children*, and various books and pamphlets that include articles and book reviews relating to many areas of infancy and caregiving. The association has regional, state, and local affiliates.

Ecumenical Child Care Network
National Council of Churches
475 Riverside Drive, Room 572
New York, New York 10115
phone: 212-870-3342
It links church-housed child caregivers, early childhood educators, advocates, and church leaders nationwide.

National Head Start Association
1309 King Street, Suite 200
Alexandria, Virginia 22314
phone: 703-739-0875

REFERENCES

Adams, D. 1982. Family day care regulations: State policies in transition. *Day Care Journal.* 1(1), 9-13.

Burud, S. L., Aschbacher, P. R., and McCroskey, J. 1984. *Employer-Supported Child Care.* Boston: Auburn House.

Click, M. H. 1981. The growth of family day care associations. *Day Care and Early Education.* 8(3), 39-41.

Corsini, D. A., Wisensale, S., and Caruso, G. 1988. Family day care: System issues and regulatory models. *Young Children.* 4(6), 17-23.

Lindner, E. W., Mattis, M. C., and Rogers, J. R. 1983. *When Churches Mind the Children.* Ypsilanti, Michigan: High/Scope Press.

Morgan, G. 1984. Change through regulation. In J. T. Greenman and R. W. Fuqua, eds. *Making Day Care Better.* New York: Teachers College Press, 163–84.

National Association for Family Day Care. 1988. *New Accreditation for Family Day Care Homes.* Washington, D.C.: Author.

National Association for the Education of Young Children. 1987. *Accreditation by the National Academy of Early Childhood Programs.* Washington, D.C.: Author.

National Council of Churches. 1984. *Policy Statement of Child Day Care.* New York: Governing Board of the National Council of Churches.

National Council of Jewish Women. 1988. *Employer Supports for Child Care.* New York: National Council of Jewish Women Center for the Child.

Pearson, David. 1987. Interview Cris Ros-Dukler. *Child Care Review.* 2(6), 14-21.

Siegel, P. and Lawrence, M. 1984. Information, referral, and resource centers. In J. T. Greenman and R. W. Fuqua, eds. *Making Day Care Better.* New York: Teachers College Press, 227–43.

Torres, Y. 1981. A hospital-based family day care network. *Day Care and Early Education.* 9(1), 44–45.

U.S. Department of Labor. 1988. *BLS Reports on Employer Child Care Practices.* Washington, D.C.: U.S. Dept of Labor Bureau of Labor Statistics.

STUDENT ACTIVITIES

1. Compare a family day care home and a day care center in your area using the following categories:

	STAFFING	NUMBER AND AGES OF CHILDREN	REGULATION
Family Day Care Home Day Care Center			

2. Interview one family day care mother and one day care center caregiver.
   a. What are the goals of the program?
   b. What are the caregiver responsibilities?
   c. What is planned for the children?
3. Make a list of local and state organizations which provide phone contacts, meetings, workshops, or conferences for caregivers.

REVIEW

1. How are a family day care home and a day care center alike? How are they different?
2. Compare the responsibilities of a family day care mother and a caregiver in a day care center.
3. Describe a "holistic" day care program emphasis.
4. Describe a "developmental" day care program emphasis.

3

Communicating with Parents and Staff

Communication is essential to a child care program. For communication to be effective, the people involved must actively listen, think, and express their ideas and feelings in a meaningful way.

WHY COMMUNICATE WITH PARENTS AND STAFF?

Caregivers and parents seek a common goal: to provide high-quality experiences for children. In order to achieve this goal there must be communication between caregivers and parents and among the caregiving staff. Communication is a two-way process. It requires both active listening and effective expression. The attitudes caregivers and parents have toward each other shows up in the communication process. Mutual respect is reflected in the way each person treats the other, shares information, and raises questions. Suspicion and competitiveness between people may block or cloud their understanding of each other.

HOW TO COMMUNICATE WITH PARENTS AND STAFF

Communication includes the following processes:

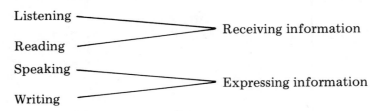

The information communicated may be facts, ideas, questions, or feelings. It may be expressed in spoken or written words or nonverbally in facial expressions, gestures, or other body movements. The caregiver needs skill in all communication processes.

TYPES OF COMMUNICATION

Communicating with Parents

LISTENING TO PARENTS

Parents often need to express their concerns and raise questions about parenting. Parents are often isolated from other family members and may be too busy to talk about these things with neighbors. They want the caregiver to listen to them (see Figure 3–1).

Parents may want the caregiver to agree with them or reassure them, to confirm or reject ideas and pressures from family and friends. For example, Mabel rushed in one morning with her son and said, "I called my mother last night and told her I went back to work this week and she had a fit. She said it was too soon and that right now my place was at home." Listen to Mabel's words, her tone of voice; read her nonverbal cues, her facial expressions and degree of tenseness. She may be telling you that she is feeling frustrated and guilty, or she may be stating her mother's view while feeling fairly comfortable with her own choice of going back to work. You must listen to the whole story (words, tone, cues) to interpret accurately what Mabel is telling you.

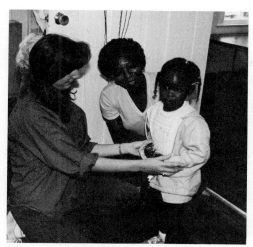

Figure 3-1 Parents and caregivers need to communicate in order to ensure the best care for the child.

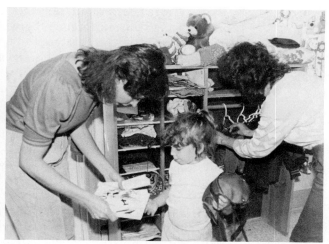

Figure 3-2 Parent and caregiver assist the child in making the transition between home and the child care program.

Parents express their desires for their children. Phyllis said, "I want Velma to be happy. It bothers me to see her cry when I leave." Arlene stated, "I want Pearl to get used to babies because my baby is due next month." Listen to what the parent is saying not only about the child but also about the parent's own needs.

Listen to parents when they tell you what care they expect you to provide. Some parents have very definite ideas and will tell you about them. Other parents do not say anything until they disagree with something, and then they may express frustration or be angry with you. Take in the parents' emotions as well as what they say to you.

Parents tell you much information about their children and themselves. Details about what the child does at home are needed by the caregiver each morning (see Figure 3-2). Listen carefully and record the information as soon as possible (see Chapter 5, Message Board).

SHARING WITH PARENTS

Information Parents need information about the daily experiences their child has in your care. The Message Board and Care Sheets (see Chapter 5) help you organize and record important things the child has done to share with the parent. Special experiences, like the child's excitement about a visiting rabbit, may go into the written record or the caregiver may tell the parent orally.

The child's rate and pattern of development can be shared with parents. Refer to the child's developmental profile (see Appendix A) to focus on recent developments and identify developmental tasks the child may soon be mastering.

CDA
IV . 11

Share ideas for stimulating the child's development (see Chapters 8–14), emphasizing the difference between facilitating and pushing the child. Parents are often very interested in written directions for and drawings of age-appropriate activities and homemade toys (see Chapters 7–14).

Share with parents information relating to their concerns about their child. Mabel may be interested in information relating to the effect of day care on 2-month-old children. Phyllis may be ready for information about separation anxiety. Arlene may need information which helps her understand that Pearl's sharing Mommy with the new baby involves much more than practice in getting used to babies. Changing sleeping and eating patterns and toilet-training are also areas which parents frequently raise questions about with caregivers.

Parents need information about the child care program in which their child is enrolled. Before the child is admitted, the program director shares program goals, policies, and a description of the daily program with parents. Many situations arise which parents need to clarify and discuss with caregivers. For example, Dale wants his 23-month-old daughter to stop using her fingers when she eats. To help him understand the bad emotional effects of undue pressure to perform physical activities the child has not yet mastered, the caregiver can discuss with Dale the holistic goals of the program as it relates to his child's development.

Feelings Caregiving involves feelings and emotions. Parents want to know that you are concerned about their child and about them. In different ways let parents know you like and respect their child. Parents look for caregivers who can and do accept and like their child and who provide emotional security.

Share the excitement of the child's new developments with the parent. The first time you see children pulling themselves up on the table leg, or teetering two steps, or holding utensils, or riding a tyke bike, or turning book pages, or hugging a friend, or asking to go to the toilet, or catching a ball, you are excited and pleased with their accomplishments. When you share these experiences with the parents, let them know how excited you are.

Express sympathy for the child or parent in situations where there is hurt. Express empathy with the parent in some of the trying, frustrating experiences which they encounter with children.

Expectations Share your goals and expectations of the child care program with parents in informal ways. Your casual statements may take on more meaning than written goal statements. Ms. Horsely describes a situation where she encouraged a child's independence; "We want to help children become as independent as they can, so when Louella resisted my helping her take off her bib, I let her try to take it off by herself. She got stuck once, and I helped her lift one arm out, and then she could do the rest by herself. Her big smile and chatter showed me how pleased she was."

Parents are interested in what you expect of yourself as a caregiver. What kinds of things do you do? How committed are you? How friendly are you? Do you think you are more important than parents? Do you extend and supplement parents or do you expect to supplant them? You communicate these expectations through your words, attitudes, mannerisms, and interactions with children and parents.

What do you expect of the children in your care? A child care program emphasizing the development of the whole child and individuality among children is supported by caregivers who facilitate that development. Assure parents that development does not follow a rigid schedule and is not identical among children. Parents often compare their child's development with another child's and gloat or fret at what they see. Caregivers who show that they believe children behave differently within a broad range of normal activity let parents know that you can challenge children without putting harmful pressure on them.

Caregivers expect many things of parents. Some expectations you may express; others you should keep to yourself. You might expect parents to

- love and like their child.
- want to hear special occurrences in their child's day.
- want to learn more about their developing child.
- be observant of the child's health or illness.
- be willing to share information about the child with the caregiver.
- respect the caregiver.

Some parents will not meet your expectations. Because caregiving occurs in the family as well as in the child care program, you will need to resolve your differences with the child's parents.

You may need to change your expectations of parents. We speak of accepting children as they are. You need to take the same attitude toward parents. They come to the child care program because they need care for their child outside the home. They usually are not looking for situations which place additional demands and expectations on them as parents. So long as parents abide by the policies relating to health, attendance, and fee payment, they are doing their part to support the program. Information to help parents grow can be offered but not forced upon them.

INVOLVING PARENTS

In Decision-Making Some programs involve parents in decision-making. Many not-for-profit child care centers have policy boards which include parents. These boards may make recommendations and decisions about center policy. Sometimes parents even serve on boards which make administrative decisions about hiring and firing staff and selecting curricula. However, few family day care homes and for-profit child care centers involve parents in decision-making about policy, staff, or curricula.

Parents of infants and toddlers must be involved in some decisions relating to their child's care. The parent or pediatrician selects the infant's milk or formula; the caregiver does not make that decision. Parent and caregiver must share information about the child's changing eating and sleeping schedules. The length of time from afternoon pick-up to mealtime to bedtime varies among families. Since late afternoon naps or snacks may improve or disrupt evening family time, parents should discuss with you what schedule is best for the child and its family. Toilet-training must be coordinated between parent and caregiver. Both share information about the appropriateness of timing, the failures and successes of the child, and the decision to discontinue or continue toilet-training. If a parent insists that toilet-training be started or continued when you think the child is not ready, share with the parent information about the necessary development of the child before training can occur. Tell the parent about actions children take when they are showing an interest in or a readiness for toilet-training. Share with the parent the harmful effects on children of consistent failures and parental pressures. When the child is ready for toilet-training, the procedures at home and in child care must be the same so that the child does not become confused.

With Children Most parents of infants and toddlers in child care are employed. Therefore, parental involvement during the child care day is often limited to arrival and pick-up time. The parent can help the child take off a coat or unpack supplies when leaving the child in the morning, and can share with the caregiver information about the child's night, health, or special experiences. At pick-up time the caregiver initiates conversations about the child's experiences and projects during the day, while the parent helps the infant or toddler make the transition back to being part of the family by hugging the child or helping put on outdoor clothes.

PARENT-CAREGIVER CONFERENCES

Employed parents often have difficulty scheduling formal parent-caregiver conferences. To make the most efficient use of time, plan the conference thoroughly. Identify the major purpose of the conference. If the parent requests a conference, ask at that time what the parent's concerns are so you can prepare for the conference. If the caregiver requests the conference, tell the parent why, so the parent has time to think about it before the conference begins. Gather any background information needed to discuss the topic. Caregiver records of observations, both formal and informal, may be helpful (see Chapter 5 and Appendix A). Outside sources such as articles, books, pamphlets, tapes, and filmstrips may provide information for the caregiver and may be appropriate to share with the parent. You may also need to refer parents to organizations in your community or region.

Plan the conference agenda:

1. State the purpose for the conference.
2. If initiated by a parent, state your interest in listening to the parent.

a. LISTEN.

b. Present information and those of your ideas and feelings which you think are appropriate and helpful to the discussion.

3. If initiated by the caregiver, state your information, ideas, and concerns.

a. LISTEN to the parent's responses.

b. Explain your points further if you think it will help the parent understand.

4. Provide additional outside information if needed.

5. Discuss the issue(s) with the parent.

6. Emphasize that both you and the parent are working together for the welfare of the child.

HOME VISITS

Home visits are a regular part of Head Start programs, but few other child care programs make them. Home visits can be valuable opportunities for the parent and the caregiver to learn more about each other and the child. The caregiver can see how the parent and child relate to each other in their own home. Home visits must be planned carefully.

Identify the purpose for the visit. Is it to get acquainted? Is it to gather information? Is it to work with the parent, child, or both?

Gather whatever background information the visit requires. Do you need to take along any forms to be filled out? Will you be sharing your program goals? If so, do you have a flyer or pamphlet or will you just tell them? Are there specific problems or concerns you want to discuss? Do you have written documentation of the child's behavior, such as daily reports or notes, to share as well as resource and referral information which might be available?

When you make a home visit, you are a guest in the parent's home. You are there to listen and learn. Discuss the purpose of the conference. When you have finished talking about the issues, thank the parent or parents for their interest, time, and hospitality, and then leave. A home visit is not a social visit.

Communicating with Staff

When more than one person works in a child care program, effective communication among staff is essential. Although family day care providers often work alone in their own home, even they are in contact with licensing staff and sometimes with other family day care providers. Group family day care arrangements employ at least two people, who work with a larger group of children in the home. Child care centers usually have a staff which includes at least a director and one or more caregivers. The size of enrollment determines the number and kind of additional staff; these may be caregivers, cooks, custodians, bus drivers, or education, social service, and health personnel.

LISTENING TO STAFF

Each caregiver needs to be a listener. Staff can exchange information and discuss program issues in a reasonable way only if all are active listeners. How you listen to one another reflects how you respect each other.

SHARING WITH COLLEAGUES

Share information with colleagues. What you know and your experiences give you information, insights, and perspectives which will help others understand issues and deal with problems.

Share your feelings. Express your excitement and joy with those who work with you. As a part of a team, you all can benefit from sharing pleasurable experiences. Tactfully express frustrations, disappointments, and anger. Keeping those feelings bottled up can harm you and those with whom you work, but exploding can also harm all of you. Determine what is distressing you and discuss the issue. Focus on how staff activities are affecting program goals. You will be more likely to clear up misunderstandings and misperceptions if you focus your discussion on issues rather than on personalities.

Share feedback. Both informal and formal observations about what you and your colleagues are doing provide you with information to share with your colleagues (see Chapter 5). This kind of information is called feedback. Noting how other caregivers behave with people and materials in various settings, schedules, and routines can help the entire staff evaluate the current program and to make necessary adjustments. Feedback can highlight caregiver actions which are helpful and effective, but you should use tact when commenting on a situation where you believe your colleagues might act differently. Focus on what is best for the children and what changes can provide a better situation. Do not focus on what a caregiver did "wrong." Actions are more often "inappropriate" than "wrong." Since all caregivers are developing their skills, comments which make colleagues feel incompetent are not helpful. It is more productive to focus on appropriate alternative actions to learn and use.

Share responsibilities with your colleagues. Your colleagues will notice whether you are willing to carry your load. Even when people work under written job descriptions containing specific tasks, the total responsibilities often do not fit neatly into separate categories. Martha is responsible for getting snacks ready, but today she is rocking Natalie, who after crying and fussing has finally settled down but does not seem quite ready to be put down to play. If another caregiver volunteers to set up snacks, Natalie will not be disturbed again and so will not disturb the other children.

Share your expertise. Each person has special talents and unique insights to share with colleagues, children, and parents. Nobody appreciates know-it-alls, but we all benefit from people who are willing to share ideas which can be discussed, accepted, modified, or rejected.

Figure 3–3 Supportive relationships are necessary among caregivers who work together in a child care program.

SUPPORTING COLLEAGUES

Caregiving is physically and emotionally draining. Assisting a colleague when extra help is needed reduces that stress. You can provide positive emotional support by listening, using honest compliments, giving credit, assuring and reassuring colleagues about ideas or actions of theirs which you think are appropriate. Your colleagues' knowing that you are working with them rather than against them is in itself a powerful emotional support (see Figure 3–3).

MAKING DECISIONS

Caregivers need information to make intelligent staff decisions. Study and learn about issues when necessary so that you will be able to discuss subjects intelligently and make wise decisions. Identify the issue and factors which affect the decision. Raise questions with colleagues; listen, think, and take an active part in making decisions relating to caregiving.

RESOURCES FOR PARENTS AND STAFF

Governmental:
Centers for Disease Control
1600 Clifton Road, N.E.
Atlanta, Georgia 30333 *(continued)*

National Hotline for AIDS
1-800-342-2437

Bureau of Community Health Services
Office of Maternal and Child Health
Public Health Service
U.S. Dept of Health and Human Services
5600 Fishers Lane
Rockville, Maryland 20857

Children's Bureau
Office of Human Development Services
Administration for Children, Youth and Families
U.S. Dept of Health and Human Services
Washington, D.C. 20201

Head Start Bureau
Office of Human Development Services
Administration for Children, Youth and Families
U.S. Dept of Health and Human Services
Washington, D.C. 20201

National Caries Program
National Institute of Dental Research
Westwood Building
5333 Westbard Avenue
Bethesda, Maryland 20205

Food and Nutrition Services
U.S. Dept of Agriculture
Washington, D.C. 20250

State Departments of Health

County Health Departments

State and regional Poison Control Centers

State and County Cooperative Extension Services

Professional:
American Academy of Pediatrics
141 Northwest Point Boulevard

P.O. Box 927
Elk Grove, Illinois 60009
phone: 1-800-433-9016

American Academy of Dermatology
1567 Maple Avenue
Evanston, Illinois 60201

American Dental Association
211 East Chicago Avenue
Chicago, Illinois 60611

American Optometric Association
243 North Lindbergh Boulevard
St. Louis, Missouri 63141

Health Related:
National Center for Clinical Infant Programs
733 Fifteen Street, N.W., Suite 912
Washington, D.C. 20005
phone: 202-347-0308

Johnson and Johnson Baby Products Company
Skillman, New Jersey 08558
phone: 1-800-526-3967

Parents' Pediatric Report
Child Health Care Newsletter
Box 155
77 Ives Street
Providence, Rhode Island 02906

U.S. Consumer Product Safety Commission
Office of Information and Public Affairs
Washington, D.C. 20207
1-800-638-2772

American Automobile Association
8111 Gatehouse Road
Falls Church, Virginia 22047
703-222-6000

American Red Cross
1-800-322-8349

Ross Laboratories
Columbus, Ohio 43216

Health & Welfare Division
Metropolitan Life
One Madison Avenue
New York, New York 10010

ADDITIONAL RESOURCES

Ardell, Donald B. and Tager, Mark J. 1981. *Planning for Wellness.* Portland, Oregon: Wellness Media, Ltd.

Dawley, Gloria, and Sorger, James. 1982. *What To Do. . .Until the Doctor Calls Back.* Plainfield, New Jersey: Bayberry Books.

Greater Minneapolis Day Care Association. 1983. *Child Health Guidelines.* Minneapolis, Minnesota: Author.

Horowitz, Alive M. 1981. *Preventing Tooth Decay: A Guide for Implementing Self-applied Fluorides in School Settings.* (NIH Publication No. 82–1196). Bethesda, Maryland: National Institute of Dental Research.

National Institute of Dental Research. 1983. *Snack Facts.* (NIH Publication No. 83–1680). Bethesda, Maryland: Author.

National Institute of Dental Research and the National Association of Community Health Centers, Inc. 1979. *Good Teeth for You and Your Baby.* (NIH Publication No. 79–1255). Bethesda, Maryland: Author.

National Institute of Dental Research and the National Association of Community Health Centers, Inc. 1979. *Una buena dentadura para usted y su bebe.* (NIH Publication No. 79–1465). Bethesda, Maryland: Author.

Public Health Service. 1980. *Healthy Children.* Effective public health practices for improving children's oral health. (DHHS Publication No. [PHS] 80–50136). Washington, D.C.: Author.

STUDENT ACTIVITIES

1. Listen to a parent-caregiver dialogue when the child arrives in the morning. Write down the statements and then categorize them.

	PARENT	CAREGIVER
Information Questions Affirmation		

2. Conduct one simulated parent-caregiver conference initiated by the caregiver and one initiated by the parent.
3. Interview a caregiver who has made a home visit. Determine the purpose and procedures for the visit.
4. Role-play a child care center staff meeting which is discussing problems of sharing play yard space.
5. Identify the responsibilities of one caregiver in a setting with which you are familiar. Categorize the activities according to whether the caregiver attends to them independently or in cooperation with other staff.

TASK	ACCOMPLISH INDEPENDENTLY	NEEDS COOPERATION OF OTHER STAFF

6. List your perceived strengths in interrelationships with parents and staff. List areas where you need to set growth goals.

REVIEW

1. Why is effective communication with parents important?
2. Why is effective communication with staff important?
3. Write an agenda for a parent-caregiver conference initiated by the caregiver to discuss the child's toilet-training.
4. Describe two situations in which caregivers interact with each other. Identify the interpersonal skills needed.

SITUATION	SKILLS NEEDED: CAREGIVER 1	SKILLS NEEDED: CAREGIVER 2

5. How can you contribute to effective, positive staff relationships?

II

Designing Infant and Toddler Curriculum

Caregivers must understand infant and toddler development and be familiar with the development of each child in their care. They must know about materials and equipment and how to arrange and manage space in ways that will enhance the development of each child. They must know what caregivers can and should do to facilitate each child's development. Caregivers exert a strong influence on the quality of the infant and toddler curriculum.

The child actually helps determine his or her own curriculum. While all children develop in similar ways, each is unique. Children are natural learners. Born learners, they maintain the drive to learn. Moreover, children engage energetically in activities which contribute to their development.

An infant and toddler curriculum cannot be fit into a kit. Some experiences are planned and some are spontaneous. Some experiences are initiated by the child and some by the caregiver. Each new skill achieved or concept developed provides a foundation for the child's continuing development. The knowledge caregivers have enables them to recognize and reinforce appropriate experiences for each child.

4

What Is Curriculum?

OBJECTIVES

After completing this chapter, the caregiver shall
   Identify major influences on the curriculum.
   Examine the caregiver's role in curriculum development.
   Write an integrated unit plan.

CHILD DEVELOPMENT ASSOCIATE FUNCTIONAL AREAS

I. 3 Learning Environment
IV. 11 Families

V. 12 Program Management
VI. 13 Professionalism

INFANT-TODDLER CURRICULUM

Scope of Curriculum

Every experience and every minute in the day are a part of the infant and toddler curriculum. Diapering, feeding, washing, and comforting are elements of the curriculum, as are singing, playing, watching, and moving.

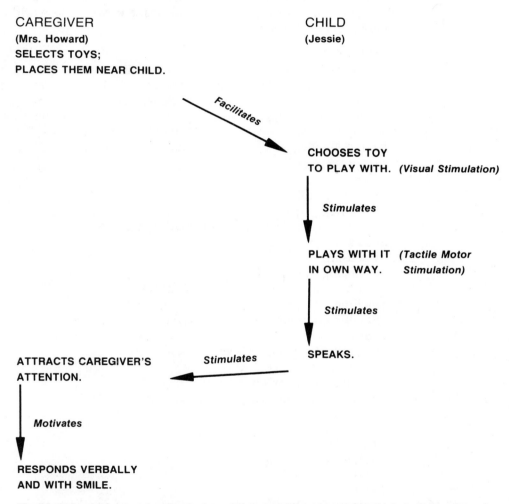

Figure 4–1 An example of caregiver-child-material interaction which individualizes the curriculum.

Infants and toddlers participate actively in selecting their curriculum and initiating their activities. When Jessie babbles sentencelike sounds and then pauses, Ms. Howard looks over to her, smiles, and answers, "Jessie, you sound happy today. That is a pretty ring in your hand." Jessie is playing with a large colored plastic ring that Ms. Howard has set near her. Jessie determines what she will do with the ring and what she will say. Her sounds stimulate Ms. Howard to respond to her (see Figure 4-1). Daily experiences can provide a very integrated curriculum, for children are actively involved with their whole being, with themselves, and with the world around them. All are parts of the curriculum.

EXAMPLE 1

The caregiver is holding 4-month-old Lisa, patting her, and singing and talking to her. While the infant greedily drinks milk from her bottle, she pats the flowers on the caregiver's blouse and looks at the flowers, the buttons, her own hand, the caregiver's face. Lisa stops eating, talks to the caregiver, smiles, and then starts eating, patting, looking, and listening again.

Here is an analysis of this situation:

Infant Behaviors
Motor
  Drinking milk
  Reaching
  Coordinating eye and hand to pat the flowers
Seeing
  Focusing
  Changing focus
  Looking at attention-catching features
Smelling
  Smelling familiar odor of caregiver
Hearing
  Listening to caregiver's voice
  Hearing own voice
  Hearing caregiver's heartbeat
  Hearing own and caregiver's breathing
Emotional
  Satisfying self
  Touching
  Achieving closeness
  Gratifying needs
Social
  Gaining familiarity with and acceptance of another person
  Smiling
  Interacting with another person
Cognitive
  Paying attention to details

Noticing one object, then moving on to another and another
Language
  Listening
  Talking
  Responding to another's talking, singing

Caregiver Behaviors
  Observing
  Holding
  Feeding
  Rocking
  Talking
  Singing
  Listening

EXAMPLE 2

One-month-old Roger awakens from a nap and cries with intense body jerking movements. The caregiver immediately lifts him up, holds him close, changes his diaper, prepares a bottle and feeds him, smiles and talks quietly to him while doing so.

Infant Behaviors
Physical
  Moves reflexively
  Begins to control movements
Emotional
  Shows distress
  Calms down
Language
  Cries

Caregiver Behaviors
  Listens
  Responds to infant's cries by physically comforting him
  Determines cause of distress
  Responds to infant's schedule—need for food
  Initiates and continues interacting by looking, smiling, talking

Since infant and toddler curriculum involves the whole child, the child should have experiences which will enhance the child's physical, emotional, social, and cognitive development. The caregiver is responsible for planning and facilitating this holistic curriculum.

Each child is a distinct being, differing from others in some ways, yet sharing many of the same basic needs. **There is no one curriculum for all infants.** Caregivers have a special responsibility to design each child's curriculum by observing, thinking, planning, and putting many different skills and information together.

Purposes for Curriculum

Designing curriculum serves several functions in child care.

1. The providers (caregivers) and the consumers (parents and children) contribute to the decisions on curricula.
2. The process of curriculum development helps the caregiver understand and plan so that curriculum goals and objectives are realized through daily experiences.
3. The curriculum reflects the interrelationship of the caregiver and child in determining and initiating the curriculum.
4. Analysis of the curriculum highlights a balance or a need for balance in the experiences offered to children.
5. Analysis of the ever-changing needs of the developing young child supports the need for an individualized curriculum.

INFLUENCES ON THE CURRICULUM

Society, the setting, the child, and the caregiver all influence the infant and toddler curriculum. Each affects what is done to the young child and with the young child.

Influences of Society

PARENTS

Parents place children in child care outside their own home for a variety of reasons. The majority of parents do so because they work. Their primary goal is to make sure their children are safe in a stable situation which the parents can trust. Therefore, parents are concerned about the physical environment and how it is used.

Parents may share with caregivers their own expectations of themselves as parents. One aspect of curriculum is for caregivers to help parents meet their needs as they relate to child-rearing and child care. Different parents have different ideas about child-rearing and parenting techniques. The following questions can stimulate varying responses from parents:

- Should a mother breast-feed or bottle-feed?
- How frequently should a parent hold and cuddle the infant?
- Should parents respond immediately to the crying infant?
- When and how should parents talk, sing, play with the infant?
- What are appropriate mothering behaviors?
- What are appropriate fathering behaviors?

Parents also look to caregivers to reinforce and extend their own child-rearing practices. They usually convey to the caregiver their expectations for their children and their attitudes concerning parenting roles and children's behaviors.

Parents view themselves in various ways. Some parents expect to be "perfect" parents. The realities of parenting often cause them to feel guilty when they fall short of perfection or when they turn the child over to the caregiver. Their frustrations may affect their attitudes about themselves and their interactions with their children and their children's caregivers. Sometimes jealousies develop. The child care staff can help these parents establish more realistic expectations (see Chapter 3).

Some parents seem very casual. They go in a very off-hand way from one parenting task to the next that pops up with seemingly little thought of goals or consequences. Some of these parents seem to place their children into child care with the attitude of "do what you want to with them; just keep them out of my hair." The caregiver may need to emphasize the worth of the child and the importance of parents and caregivers in enhancing this worth. Between these two extremes are parents who to varying degrees want to be good parents and who look to caregivers to assist them and their children.

Parents have ideas about what the caregiver should do. They express these positive and negative expectations both verbally and nonverbally, in direct and indirect ways. Parents expect caregivers to help their children learn the parents' values. They expect caregivers to find out and to reinforce behaviors the parents approve. Parents expect caregivers to be competent. They place their trust in the caregiver to provide safe, healthy, reliable, affectionate, concerned, and intelligent care for their children. Parents have their own ways of judging caregiver competence. Some judgment is intuitive, based on listening to and watching the caregiver with their child. Some of it is based on what parents think would be responsible caregiver behavior.

Parents expect their children to cope with the child care setting. Working parents need to use child care and want it to be an arrangement where the child will have satisfying as well as safe experiences. Parents expect their children to learn socially acceptable behavior. Parents define for themselves what is socially acceptable. They do not want their children to learn behaviors which are contrary to their own values and beliefs.

CULTURE

Parents feel the pressures of family and society upon their own child-rearing activities. They receive comments, praise, suggestions, scolding, and ridicule on a variety of topics. Sometimes they hear mixed opinions on the same topic. Some conflicting comments they are likely to encounter are the following:

- The parent should stay home with the newborn and very young infant vs. It is acceptable for the parent of any aged child to work outside the home.
- The newborn and very young infant should stay home and not be taken visiting vs. The infant may be taken visiting occasionally.

- The parents are wasting their time when talking to and playing with a young baby vs. The parents should talk to and play with the infant.
- The infant needs lots of clothes and blankets to keep warm vs. The infant needs only moderate covering.
- The infant should start solid foods at 4 months of age vs. The infant should start solid food at a later age.
- The infant's solid food should be commercially prepared food vs. The infant should eat only mashed table food.

The behaviors of parents and babies are a compromise between what society expects and what the parents feel comfortable with.

What one considers proper language and food are unique to one's subculture. The caregiver can draw attention positively to the similarities and uniquenesses of others. Expansion of language usage and food preference can be a part of the curriculum without negating the parent's cultural expectations.

Each caregiver brings unique cultural experiences and expectations to the caregiving role. Be aware of how these are similar to or different from those of the parents and other staff in order to plan and provide a curriculum which is acceptable to all.

For example, an infant will initiate visual, social, and language interactions but will stop if no one responds. If the caregiver feels uncomfortable or believes it is wrong to interact with the infant, that infant will gradually cease to initiate language or other interactions. But if the caregiver also initiates stimulation of visual, social, emotional, or language interactions, the infant will be challenged to respond and to do the same.

Most caregivers have frequent physical contact with the infant, because they feel comfortable doing it and because they know it is comforting to infants. When feeding the baby, most caregivers not only hold the infant and the bottle, but they also pat the infant and talk and sing. These activities meet several of the infant's needs: touching, holding, and patting help the infant feel secure and cared for; holding the bottle, talking and singing to the infant provide a positive interaction between the caregiver and infant which stimulates the infant to look around, listen, and talk. The infant whose culture expects limited physical contact will have different experiences from the infant who has received much physical contact.

TELEVISION

Television is having an impact on families and caregivers. Parents see role models of what parents "ought" to be or do. They compare their own children to those they view on television. Toddlers watch television and imitate repeatedly language and behavior they do not understand. They lack the judgment to determine whether what they are doing and saying is appropriate. Caregivers see on television role models in adults and come to expect from watching it certain adult and child behavior regarding learning, achievement, and excellence. These pressures may affect their selection of curriculum.

The ease with which television becomes an instant babysitter may tempt the harried caregiver at times, but hopefully the caregiver will not give in to the temptation. The caregiver needs to be aware of how television can both expand and limit infants' and toddlers' experience. Very few television programs are appropriate for infants and toddlers. Television does not permit the child's active interaction with it, and the child under 3 years of age cannot understand most of what is on. Special programs should be carefully selected, and the caregiver should actively view them with the toddler. The television set should **not** be left on through adult programs. Not only is the content inappropriate for toddlers but also the children need some peace and quiet when no extra noises are intruding.

Influences of the Setting

DAY CARE HOME

Family day care homes provide a homelike situation for the infant or toddler. Because the child must adjust to a new caregiver and a new situation, the caregiver should quickly establish the child's familiarity with a similar setting: crib, rooms, and routines of playing, eating, sleeping. A warm one-to-one relationship between the family day care provider and the child provides security in this new setting.

DAY CARE CENTER

Some day care centers care for infants 6 weeks of age and older, and a few centers are even equipped to care for newborns. The very young infant must receive special care. One caregiver in each shift needs to be responsible for the same infant each day. The caregiver should adjust routines to the infant's body schedule rather than trying to make the infant eat and sleep according to the center's schedule. The caregiver will need to work closely with the parent to understand the infant's behavior and changing schedule of eating and sleeping. Consistently recording and sharing information with the parents is necessary to meet the infant's needs and also to involve the parents in their child's daily experiences.

TIME

The number and age of children in a group will affect the amount of time the caregiver has to give each child. The needs of the other children also affect how the time is allocated.

Schedules in the day care home or center are adjusted to the children and the parents' employment schedules. For instance, if three school-aged children arrive at 3 P.M., the infant's feeding may be disrupted. But it also can mean there are three more people to talk and play with the infant.

If the parent works the 7 A.M. to 3 P.M. shift, the infant awakening from a nap at 2:45 may need a more hurried feeding to be ready when the parent arrives. The quality of interaction can remain high even when time for interactions is limited. Caregivers should determine what earlier activities will let them spend more time with the infant on this nap schedule.

Influences of the Child

Every child has an internal need to grow, develop, and learn. During the first years of life children's energies are directed toward those purposes both consciously and unconsciously. Though children cannot tell you this, observers can see that both random and purposeful behaviors help children.

The children look, touch, taste, listen, smell, reach, bite, push, kick, smile, and take any other action they can in order to actively involve themselves with the world. The fact that children are sometimes unsuccessful in what they try to do does not stop them from attempting new tasks. Sometimes they may turn away to a different task, but they will keep seeking something to do.

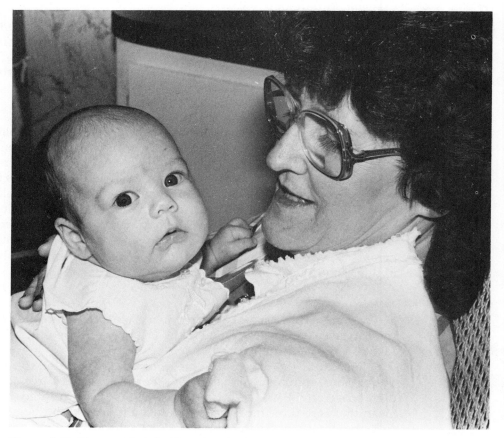

Figure 4–2 The caregiver facilitates each child's development by making him or her feel secure.

Some experiences please children, as when the bells jingle when they shake them. Some are frustrating experiences, as when children try to capture peas with a fork or spoon and steer them into their mouths.

Infants learn from the kinds of response they get to their actions. When the caregiver consistently "answers" cries of distress immediately, infants begin to build up feelings of security (see Figure 4–2). Gradually these responses will help infants learn to exert control over their world. If caregivers let infants cry for long periods of time before going to them, the infants remain distressed longer. They may have difficulty developing a sense of security and trust.

THE PROCESS OF CURRICULUM DEVELOPMENT

Curriculum development is on-going. A development cycle helps ensure that the curriculum is appropriate and relevant. The process involves setting goals, selecting objectives, determining appropriate methods, selecting materials, evaluating the attainment of objectives, gathering feedback on the above components and making necessary adjustments (see Figure 4–3).

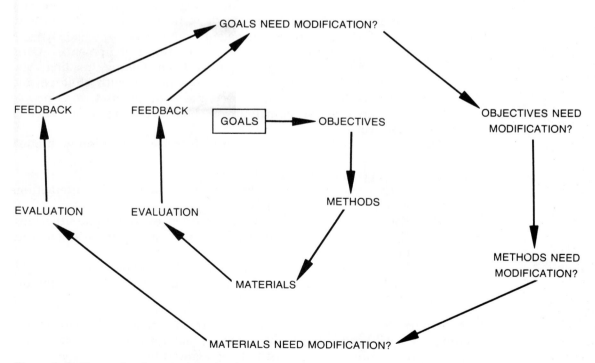

Figure 4–3 The cycle of curriculum development.

Purposes and Philosophy

The purposes for providing child care and the philosophies of the parents and caregivers relating to that care need to be identified and discussed. This text reflects the following particular view.

1. The purposes of child care
   a. for children: to provide a supportive environment, trained staff, and experiences where the children can develop to their fullest potential physically, emotionally, socially, and cognitively.
   b. for parents: to provide a mutually supportive environment with a variety of materials and experiences and a staff with diverse abilities where the parents can place their children for high-quality care and where they can also receive guidance and resources for parenting.
   c. for caregivers: to provide a work environment which addresses the needs of infants and toddlers and staff and to create a positive team effort to meet the needs of the families being served.
2. The philosophy
   a. All people are viewed developmentally.
      (1) Each infant and toddler is progressing through specific sequences or stages of development.
      (2) Each parent is in a phase of parenting the experiences of which contribute to the parent's knowledge and skill. Some are new parents, some are experienced, some anxious, some relaxed, some informed, some nonchalant, some eager.
      (3) Each caregiver has his or her own level of competence. Caregivers have knowledge obtained from talking, reading, and studying; they have individual experiences with children and parents; their views and expectations of themselves as people and caregivers all contribute to their increasing competence as caregivers.
   b. Development and change occur through active interaction with one's environment.
      (1) Each person is an active learner.
      (2) Each person constructs knowledge through active interactions with people and materials.
      (3) Each person adapts previous experiences to current situations.
      (4) Each person builds on the knowledge and skills learned from previous experiences.
      (5) Each person initiates interactions with other people.
      (6) Each person initiates interactions with materials in the environment.

These purposes and philosophy serve as the foundation for curriculum development. All goals, objectives, methods, materials, and evaluations are built upon them, providing a consistent, integrated program. Parents, children, and caregivers all participate in the process of curriculum development.

Goals

Goals are broad generalizations about what you want a program to provide. The program's purposes and philosophy shape determination of the goals.

As an example, the Infant and Toddler Caregiver Competencies developed for the Child Development Associate (CDA) Credential appear in Table 4–1. These competencies state the purpose or goal of the caregiver's behaviors. Program goals can be matched with goals for caregivers.

Mrs. Jalimek is an elementary school teacher with a 2-year-old son, Leon. Her caregiver is moving, so she is looking for a new child care arrangement. She has visited several child care centers and family day care homes and interviewed the directors and caregivers. She wants a program where a caregiver will provide strong emotional support for Leon, will learn about him and adjust to his needs, will help him have happy, satisfying experiences, will allow him to grow at his own rate, and will listen to her concerns and share information with her as a parent.

Mrs. Jalimek has seen situations where 2-year-olds are seated at tables working on worksheets and struggling with numeral and alphabet flashcards. She has observed classrooms and homes where the children play among themselves while the caregivers sit apart talking with other adults and only occasionally interact with the children, and then mainly to reprimand them. She finally chose a program where the caregiver stated:

> I try to make this as much like a home as possible. I am available to each child. I snuggle and love them. We play and sing and laugh and sometimes cry. We cook and help with clean-up chores. When an infant is hungry, I feed him. The children know each other and watch, touch, hug, and talk with each other. They watch in the morning for each child to arrive and greet each with big smiles and waves. They recognize mommies and daddies and watch afternoon greetings and then wave and call out good-byes in the language they use. The children act like they are comfortable here with me and with each other.

TABLE 4–1
CDA PROGRAM AND CAREGIVER GOALS

PROGRAM GOALS	CAREGIVER COMPETENCY GOALS
I. Safe, healthy learning environment	I. Establish and maintain a safe, healthy learning environment
II. Physical and intellectual competence	II. Advance physical and intellectual competence
III. Positive social and emotional development	III. Support social and emotional development and provide positive guidance
IV. Positive and productive relationships with families	IV. Establish positive and productive relationships with families
V. Well-run, purposeful program	V. Ensure a well-run, purposeful program responsive to participant needs
VI. Professional relationships and development	VI. Maintain a commitment to professionalism

Objectives

Objectives describe specific achievements that lead to attainment of a goal. Several objectives may be directed toward the same goal.

The Child Development Associate (CDA) Infant and Toddler Caregiver Competencies are organized into Competency Goals I-VI, which are subdivided into Functional Areas One-Thirteen. Each of the Functional Areas lists examples of caregiver behaviors. Each behavior addresses a specific objective for the child, parent, and caregiver. (See Appendix B for the complete CDA Infant and Toddler Competency Standards.) Table 4-2 shows the interrelationships of the child's needs, parents' needs, and caregiver behaviors.

Methods

Methods are one of the means by which the curriculum occurs. The caregiver has several tasks relating to methods.

1. Knowledge:
   a. of a variety of caregiver behaviors and strategies
   b. of the child's needs
   c. of how to match caregiver behaviors and strategies to the needs of the child
2. Application:
   a. to identify specific needs of the child in specific situations
   b. to select appropriate caregiver behaviors and strategies
   c. to use selected caregiver behaviors and strategies
3. Evaluation:
   a. to judge whether caregiver behaviors and strategies "match" the child's needs appropriately

The caregiver behaviors and strategies should be consistent with the objectives, goals, and philosophy of the program. For example, one facet of the caregiver role is to act as organizer (see Chapter 5). When the caregiver views the child developmentally and as one who needs to have active interaction with materials, the caregiver may select several toys which are developmentally appropriate for the child and then allow the child to choose which toys to use. The caregiver facilitates the child's development by encouraging the child to make the choices among appropriate materials.

Materials

Materials are a vital part of the curriculum. The infant and toddler learn by interacting with materials. The child constructs knowledge by holding, tasting, shaking, hitting, throwing, looking, smelling, and listening to objects.

Some materials provide a variety of experiences; sand has texture, weight, color, smell and can be formed, shaped, dropped, thrown, and so forth.

TABLE 4–2
RELATIONSHIP OF THE CDA OBJECTIVES TO THE CHILD, PARENT, AND CAREGIVER

FUNCTIONAL AREA	TO CHILD	TO PARENT	TO CAREGIVER
ONE: Safe	Safe environment	Reliable, safe environment for child	Provide safe environment for child
TWO: Healthy	Good health and nutrition	Healthy and nutritious environment for child	Promote good health and nutrition
THREE: Learning Environment	Access to stimulating learning environment	Appropriate, stimulating learning environment	Plan, organize, and set up appropriate stimulating learning environment
FOUR: Physical	Development and coordination of physical movements and senses	Opportunities for stimulating physical development	Provide equipment and interaction to stimualte physical development
FIVE: Cognitive	Development of thinking and problem solving	Appropriate stimulation of thinking	Provide appropriate cognitive stimulation
SIX: Communication	Communicate by verbal and nonverbal means	Active involvement in communicating	Model communication through interaction with child and adult
SEVEN: Creative	Explore sights, sounds, and materials	Individualized, flexible materials and activities	Encourage child's unique explorations and creations
EIGHT: Self	Emotional security	Trustworthy, responsive care for child	Provide love, affection, and security
NINE: Social	Social interactions and social awareness	Appropriate social support and stimulation for child	Model and stimulate positive social interactions
TEN: Guidance	Use acceptable behaviors	Support and reinforce child's appropriate behaviors	Establish and maintain management rules and routines and nurture child's self-control
ELEVEN: Families	Stability between environments at home and child care	Partnership with caregiver, exchanging information and support	Communicate with parent, sharing child's experiences and mutual concerns
TWELVE: Program Management	Participate in consistent, appropriate, quality program	Predictable, appropriate, quality program	Plan, coordinate, implement quality program
THIRTEEN: Professionalism	Appropriate care	Informed, learning caregiver for child	Attitude and behavior seeking continued learning

Other objects have very limited use; a wind-up dancing doll provides little stimulation for varied and continued use.

Materials can contribute to or impede the child's development. The caregiver's selection of appropriate materials for each child facilitates that child's development (see Part III). Materials which are too easy can be boring, and those which are too difficult can be frustrating.

Caregivers should select materials which contribute to the attainment of program goals and objectives. Currently popular materials or those labeled "educational" may or may not be appropriate and effective.

Evaluation

Curriculum evaluation is on-going in an infant and toddler program. The caregiver must continually examine the daily experiences to determine whether the curriculum is individualized, is balanced (for the whole child), is relevant, is realistic, and implements the program goals and objectives.

Evaluation should always relate to the identified goals and objectives of the program. Were the goals and objectives attained? If so, what contributed to their attainment? If not, were some or parts of them attained? Satisfactorily or unsatisfactorily? What reasons or factors caused less than full attainment?

Statements of goals and objectives for the day care home or center serve as guidelines for evaluation. Curriculum evaluation can be informal or formal. Recorded data about children and activities may be selected to provide needed information for evaluation (see Chapter 5 and Appendix A Developmental Profiles).

Feedback

Feedback is a critical step in curriculum development. Feedback comes from the parents, caregivers, and the children themselves.

Feedback uses information from each of the parts of the process of curriculum development. Are the goals and objectives still appropriate? Do new influences make it necessary to modify them? Were some methods and materials more effective than others? Do they need to be changed if the goals and objectives are modified? Was the curriculum evaluated periodically and accurately, or was it a one-time evaluation which missed several influencing factors?

Feedback from the total process is necessary to determine whether changes need to be made. Feedback also provides guidance for selecting the kinds of changes which will improve the curriculum.

DESIGNING CURRICULUM

Your selection of a curriculum for an infant or toddler is based on what you know about that child's development, that is, what the child can do now and what the next step is. Your caregiver strategies should reinforce the child's present level of development and challenge the child to move toward the next level. Appropriate planning will help the child do so.

Schedule

FLEXIBILITY

There are two kinds of schedules:

1. The infant's schedule: each infant has an individual physical schedule
2. The caregiver's schedule: each caregiver designs a schedule which coordinates caregiving duties with each infant's schedule.

Andrea arrives at 7:45 A.M.; Kevin is ready for a bottle and nap at 8:00 A.M.; Myron is alert and will play until about 9:00 A.M., when he takes a bottle and a nap; and Audrey is alert and will play all morning and take a nap immediately after lunch. As caregiver, write a list of expected activities in each time block. This also will provide you with guidelines for your time.

The daily schedule must be individualized in infant and toddler care. It focuses on the basic activities: sleeping, feeding, playing. During the first months the infant is in the process of setting a personal, internal schedule. Some infants do this easily; others seem to have more difficulty.

First of all, ask parents what the infant or toddler does at home. Write this down to serve as a guideline. Next, observe the child to see whether he or she follows the home schedule or develops a different schedule.

TIME BLOCKS

The daily schedule in an infant and toddler program is organized around the child's physical schedule. As the infant spends more time awake, the schedule will change. Toddlers also differ in how much time they spend asleep or awake. Their morning and afternoon naps often do not fit into a rigid "naptime from 12 to 2 P.M." schedule. The caregiver can identify blocks of time for specific types of activities, but should keep in mind that no clock time fits all children.

Arrival Time During this special time the primary caregiver greets the parent and child and receives the infant or toddler. This is the time the caregiver should listen to the parent tell about the child's night and about any joys, problems, or concerns. The parent should write down special information on the message board, for example, "exposed to measles last night."

Arrival time is also a time to help the infant or toddler make the transition from parent to caregiver. The caregiver's relationship with the child should provide a calming, comfortable, accepting situation so the child will feel secure. Touching, holding, and talking with the child for a few minutes helps the child reestablish relations with the caregiver. When the child is settled, the caregiver may move on to whatever activity the child is ready to do.

CDA II.4

Sleeping Most of a newborn's time is spent sleeping, although the time awake gradually lengthens. Some infants and toddlers fall asleep easily; others need to be fed, rocked, and then held for a short time even after they are asleep. If you are responsible for several infants or toddlers, plan your time carefully so you are available to help the child fall to sleep. Provide quiet, calming holding, talking, singing, rubbing, rocking. Provide toys for the other children who are awake so they will be productively occupied.

Record the child's sleeping time. Parents need to know how long and at what time their child slept. The caregiver needs to know when each infant or toddler will usually be sleeping. Each infant or toddler in your home or room may have a different nap time.

Each month infants sleep less. This affects when they will eat and when they will be alert. As each infant changes his or her sleeping schedule, the caregiver has to change the infant's feeding and playing times.

Some infants and toddlers wake up alert and happy. Others awaken groggy and crying. You can help ease the infant or toddler into wakefulness. Some you can pick up and cuddle. Talk quietly to them, and move them around so they see other things in the room which may be interesting. Usually infants and toddlers need to have their diapers changed or need to go to the bathroom when they wake up. Some infants will be hungry and need a bottle at this time.

CDA I.2

Eating The very young infant may eat every 2 to 4 hours. Ask the parent how often the baby eats at home. Infants will tell you when they are hungry by fussing and crying. Learn their individual schedules, their physical and oral signals, so you can feed them before they have to cry. Record the time of feedings and the amount of milk or formula the baby drank.

Hold the infant when you are giving a bottle. This is not only feeding time; it is a time to nurture physical, emotional, social, cognitive, and language development.

The parent and pediatrician decide on what milk or formula to give the infant; the caregiver feeds the infant what is prescribed. If you think changes need to be made in the diet, discuss the matter with the infant's parent and a health professional. Many pediatricians recommend that during the first six months or so of life the infant receive only milk or formula and fluids, thus giving the child's body time to mature so that it can more efficiently process solid foods.

Once solid foods are started, the infant can be introduced to a variety of foods. This is the beginning of life-long food preferences and eating habits. Providing a variety of attractive and tasty foods in all food groups can be a special help to the infant.

The toddler usually has established regular eating times. Breakfast, morning snack, lunch, and afternoon snack may be scheduled at specific times. However, individual adjustments may need to be made as a child gradually changes naptime.

Elimination Often infants need their diapers changed after eating. Check an infant's diaper after you have cleaned up from feeding. Check periodically during the time the child is awake. Talk and sing while you are changing the infant. Make this a pleasant time for both of you. Your positive feelings about diapering are reflected to the child. The toddler who is being toilet-trained may need special attention after meals, nap, and during play. Toilet-trained children can be helped to anticipate when they will need to go to the bathroom (e.g., after the nap).

Alert Time In between sleeping and eating infants and toddlers have times when they are very alert to themselves and attracted to the world around them. This is the time when the caregiver does special activities with them (see Part III for suggestions). The infant or toddler discovers him or herself, plays, and talks and interacts with you and others. Children have fun at this time of day as they actively involve themselves in the world.

Determine the times when the infants and toddlers in your care are alert. Decide which times each individual child will spend alone with appropriate materials you have selected and which times you will spend with each. Each infant or toddler needs some time during each day playing with his or her primary caregiver. This play time is in addition to the time you spend changing diapers, feeding the child, and helping the child get to sleep.

As you play with the infant or toddler, you will discover how long that child remains interested. Stop before the child gets tired. The child is just learning how to interact with others and needs rest times and unpressured times in between highly attentive times. With an infant you might play a reaching-grasping game for a couple of minutes, a visual focusing activity for about a minute, a directional sound activity for about a minute, and a standing-bouncing-singing game for a minute. Watch the infant's reactions to determine when to extend the minute to two minutes, five minutes, etc. Alternate interactive times with playing-alone times. Infants will stay awake and alert longer if they have some times of stimulation and interaction.

Toddlers spend increasing amounts of time in play. There should be opportunities for self-directed play as well as challenge and interaction with the caregiver. Toddlers also need quiet, uninterrupted time during their day. Constant activity is emotionally and physically wearing on them.

End of the Day At the end of the child's day in your care, collect your thoughts to decide what to share with the child's parent. To help you remember, or to gather information from caregivers working earlier in the day, review the notes on the message board or on the report sheets for the parent. This sharing time puts the parent into the child's day and provides a transition for the child from you to the parent.

Routines

PURPOSES

Routines give the infant or toddler a sense of security. The infant learns to trust repetition and lack of change. The child may not **think** about these routines but does **feel** the security of familiar activities.

IMPLEMENTATION

Many daily routines foster physical health, particularly those related to cleaning hands, face, teeth; to eating, sleeping, and toileting. With infants and toddlers the caregiver must care for or assist with these needs. With washing routines, the task is to remove all dirt and microorganisms as well as possible. Excellent charts and suggestions are provided in the manual, *What YOU Can Do to Stop Disease in the Child Day Care Centers.* (Centers for Disease Control 1984).

CDA
I . 2

Face Washing Wet a paper towel or clean washcloth with warm water. Add soap. Liquid soap in a dispenser is more sanitary than a bar of soap because dirt and germs may remain on the soap bar. Keep dirt off the dispenser plunger. Wipe the face gently. Rinse the paper towel or washcloth thoroughly in warm water. Wipe the face gently, patting areas around the eyes.

CDA
I . 2

Handwashing Handwashing is a procedure directly related to health and the occurrence of illness. Handwashing procedures should be thorough. A quick rinse through clear water does not remove microorganisms. Frequent handwashing is a vital routine for caregivers and children to establish.

1. *Caregiver:*
   a. Wash hands before
      (1) Working with children at the beginning of the day
      (2) Handling bottles, food, feeding utensils
      (3) Assisting child with face and handwashing
      (4) Assisting child with brushing teeth
   b. Wash hands after
      (1) Feeding
      (2) Cleaning up
      (3) Diapering
      (4) Assisting with toileting
      (5) Wiping or assisting with a runny nose
      (6) Working with wet, sticky, dirty items
2. *Child:*
   a. Wash hands before
      (1) Handling food, food utensils
      (2) Brushing teeth
   b. Wash hands after
      (1) Eating

(2) Diapering or toileting

(3) Playing with wet, sticky, dirty (sand, mud, etc.) items

Wet the whole hand with warm water, soap it, and rub the whole hand—palm, back, between fingers, and around fingernails. Rinse with clean water, rubbing the skin to help remove the microorganisms and soap. Dry hands on a disposable paper towel which has no colored dyes in it. Throw away the towel so others do not have to handle it. You can also use small washcloths as towels with each child using his own once and then putting it in the laundry basket.

Toddlers who can stand on a stepstool at the sink can be assisted in washing their own hands. You can turn on the water, push the soap dispenser, verbally encourage them to use their hands to wash and rinse each other, turn off the water, and if necessary hand them a towel.

Toothbrushing Help toddlers step up on the stepstool at the sink if they need assistance. Turn on the faucet so a small stream of water is running. Wash your hands. Assist in the child's handwashing.

Allow the toddlers to wet their own toothbrush. Shut off the water. Put a small amount of toothpaste on the toothbrush and then encourage toddlers to brush all their teeth (not just the front ones).

Fill a paper or plastic cup half full of water. Encourage the toddlers to rinse their mouths well. Give them more water if needed. Turn on the faucet and allow the toddlers to rinse their own toothbrush and rinse out the plastic cup. Have the children wipe off their mouths with a tissue. Return the toothbrush and plastic cup to their proper place or throw away the paper cup.

CDA
I.2

Eating Eating routines should have a positive effect on children physically, emotionally, socially, and cognitively.

Bibs protect infants' clothes when they are drooling during the first year or so of life. A little cloth bib can be changed during the day when it becomes wet and soiled. These bibs should be laundered rather than just rinsed out.

Infants and toddlers eating solid food need to wear bibs to protect their clothes and the area around them. Bibs with pockets to catch the spills are helpful. Each child needs a separate bib. The bib should be wide enough to cover the child's shoulders and reach the child's sides. It should be long enough to reach the lap; however, if it is too long, it will wrinkle the pocket so spills will not be caught. Plastic bibs should be immersed in soapy water, rinsed, and towel or air dried. Fabric bibs should be shaken, and if wet or soiled, they should be put in the laundry.

Bottle procedures are simple and need to be consistent. Infants let you know when they are hungry. Wash your hands and the infant's face and hands. Prepare the bottle (ask the parent whether it should be warm or cold). Put a bib on the infant. Hold the infant while giving the bottle.

Emotionally the baby needs your closeness. Also, choking, tooth decay, and ear infection are more prevalent among babies who lie down when drinking from the bottle.

Stop periodically to burp the baby. Support the infant's head until the infant has enough neck strength to control head movements. Set the infant upright or up to your shoulder. Press firmly upward or pat on the baby's back until the burp comes. Because the baby may spit up when burping, keep a towel under the infant's mouth to keep both of you dry and to wipe off the baby's mouth. When the baby has finished drinking and burping, remove the bib if it is soiled.

An unfinished bottle should be refrigerated immediately. It may not be saved for use the next day.

After feeding infants a bottle, hold them to put them to sleep, or play with them, or put them down to play with toys and watch or play with other children (see Figure 4–4).

Baby food requires one bowl and spoon per baby. If you anticipate that the baby will not eat a full jar, spoon the desired amount into a dish and put the remainder in the covered jar into the refrigerator. If the spoon is dipped into the jar during feeding, the spoon leaves saliva in the food which can contaminate the rest of the jar of food.

Wash your hands and the infant's face and hands. Put a bib on the infant.

Plan something to keep the infant's hands busy: use one of your hands to play with the baby's hands or give the child a small toy or feeding tool to grasp. Infant muscular coordination is still erratic, so waving arms and grasping hands often collide with a spoonful of food. The infant does not mind the mess, but gradually you may become frustrated, and the infant can pick up your negative feelings.

When food is spilled (hit, tipped, etc.), don't spoon it up to feed to the infant. The tray and clothes surfaces are not kept as clean as the dishes and spoons; they have dirt and germs which would be spooned up with the spilled food. When infants stop eating, stop trying to feed them. **Do not force food!**

Wash the infant's face and hands while you talk and sing to the child, take off the bib, and put the child down to play. Put the dish, spoon, and bib in the kitchen to be washed. Wash off the tray with soapy water and rinse. Wash spills off surfaces.

Finger food affects space as well as eating. Prepare the area by clearing the table and clearing or covering surrounding floor space. Wash your hands and the infant's face and hands. Put a bib on the child. Wash the eating surface; finger foods often are pushed off plates and bowls onto the tray or table.

Set the finger food in front of the infant, say what it is, and encourage the baby to take the first bite. Talk with the infant, using descriptive words as the child eats. Praise the child's competence. Emphasize how special it is that the child can feed him or herself (see Figure 4–5).

CDA
I.2

Figure 4–4 The infant's feeding may be interrupted and enriched by older children who come to talk.

Figure 4–5 The infant soon becomes competent in eating finger foods.

Wash the infant's face and hands, take off the bib, and put the child down to play when he or she has stopped eating. Pick up any remaining food on the tray, table, and floor. Take dish and bib to the kitchen to be washed. Wash the eating surface. Sweep or vacuum the floor. Wash your hands.

Table food is prepared for the young child. Wash your hands and assist the toddler to do likewise. Put a bib on the child. Serve small portions of food. Cut up meat and firm foods into bite sizes of about a half inch.

Allow the child to pick up and use a child-size spoon with whatever hand the child chooses. Since most people are right-handed, you can place the spoon on the right side of the plate. But if the child puts the spoon in the left hand, leave it there. Provide a child-sized spoon and help the child grasp it with palm and fingers. The toddler will use **both** hands when eating. The hand without the spoon is sometimes used to put food in the mouth and sometimes to put food on the spoon. Do not try to keep one hand in the child's lap. When children develop the coordination needed to use utensils, they use their whole body by leaning, twisting, pushing, and grasping. Muscular control must develop before manners can be stressed.

Do not put dropped food back on the child's plate. This food should be thrown away.

Talk with children when they are eating. Name foods, tastes, and textures. Praise the children's competence in eating. Listen and enjoy their talk with you and with others.

When a child has stopped eating, wash the infant's face and hands and help the toddler to do this job.

Remove the bib and allow the child to leave the eating area and go to a play area while you complete the remaining tasks. Put the dishes, utensils, and bibs on a cart or in the kitchen to be washed. Pick up dropped food. Wash the eating surface and table and chair surfaces where sticky hands and food have touched. Sweep or vacuum under the eating area. Wash your hands.

Sleeping You control the sleeping conditions of the infant and toddler. Each child has preferences which you need to learn.

(CDA I . 1-2)

Each infant needs a separate crib with a sheet and blanket. If another infant sleeps in the crib later in the day, remove the sheet and blanket of the first child and store them or put them into the laundry. Spray the crib with disinfectant before putting on the sheet and blanket of the next child. Keep the sheet and blanket sets in cubbies or on a labeled shelf.

Licensing requirements will indicate the space needed between cribs. Many require two feet of space between cribs.

"Cribs and playpens with slats spaced no wider than 2 3/8 inches apart must be used. Crib sides must remain up at all times and cover at least 3/4 of the child's height. The mattress must fit the crib snuggly. If there is more than one inch between the crib sides or ends and mattress, the mattress is too small. Bumper pads must extend around the entire crib and tie into place with at least six ties; they need to be used until four months of age" (Greater Minneapolis Day Care Association 1983). Check older cribs to cover slats that are too far apart.

(CDA II . 4)

Some infants will be sleeping while others are awake. Use sheets or blankets to hang over the crib side to create a visual barrier if you use the room for sleeping and playing.

Infants have their own schedules for sleeping. Ask parents what schedule their infants had before coming to child care. Allow children to sleep when they indicate they are sleepy.

Some infants awaken at dawn and may be ready for a morning nap by 8:30 or 9:00 A.M. As they get older, naptimes change to later and later in the morning. At some point it is necessary to adjust so that naptime and lunch time do not coincide, or you will find the infant falling asleep in his lunch. During these months either feed the infant before the nap or postpone lunch until after the child awakens. Falling asleep in the potatoes is no fun. In the process of being cleaned up the infant usually awakens and cries and fusses at the interrupted nap.

Some infants and toddlers like to be rocked to sleep; some enjoy back rubs. Some prefer to lie on their stomachs to go to sleep; some prefer to lie on their backs. Ask parents what their children prefer. Coordinate your routines with what is done at home. Share information with parents about how the infant or toddler responds with you.

Allow infants or toddlers to awaken on their own schedule and give them time to adjust to wakefulness. Change their diapers, take them to the bathroom, and talk softly to them, helping them make the transition gently. Some children are "on the move" immediately upon awakening. Provide a place and quiet activities for them.

Cribs are for sleeping; they are not play pens. When infants wake up, they should be removed from the crib to enjoy activities in other parts of the room.

Record the time the child slept. The time of day and length of time are important information for you during the day and for parents in planning activities and in noting symptoms of possible sleep problems.

If the sheet is wet or soiled, change it now so it will be ready when the child needs to sleep again.

Infants' afternoon naps depend on the time and length of their morning nap. Some infants may be awake and ready to play while the other infants and toddlers are napping. Provide space and time for these infants to be involved in meaningful activities.

Afternoon naptime may be similar for many toddlers. After lunch and diapering or toileting, toddlers can remove their shoes and lie down on a cot with their own sheets and blankets. Put the shoes in the same place under the cot each day so each toddler learns where to put them and where to look for them. If possible, reduce the light and noise level at least slightly.

Some toddlers like to have their backs rubbed or arms or legs stroked. Some like to listen to music. Hum or play quiet music without words so children can relax rather than remain alert to the words (see Figure 4–6).

Toddlers will wake up at different times. Assist with diapering or toileting and putting on shoes. Designate a room or an area of the sleeping room as a quiet play area until others awaken.

Some infants and toddlers have difficulty relaxing and falling asleep. Schumann described relaxation techniques she has used with children as young as 18 months old. After creating an environment conducive to sleep, she uses the following procedures. A quiet, steady voice along with stroking facilitate relaxation even when the child may not understand all the words being used.

CDA
II.4

> Use a quiet even voice to help the children relax each part of their bodies. Repeatedly (six to eight times) state that the body part is "heavy." For some children it may help to stroke firmly with two hands over the body part to be relaxed. Begin with the toes and work up the body in the following fashion: toes, feet, legs, back (or abdomen, depending on position), fingers, hands, arms, shoulders, neck, eyes, lips, and chin. After relaxing each body part, check it to see how successful each child has been. Tenseness is indicated by a raised bulging or rigid muscles or by movement of a muscle or body part. Using firm hands, strive for being able to move the body part yourself at the joint without the child's helping or keeping the area stiff. Give POSITIVE reinforcement for the way you want the body part to be. Explain to the children to let the feet stay "heavy" while you are checking that part. As you move from talking about one body part to the next, keep your voice a continuous monotone rather than pausing. After doing two or three body parts, repeat the idea that the previous ones are still "heavy" also.

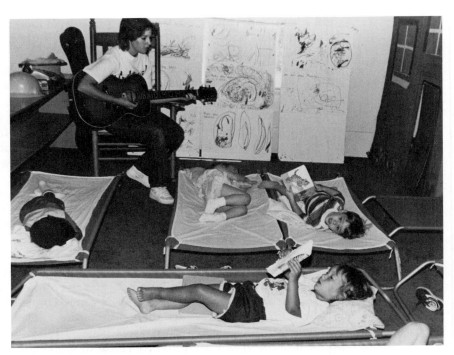

Figure 4–6 The caregiver assists children who need help relaxing by playing soothing music.

For example, "Your toes are heavy. Your toes are heavy. Your toes are heavy. Your toes are heavy." (Check for relaxation, insert positive reinforcement) "Your feet are heavy. Your feet are relaxed. Your feet are heavy. Your feet are heavy." (Check for relaxation, insert positive reinforcement) "Your toes are heavy. Your feet are heavy. Your legs are heavy." By the time each child is told his eyes are heavy, it is likely that he will either already have them closed or be willing to close them at your request. ... If a child still seems fairly alert at the end of the toe-to-head release sequence, try repeating the sequence but eliminating touch and checking of the body for relaxation. Some children might require or seek more body contact than others. For some the continued manipulation interferes with their relaxation (pp. 17–18).

Toileting Diapering requires planning. If you use a changing table, have all supplies within reach. It is desirable to have the changing table next to a sink with hot and cold running water. If you do not use a changing table, use a piece of heavy plastic large enough to hold the infant's back and legs as well as the container with the supplies and a place to put the soiled diaper. Remove the infant's clothes or pull them up to chest level. Remove the soiled diaper. Put a disposable diaper in a covered, plastic-bag-lined container. Put a cloth diaper in a plastic bag which will be closed with a twisty when you are finished.

Keep one hand on the infant at all times.

CDA
I.1–2

Wipe off bowel movement with toilet tissue, going from front to back. Put the tissue on the soiled diaper or drop it into the toilet stool if it is next to your changing area. Use separate toweling or tissue when turning the faucet on and off so feces will not contaminate the faucet. Use a plain paper towel or washcloth with warm water and soap to wash the infant's bottom thoroughly. Rinse the towel or cloth and rinse the baby's bottom. Throw the paper towel away, or put the washcloth in the laundry. Pretreated paper wipes are not necessary, and they sometimes irritate an infant's skin.

Put on a clean diaper, fitting it snuggly around the legs and waist. Re-dress the infant, wash the child's face and hands, and take the child to the next activity. Wash off the changing table or plastic sheet and spray with disinfectant. **Wash your hands thoroughly** before you do anything else.

Record the time and consistency of bowel movements. You and the parents need this information to determine patterns of normalcy and to look for causes of irregularity.

Toilet-training may begin when the toddler is ready. Toddlers will indicate when they are ready to be toilet-trained. Their diapers may be dry for a few hours; they may tell you they have urinated or had a bowel movement **after** they have; they may watch other children use the big toilet—a motivation available when you have children who are already toilet-trained (see Figure 4–7).

Discuss the timing with the toddler's parents. Both the home and child care program need to begin at the same time and use the same procedures. Frequent, regular dialogue between parents and caregivers is needed to determine whether to continue toilet-training or to stop and begin again a few months later.

It is often difficult for parents to resist cultural pressures for early toilet-training even when they know the toddler is not ready and is unsuccessful in attempts. The caregiver can help parents understand the needs and development of their toddler.

The toddler needs two major functions for toilet-training—biofeedback and muscular control. Toddlers learn to recognize the feelings their bodies have before they urinate or have a bowel movement. They can use this biofeedback to decide what to do. At first they seem to "observe" the feelings and afterward label what has happened. When they decide to go into the bathroom **before** elimination, they need to use muscular control until they are safely on the toilet. Timing and control must be coordinated. Toddlers may have some control but not enough to last as long as it takes to get into the bathroom, get clothes out of the way, and get seated or standing. Through trial and error, feedback and adjustments, toddlers learn what their bodies are doing and what they can control and plan.

When it has been determined to start toilet-training, use training pants at home and at the child care program. Do **not** put diapers on the toddler during naptime. Diapers confuse toddlers who are attempting to gain muscular control. Outer clothes must be loose or easily removed to facilitate self-help.

CDA
II . 4

CDA
II . 4

Figure 4–7 Toilet-training is often motivated by the presence of older children.

Take the toddler to the bathroom and demonstrate how to pull down necessary clothes and how to get seated on the adapter seat or potty chair. For the boy who can reach standing, determine where he should stand and where he should direct his penis. Wait until the child goes to the toilet, or wait a few minutes. Demonstrate how to get toilet paper and how to wipe from the front to back. Then let the child try to do it alone. Check to see if assistance is needed in cleaning the child's bottom. Assist in getting clothes back up. Assist in washing the child's hands with soap and water.

Wipe off the toilet seat and spray with disinfectant if there is urine or feces on the seat or sides.

Wash your hands thoroughly before doing anything else.

Occasionally during play time ask children whether they need to go to the bathroom. Ask them to go after lunch and before naptime. As soon as they get up from their naps, have them go to the bathroom.

Toilet-training should be a positive developmental experience. It should take a very short period of time. Problems in toilet-training most often arise when adults do not pay attention to the child's lack of readiness. They pressure the child through weeks of unsuccessful experiences during which they blame the child for the failure rather than blaming themselves for wrong timing. Help parents understand that timing for toilet-training is individual, as is learning to walk. There is no **right** age by which all children should be toilet-trained.

Daily Activities Routines are ready guides for caregivers so that important details of caregiving are attended to. Some routine tasks can be accomplished by the toddler alone, some can only be accomplished by the caregiver, while some tasks involve the caregiver's facilitating the toddler.

Hang outside clothes on a hook or put in the cubbie. Leave those clothes there until it is time to go back outside.

Encourage children to hold books with both clean hands and to turn the pages carefully. Help them learn to put the book back on the shelf or table when they finish looking at it.

Encourage children to take out, or off the shelf, only the toy they are going to play with. At clean-up time before lunch and before going home, have the children help put the toys where they belong.

Have the children put on a smock when painting or gluing (they should ask for help if they need it). Have them stand at the easel or table while working, and keep the supplies at the easel or table. Teach them to wash their hands while the smock is still on (in a nearby sink or in a water-filled basin or pail at the table). They should then dry their hands and throw away the towel in the nearby wastebasket. The children can then take off the smock (asking for help if they need it).

Written Plans

A written plan helps you organize your activities. It also becomes a record you can review to see which behaviors of the child have been reinforced and which materials and strategies have been used.

DAILY AND WEEKLY PLANS

Plans can be daily and weekly. To make a daily plan, decide after your special time with the infant or toddler which of the things you did together today you can build on tomorrow. Review and if necessary revise the plans you had made for tomorrow. Weekly plans should provide experiences in all areas of development. You can add additional information during the week so that you adequately reinforce the behaviors which actually occur during that week (see Table 4–3).

Look at the child's developmental profile (see Appendix A) to determine which behavior is new and to select one behavior to reinforce. List the appropriate materials and strategies to use with the child (see Part III).

TABLE 4–3
WEEKLY PLAN FOR AN INDIVIDUAL CHILD

		CHILD'S NAME:		WEEK:
		Area of Development*	Materials	Caregiver Strategies and Comments
MONDAY				
TUESDAY				
WEDNESDAY				
THURSDAY				
FRIDAY				

Behavior — R = Reinforced   N = New

EXAMPLE:

		CHILD'S NAME:		WEEK:
		Area of Development	Materials	Caregiver Strategies and Comments
TUESDAY		Physical: Vision R: Visual tracking	Red Ribbon bow	Hold bow where infant can focus. Slowly move bow to side, to front, to other side. Observe eyes holding focus. Stop. Talk to infant. Repeat moving bow.
		N: Changing focus	Red and blue ribbon bows	Hold red bow where infant can focus. Lift up blue bow and hold a few inches to side of red bow. Observe eyes changing focus. Continue changing positions with both bows.

UNIT PLANS

Long-term planning involves your choosing appropriate themes for the next weeks and months. When you have selected your themes, you can collect materials and decide on activities long before you will need to use them. Careful long-term planning means you do not have to rush to get the information and material you need for your daily and weekly plans.

When you write down your unit plan, you can think more clearly about your ideas, add to them, revise them, and get yourself, your materials, and your room organized before you begin the unit with the children. The following outline has five major parts which must relate to each other. The materials, preparation, procedures, and evaluation all must implement the objectives. If you have a clever idea or some cute material, but they do not fit the unit objectives, do not include them in that unit.

1. Unit Objectives
2. Materials
   a. Select equipment, furniture.
   b. Select manipulatives, art, books, toys.
3. Preparation
   a. Identify materials which need to be ordered or made.
   b. Collect and organize materials and space.
   c. Set up Learning Centers, if used.
   d. Determine caregiver's schedule for specific involvement with individual children.
4. Procedures
   a. Facilitate individual child's involvement with materials and children.
   b. Facilitate the child's use of new behaviors.
   c. Interact with the child or children.
5. Evaluation
   a. Of learning
      (1) Observe each child's behaviors and compare to the unit objectives.
   b. Of the unit
      (1) Observe each child's behaviors to determine whether the unit objectives, materials, and procedures matched the child's ability to learn physically, emotionally, socially, and cognitively.
      (2) Observe each child's beginning, continuing, and failing interest in the topic.

THEMATIC UNITS

Unit themes can be planned to provide new and interesting experiences for the children. You must give much thought to whether the topic is one the children can deal with physically, emotionally, socially, and cognitively.

Objectives Unit objectives for infants and toddlers differ from objectives for older children. Objectives for infants and toddlers focus on involving the child with materials and people so that the child can construct knowledge. Children of this age derive much of the information from the material itself rather than from being told something about it by or telling something about it to the adult. Therefore, the materials themselves and the child's actual use of them are more important than "making" and "talking about" something.

A thematic unit may have some objectives which are appropriate for all children and some which are appropriate for specific children. A Bumpy Unit may have the objective that the child will touch and hold bumpy and smooth objects. Both a 9-month-old and a 27-month-old can do this. An additional objective for the 27-month-old may be to say verbally which object is bumpy and to find another bumpy object.

A theme or topic may last a week or be extended as interest continues. It can be integrated into many experiences.

The Environment Room arrangement may reflect the theme. Furniture placement and tape on the floor can enrich a unit. You can arrange chairs in rows like a bus or train. A large cardboard box can be painted to look like a house when you talk about families. Use wall and hanging space for pictures, mobiles, floor-to-ceiling projects, bulletin boards, and displays.

Learning Centers Learning centers integrate a theme by organizing the room, materials, and encouraging specific uses of a particular space. Tables, shelves, containers, floor and wall space all form part of a learning center. You can change learning centers to fit new themes.

For infants and toddlers you can organize learning centers in several ways. These children use their senses to gather information to construct knowledge, so the senses can become the focus for the learning centers—you can set up a Seeing Center, Hearing Center, Touching and Feeling Center, Smelling Center, and Tasting Center. Any or all sense centers may be used in a thematic unit. For a Bumpy Unit a Touching Center could contain bumpy objects. A Hearing Center could have bumpy and smooth objects and items which make contrasting sounds when rubbed. A Seeing Center could have clear plastic bags of gravel, corn, and flour to look at and then feel.

You can also organize centers around room-use areas. You can have a Construction Center, a Wet Center, a Reading and Listening Center, a Home Center (see Figure 4–8).

Materials The theme will stimulate ideas for materials. A Bumpy Unit would need all kinds of materials which are bumpy and a few materials which are smooth.

Many household items make good materials for infant and toddler units. Each chapter in Part III contains several ideas for easy-to-make materials.

Books related to the theme can be read to one or a few children at a time when they show interest in hearing a story. For toddlers most books become more meaningful when they are talked about. The caregiver may

CDA
I.3

CDA
I.3

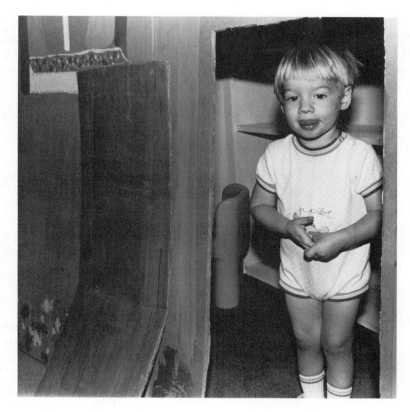

Figure 4–8 A play house can encourage imaginative and creative play.

choose to tell the story in her own words rather than read the printed story-line. She can direct attention to pictures, ask questions about them, and ask the child or children to tell what they are thinking about the story. If children lose interest, put the book down; a child may choose to use the book again at a later time either with you or alone.

Strategies Most of your strategies should focus on helping the individual child become involved. Few toddlers are ready for group experiences. The young child constructs knowledge by actively using materials and engaging in a limited amount of verbal naming of the materials. Refer to Chapter 5 and Part III for listings and examples of strategies.

Sample Thematic Unit The sample thematic unit presented here shows the planning, preparation, and relationships of the unit parts. To put this unit into actual practice, you would need to match the suggested activities with the interests and needs of your children.

SAMPLE THEMATIC UNIT ON RIDING

Riding is physical knowledge. The child constructs this knowledge by physically experiencing riding rather than being told about riding. If your children do not ride the subway (or train, airplane, etc.), do not include those activities in your unit.

1. Objectives
   a. The child shall ride in wheeled equipment.
   b. The child shall ride on wheeled toys.
   c. The child shall show pleasure when riding.
   d. The child shall be exposed to representations of riding: toys with riders, pictures, and oral language.
   e. The child shall identify riding.
2. Webbing

   Unit objectives are fostered by activities which help the child develop and use the desired concepts. Webbing is useful to help you think about the many possible concepts for a unit. Creating the webbing picture shows you the relationships of concepts to the central theme and often stimulates the development of other concepts (see Figure 4–9).
3. Learning Environment

Centers	Materials	Additional Materials
a. Riding (1) Set boundaries.	(1) Tyke bike (2) Sit and spin (3) Wagon	(1) Pictures of children, families riding in car, city bus, etc. (Display at 2-year-old's eye level.)
b. Dramatic Play	(1) Empty cardboard boxes large enough to seat 1–2 children. (2) Toy and/or child-sized stroller. (3) Pick-up.	(1) Floor-to-ceiling hanging: car (made from paper sacks cut and taped together and painted with tempera by children. The "door" opens to allow a child to enter and sit down.

   c. Language
   (1) Books (about riding on or in objects familiar to the child)
   (2) Records (songs and sounds of riding familiar to the child)
   (3) Song cards (for caregiver)
   (4) Newsprint
   (5) Paper and markers (for child's "drawings" and stories)
   (Other areas may contribute to the theme. A child playing with blocks may call a block a car and in sing-song fashion tell where he is "riding" as he pushes the "car" around.)
4. Possible Caregiver-Initiated Activities
   a. Labeling: Use descriptive words to describe a child's actions. For example, "Maria is riding in the stroller"; "Nathan is giving his babies a ride in his wagon"; "Sasha is riding the big wheel." Name objects in pictures on the wall and in books.

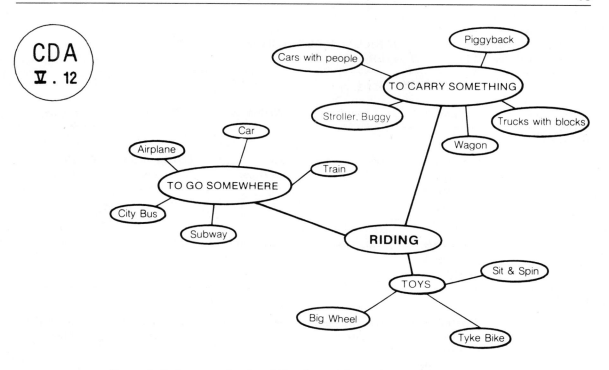

CDA
Ⅴ.12

Figure 4–9 An example of webbing for a riding unit.

b. Reading: Talk about pictures from magazines, wordless picture books. Use picture books. Children can draw their own pictures to accompany their story.

c. Listening: Listen to each child. Listen to how they make sounds and words. Respond to feelings they show. Provide verbal labels, ask questions, and listen some more.

d. Questioning: Ask questions. For example, "Who are you giving a ride?" "Where are you going riding?" "Can that box ride in your wagon?"

e. Singing: Make up your own songs to fit a child's actions. For example, "Barbara is riding, riding, riding. Barbara is riding her tyke bike." If you cannot make up a tune, say the words in sing-song fashion.

CDA
Ⅴ.12

Your record of each child's involvement provides assurance that the child has a balanced curriculum in the formal, planned times with you. Your informal times with each child are also important parts of the curriculum. Both the planned and informal involvement should provide a holistic, supporting, nurturing curriculum for each child in your care.

TABLE 4–4
WEEKLY GROUP RECORD OF CURRICULUM EMPHASIS IN
CAREGIVER-CHILD PLANNED INTERACTIONS

DATES: THEME: Riding

	Monday	Tuesday	Wednesday	Thursday	Friday
CHILD:					
	Development Area: Cognitive Recall Problem-solving	Development Area:	Development Area:	Development Area:	Development Area:
	Materials: Baby Stroller Toy truck	Materials:	Materials:	Materials:	Materials:
CHILD:					
	Development Area: Physical Large motor-riding	Development Area:	Development Area:	Development Area:	Development Area:
	Materials: Tyke bike	Materials:	Materials:	Materials:	Materials:
CHILD:					
	Development Area: Language Labeling	Development Area:	Development Area:	Development Area:	Development Area:
	Materials: Pictures of objects to ride in	Materials:	Materials:	Materials:	Materials:
CHILD:					
	Development Area: Cognitive Creative	Development Area:	Development Area:	Development Area:	Development Area:

TABLE 4–4 (continued)

	Materials: Paper, tempera, paint	Materials:	Materials:	Materials:	Materials:

CHILD:

	Development Area: Cognitive Listening, labeling	Development Area:	Development Area:	Development Area:	Development Area:
	Materials: Record, tape of sounds of car, train, airplane	Materials:	Materials:	Materials:	Materials:

CHILD:

	Development Area: Social Independence	Development Area:	Development Area:	Development Area:	Development Area:
	Materials: Stroller Dolls	Materials:	Materials:	Materials:	Materials:

REFERENCES

Centers for Disease Control. 1984. *What YOU Can Do to Stop Disease in the Child Day Care Centers*. Atlanta, Georgia: Author.

Council for Early Childhood Professional Recognition, CDA National Credentialing Program. (1987). *Child Development Associate Assessment System and Competency Standards Infant/Toddler Caregivers in Center-Based Programs*. Washington, D.C.: Author.

Schumann, M. J. 1982. Children in daycare: Settling them for sleep. *Day Care and Early Education*. 9(4): 14–18.

STUDENT ACTIVITIES

1. Obtain a written statement of the goals of a child care program. Identify the purposes and philosophy of the program.

2. Identify the time blocks in one day care program.
3. List the sequence of activities in two daily routines.
4. Use one child's developmental profile as the basis for writing a daily lesson plan.
5. Select one group of children and write one thematic unit for them.

REVIEW

1. Write a statement for a new caregiver explaining why flexibility in schedules is important in an infant and toddler program.
2. List three daily routines. Explain how each routine may be helpful to a child.

	ROUTINE	HELPFUL
1. 2. 3.		

3. List two reasons for written daily plans.
4. List the five major parts of the unit plan.
    1.
    2.
    3.
    4.
    5.
5. How can a thematic unit involve the child physically?
   emotionally?
   socially?
   cognitively?

5

What Is Caregiving/ Teaching?

OBJECTIVES

After completing this chapter, the caregiver shall

Compare characteristics a caregiver needs with his or her personal characteristics.

Identify personal goals for caregiving, for the children, for their parents.

Analyze responsibilities of the caregiver role.

Assume responsibility for continued personal growth and commitment to competence as a caregiver.

CHAPTER OUTLINE

I. Personal Characteristics of a Competent Caregiver
   A. Relating to self
   B. Relating to children
   C. Relating to adults
II. Caregiver Goals for Self
   A. Acquiring knowledge
   B. Developing skills
III. Caregiver Behaviors and Strategies
   A. Observing and recording
   B. Assessing
   C. Organizing
   D. Managing
   E. Facilitating
IV. Community Resources
V. Professional Preparation of the Caregiver

CHILD DEVELOPMENT ASSOCIATE FUNCTIONAL AREAS

I. 1 Safe
I. 2 Healthy
I. 3 Learning Environment
II. 4 Physical
II. 5 Cognitive
II. 6 Communication
II. 7 Creative

III. 8 Self
III. 9 Social
III. 10 Guidance
IV. 11 Families
V. 12 Program Management
VI. 13 Professionalism

Miss Lynn, a family day care mother, sits in a rocking chair in her den holding 5-month-old Jeremy. Nearby, 27-month-old Julian, 15-month-old Lila, 38-month-old Cameron, and 30-month-old Wanda are playing. Miss Lynn plays with Jeremy, clapping her hands and laughing; Jeremy looks at her and laughs. She lays him on his back on her lap, and he swings his arms, puts his hand in his mouth and makes sounds. He reaches and puts his hands on Miss Lynn's face, laughing and kicking his feet when she repeats his sounds. Miss Lynn is also involved with the other children. She smiles at Julian who is watching the other children. She points to Pooh Bear in response to Lila's whimpers of "Bear," and she watches Cameron and Wanda sitting on the floor, the lock blocks pail between them, constructing objects.

Mrs. Yancey sits on the floor in the toddler room in a day care center. She has her feet outstretched with Manuel sitting on her lap and three other toddlers sitting around her touching her with their hands or legs or leaning against her. Mrs. Yancey is holding a picture book, telling the story line through the pictures rather than reading the words which she decides would take too long right now. She stops and asks Manuel to point to the tree. He puts his finger on a tree and Mrs. Yancey gives him a hug, turns him so he can see her smile, and says, "That's right. That is a tree."

Miss Lynn and Mrs. Yancey provide a glimpse of what caregivers do. They are emotionally involved with the children, providing a warm, stable, supporting, confirming relationship which helps infants and toddlers develop a

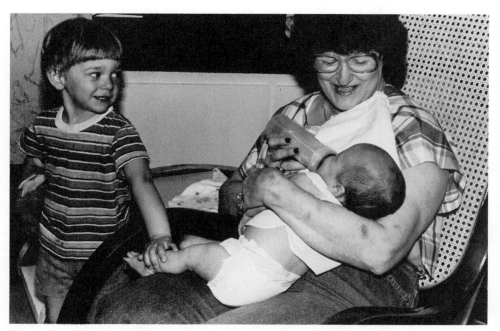

Figure 5–1 The caregiver has warm emotional relationships with children.

healthy foundation for their lives (see Figure 5–1). Caregivers anticipate needs and respond to the children. They select toys and prepare the room. They interact with other staff and with parents. And they plan for and actively stimulate the children physically, emotionally, socially, and cognitively.

The caregiver is the most influential factor in determining the quality of care children receive. As a caregiver your personal characteristics and the professional responsibilities you assume powerfully affect your care of children and your relationships with parents and staff. Caregiving is a very complex task. Becoming a competent caregiver involves acquiring knowledge and developing skills in a variety of areas.

PERSONAL CHARACTERISTICS OF A COMPETENT CAREGIVER

It takes a special person with special characteristics to be a caregiver. You draw on your interest and concern for people, your satisfaction in helping others, your feelings of goodness about yourself, your feelings of importance in being a caregiver, your physical stamina, and your knowledge and skill in working with others.

Relating to Self

CAREGIVERS ARE PHYSICALLY HEALTHY

Good health is necessary to provide the high energy level needed in caregiving. Good health is also necessary to resist the variety of illnesses to which you are exposed. The importance of a healthy staff is reflected in the American Academy of Pediatrics' recommendations that the health record for each employee contain:*

(a) evidence of freedom from active tuberculosis and an annual report of tuberculosis control measures
(b) evidence of pre-employment examination or statement from the personal physician indicating a health status permitting the employee to function in his assigned role
(c) evidence of recovery after specified communicable diseases
(d) reports of periodic evaluations

CAREGIVERS ARE MENTALLY HEALTHY

In your daily relationships you will have to provide physical closeness and nurturance for an extended time, to give emotionally more than you may feel you receive, to be patient longer than you may like, to try to resolve conflicts caused by someone else, and to be calming with one child right

---

*From *Recommendations for Day Care Centers for Infants and Children.* Evanston, Illinois: American Academy of Pediatrics, 1980.

after you have been very frustrated with another. Emotionally stable caregivers who have learned how to handle a variety of emotional demands in their daily experiences encourage greater mental health in others.

CAREGIVERS HAVE A POSITIVE SELF-IMAGE

Your feelings of self-confidence and positive self-worth show that you believe in yourself. This gives you the strength to take risks, consider alternatives, and make decisions in situations where there may be no right or obvious answer.

CAREGIVERS ARE FLEXIBLE

Caregivers do not get upset if they have to change the daily schedule, daily plans, or responsibilities. A usually quiet infant starts fussing and demanding additional attention, thus requiring you to adjust the time you spend with another infant. A substitute caregiver is unfamiliar with the routines, so for that day you must assume the additional responsibility of training the substitute as well as caring for the children. As one caregiver said, "Because the needs of the children must come first, we have a saying at our center: 'We have a beautiful schedule posted on the wall. The trouble is, the babies don't read it!'"

CAREGIVERS ARE PATIENT

Infants and toddlers seek immediate gratification, lack internal controls, are slow in developing muscular coordination, persist in demanding attention, frequently are negative, and are talkers, continually asking questions, commenting, and expecting responses. Your patience may sometimes be stretched very thin as you seek to understand the child's developing needs and behavior.

CAREGIVERS ARE MODELS FOR CHILDREN AND ADULTS

Your behavior is observed and copied by others. A caregiver should use good speech because the children learn from you. A caregiver who speaks in a loud voice stimulates children to do likewise, so try to speak in a quiet voice. A caregiver who listens to 2½-year-old Dana while she tries to tell the caregiver something helps Dana learn to listen and respond to another child. When you give serious attention to your own behavior, you share an awareness and willingness to be a model for others' learning.

CAREGIVERS ARE OPEN-MINDED

Research, common sense, and your own and others' perceptions and opinions are sources of information you can use in evaluating situations and making decisions. Awareness of your expectations of yourself and of children helps you as you think. Listening, thinking, and learning helps keep you aware of and open to ideas and information from others, which contributes to your continued growth.

CAREGIVERS ARE OPEN TO LEARNING

Caregivers develop additional skills. It is not possible to "finish" learning everything you need to know to be an effective caregiver. New information and experiences lead to new insights, understandings, and skills. Openness to learning encourages you to seek new ideas and to take advantage of new opportunities which may extend your knowledge and skill.

CAREGIVERS ARE COMPETENT

Caregivers must be competent to accomplish their tasks efficiently and effectively. Expecting competence from yourself encourages you to seek ways to develop competence. Experiences and continued learning lead to increased competence.

CAREGIVERS HAVE A COMMITMENT TO EXCELLENCE

Striving to do your best is essential to providing high quality caregiving. Read and study, visit, observe, and talk with other caregivers. Your motivation and your knowledge influence what you plan to do to continue to improve.

CAREGIVERS ENJOY CAREGIVING

There is pleasure, enjoyment, and satisfaction in providing effective, high-quality care. Though some tasks may be difficult, unpleasant, or repetitious, overall caregiving should produce satisfaction every day (see Figure 5–2). The caregiver reflects these feelings to the children, the parents, and to other staff members. Positive feelings help build good team rapport.

CAREGIVERS ARE PROFESSIONALS

Caregiving is a respected and necessary profession. You provide a very important service to children, their parents, and the community. The care you provide directly affects the child's development, both positively and negatively, at this critical time in the child's life. You will have great influence and importance in the child's life.

Relating to Children

CAREGIVERS CARE ABOUT AND ENJOY CHILDREN

You share your joy in the child's attempts and accomplishments. You show your concern for the child's well-being by planning, by playing, by listening, by comforting, and by providing physical and emotional closeness.

CAREGIVERS HAVE WARM EMOTIONAL RELATIONSHIPS

Children and their parents feel this warmth. Your attitudes and actions reveal the degree of warmth and care you have for each person.

CAREGIVERS RESPECT CHILDREN

Each child is worthy of your respect. Your accepting behavior and considerate treatment of the child show that you consider that child to be an individual who is an important person.

CAREGIVERS MAKE ADJUSTMENTS

Good interpersonal relationships call for give and take. Close daily contact requires an attitude of giving and adjusting as well as receiving.

Relating to Adults

CAREGIVERS SHARE RESPONSIBILITIES

The parents remain the primary caregivers, and the children still belong to their parents. As a caregiver you provide services to the child and the parent; you supplement rather than supplant the parents' role. You make suggestions rather than give directives to parents. You learn much from parents and are in partnership rather than competition with parents.

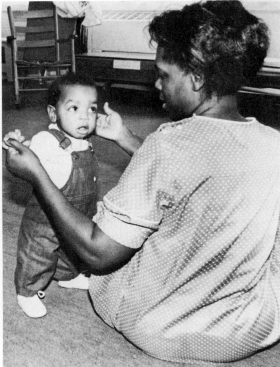

Figure 5–2 The caregiver develops skill in working with children and gains satisfaction from interacting with them.

Figure 5–3 The caregiver observes when the infant is able to stand with help.

CAREGIVERS ARE ACTIVE LISTENERS

Parents try to communicate with the caregiving staff in a variety of ways. They quickly learn whether you are listening to them or not. They will soon know what you think of them as parents, just as you will soon know what they think of you as a caregiver. They will seek approval from you in much the same way the caregiving staff will want to hear and feel parental approval for them and the program.

CAREGIVERS ENJOY INTERACTING WITH PARENTS

Providing care for a child automatically involves the caregiver with parents. Children cannot be isolated from their families; the children affect how the parents behave, and the parents affect how the children behave. Your relationships with parents need to be pleasurable and supportive, complementing your relationships with the children.

CAREGIVERS PROVIDE SUPPORT TO OTHER CAREGIVING STAFF

Each of you contributes to the care of children. Sharing ideas and information, helping accomplish a task, providing positive feedback, cooperatively planning and evaluating your program make your team effort effective. Center staff can interact with other caregivers, the cook, and the director. Family day care mothers, who very often are physically isolated, must make a special effort to locate and communicate with other family day care mothers as well as with the day care supervisor from the licensing agency.

CAREGIVER GOALS FOR SELF

The parents and 6-week-old Jasper visited for an hour with Lydia in her family day care home. The parents asked to place Jasper with Lydia when he became 8 weeks old. In their discussion they told Lydia that their pediatrician had advised them that Jasper is a Down's Syndrome baby even though "he doesn't look like it." Lydia told the parents she needed additional information before she could decide whether to provide care for Jasper. Lydia went to the library that weekend to read about Down's Syndrome. She talked with a special education professor at the local university, and she talked on the phone with her day care supervisor and with other caregivers. She considered the needs and demands of the children currently in her care. After considering all this information, she decided to accept Jasper into her family day care home. Lydia has many personal and professional goals. These goals direct her efforts and motivate her to provide excellent care. Each caregiver is a unique person in a unique day care situation. Identifying the goals which fit you in your situation provide direction to you and to your program.

Acquiring Knowledge

ABOUT YOURSELF

Why do you want to be a caregiver? What are your strengths as a caregiver? What are your weaknesses? What is your temperament? What are your interests? What are your values? What are your expectations of yourself and of others? Are you willing or unwilling to put out effort to satisfy yourself and others? How much time and effort do you think is appropriate for you to put into caregiving? What plans do you have to keep learning about yourself, about others, and about your program?

ABOUT CHILDREN

Child development research continues to provide information which you can apply to children in your care. The information helps you identify each child's individual characteristics and levels of development. Your knowledge of patterns and details of the child's physical, emotional, social, and cognitive development influence how you plan for and act with children (see Figure 5–3, page 82).

ABOUT PARENTS

Each family situation is unique and affects your caregiving. You should continually seek information from and maintain communication with parents. Parents have special needs, desires, and expectations of themselves, their children, and you.

ABOUT CAREGIVER ROLES

The term "caregiving" encompasses emotional interaction, instructional planning, and various types of teaching and learning techniques involving children, parents, and other staff. You will have to balance many roles to provide high-quality care. Understanding the responsibilities of each role will help you determine where you are strong and how to increase your knowledge and personal growth.

ABOUT PROGRAM IMPLEMENTATION

There are many successful ways to nurture, to provide care, to teach. Knowledge of these can help you adjust and individualize your caregiving procedures to meet the specific needs of your environment and the children you serve.

ABOUT MATERIALS

Caregivers must identify what materials are appropriate for different developmental levels of children and which will interest parents and staff. Resources in the outside community also may have value to the program.

Developing Skills

IN DECISION-MAKING

Making decisions and carrying them out is often difficult. Differentiating between needs and wants and being restricted by space, money, and time will affect how you make decisions. Your knowledge about the needs of young children and your program goals will influence your decisions. At times you may choose to defer decisions or refer them to someone else.

IN THE PERFORMANCE OF CAREGIVING DUTIES

Basic knowledge about children, parents, staff, and program are foundations for good caregiving. High-quality caregiving occurs when you put this knowledge into practice. The more knowledgeable and experienced the caregiver, the better the caregiving is likely to be.

CAREGIVER BEHAVIORS AND STRATEGIES

When 4½-month-old Eric, who is lying on the floor, starts to cry, Audrey, his caregiver, picks him up. She "eats" his tummy, and he laughs. She holds him up in the air, and he smiles. She gets his bottle, sits in a chair, and feeds him. Eric watches Audrey and smiles between sips. Grasping her finger, he looks around the room. Audrey stands him in her lap, holds his hands to pull him to and fro, and kisses him. He laughs. She holds him while he dances and laughs. He watches Audrey's mouth and laughs as she talks to him. He leans on her shoulder and burps. He reaches over her shoulder and fingers the afghan on the back of the chair.

The many responsibilities a caregiver has must be mixed together in a continual interaction of the caregiver with the people and environment in the child care program. Several of these responsibilities will be discussed separately to help you identify and develop specific caregiver knowledge and strategies. To support warm, emotional relationships, the caregiver needs to become a good observer and recorder, assessor, organizer, manager, and facilitator.

Observing and Recording

OBSERVER

Why Observe Caregiver observations provide important information needed for decision-making. Your observations contribute details about the child, the caregiver, the curriculum, the materials and facilities, the program, and policies. Observation must precede teaching. It is an ongoing process.

Who to Observe Each child in the day care home or center needs to be observed. All program plans and implementation start with what the caregiver knows about each child.

Each caregiver contributes unique ideas and behaviors in the child care setting, which others can identify by observing.

Each parent participates to varying degrees in the child care program. Observing how parents interact with children and adults helps caregivers understand and plan.

What to Observe Children's behavior helps us learn about the child. Infants and toddlers often cannot use words to tell about themselves. Each child is unique. Caregivers must identify the characteristics and needs of each child, because the child is the focal point of decisions and plans regarding time, space, and curriculum. Each child is continually changing. This growth and development sometimes produces expected, and sometimes unexpected, changes. Living with someone everyday, you may not notice some important emerging developments. Therefore, it is important to make periodic informal and formal observations and to record them so that over a period of time the changes in the child can be noted and shared. This information will affect your planning for and interactions with the child.

Caregiver behavior provides needed information. Ms. Sheila knew that she needed to improve her organization and planning. Every day she would discover she had forgotten to get some supplies she needed for snack time. She started making a checklist of snack items so she could make sure she had prepared everything. After snack time she noted whether she had all the supplies she needed or whether she should add something else. Other caregivers provided her feedback also. By focusing and recording in this way, Ms. Sheila was able to improve herself. Each caregiver is learning and continually developing caregiver skills. One caregiver may observe another caregiver in order to learn new strategies or to reinforce those the caregiver already uses. Other people's observations can let caregivers know whether their actual practice matches the behavior intended. Continuing evaluation and planning along with this necessary feedback can help caregivers increase their effectiveness.

Interactions involve people with people and materials. Ms. Josephine wanted to involve Monroe more when she shared a book with him. She selected a book she thought he would like; she decided on and wrote down three questions to ask Monroe which would focus his thinking and questioning on objects from the book; she set up a small cassette tape recorder where she and Monroe would be sitting; and she called Monroe over to share the book with him. Later, when Ms. Josephine listened to the tape-recording of her time with Monroe, she discovered several things she wasn't aware of. She discovered that she had talked all the time and told everything to Monroe rather than allowing him to talk, share, and question. Observations of interactions provide information about each person involved and about the kind of responses each person has to the other person or material. Observations will help you learn in what ways you have stimulated or inhibited the desired interaction (see Figure 5–4).

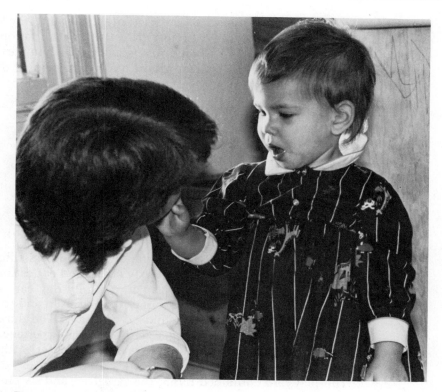

Figure 5–4 Talking and playing with a child is an important caregiver behavior.

The child care setting, with its children, equipment, materials, and arrangement of space, should be examined to determine safe and unsafe conditions; the use, misuse, lack of use, and place of use of equipment and materials; traffic patterns and much-used or little-used space; space where much disruptive behavior occurs; the separation or overrunning of quiet and active space. Make the necessary adjustments after you have evaluated how the setting works in relation to the children's needs.

How to Observe and Record Observations may be informal or formal. You may glance across the room and see Sammy roll over. You know that is the first time you have seen that happen. On the parent message board you write, "Sammy rolled from front to back this morning." Sometimes you or another staff member will arrange to spend a few minutes specifically observing a child, a caregiver, materials, or space. These observations can provide quantities of valuable information. Writing what you observe gives you and other people access to that information later.

Descriptions may consist of one word or may be very detailed and extensive. Write down the exact behavior or situation in narrative form, using as few judgmental and evaluative words as possible.

An ethnographic report describes a total situation: the time, place, people, and how they behave. Description of the total situation lets the caregiver know about things which may not be evident in one part of a specific incident. Starting with a general question "What is going on here?" Spradley identified nine major dimensions of every social situation:

1. Space: the physical place or places
2. Actor: the people involved
3. Activity: a set of related acts people do
4. Object: the physical things that are present
5. Act: single actions that people do
6. Event: a set of related activities that people carry out
7. Time: the sequencing that takes place over time
8. Goal: the things people are trying to accomplish
9. Feeling: the emotions felt and expressed (1980, 78).

Many adults unfamiliar with infants and toddlers think that the young child does not do anything. An early childhood education student observed the following during outdoor play in a family day care home one summer afternoon. She was supposed to focus on one child and to write down everything she saw and heard that child do and say. The purpose of this assignment was to identify and categorize the various experiences initiated by that 13-month-old child. The observer was not to interject her own interpretations into the narrative.

The playyard contained Lynn, the caregiver, and six children ranging from 7 months to 6 years of age. A portion of the report on Leslie, a 13-month-old girl, follows:

2:20   Lynn puts mat out and stands Leslie up in yard.
        Leslie looks around (slowly rocking to keep balance).
        Reaches hand to Lynn and baby talks.
        Looks at me and reaches for me.
        Takes 2 steps, trips on mat, so remains sitting on it.
        Turns around to face me.
        Cries a little.
        Reaches for Lynn, then to me (wants to be picked up).
        Tries to stand up.
        Looks around and watches Jason.
        Reaches hand toward Lynn.
        Watches Jason and sucks middle 2 fingers on right hand.
        Looks around.
        Tries to stand periodically, then seems to change mind.
        Swings right arm.
2:45   Takes Lynn's fingers and stands.
        Walks 2 steps on to grass.
        Swings right arm and brushes lips with hand to make sound—baby talk.

Turns toward Lynn and babbles.
Lane arrives. Leslie watches and rubs left eye with left hand.
"Do you remember Leslie?" Lynn asks Lane.
Leslie reaches out arms to Lynn and walks to her. Hugs her.
Listens and watches Lynn. Holds on to her for support.
Turns around and steps on pine straw and lifts foot to see what it is.
Watches Lynn tie Jason's shoe.
Lynn lifts her in air, then sets her on her knee.
She lies back in her lap and laughs.
Takes dress and lifts it up and down.
Holds on to Lynn's shoulder.
Leslie lifts right hand and "says" bye bye twice.
Smiles and sucks 2 middle fingers again.
Squats.
Looks at Joshua.
Sits down.
Lynn stands her up, holds her hand, and walks her to mat.
Picks up toy keys and puts them in her mouth.
Takes out and plays with. Baby sounds.
Smiles.
"Hey, hey."
Drops keys and says, "uh, oh!"
Stands up and walks.
Squats and gets keys.
Puts in mouth.
Chews on keys.
Lets keys hang from mouth.
Reaches arms for me.
Squats.
Drops keys and picks them up.
Plays with them and chews on them.
Tries to get up and looks at me.
Stands up looking at me.
Steps forward about 2 steps.
Twists top half of body.
Chews keys.
Watches Lynn fix Lane's hair.
Squats, falls, rubs gnat away from eye.
Leans over edge of mat and looks in grass.
Looks at me and baby talks.
Chews keys some more.

Analysis of these descriptive statements shows that Leslie initiates a variety of interactions with people and materials. She is physically, emotionally, socially, and cognitively involving herself in her world. Caregiver planning and facilitating can stimulate and build on Leslie's self-initiated behaviors.

RECORD KEEPING

Record keeping has several purposes:

1. for sharing information with parents
2. for planning curriculum, strategies, and program
3. for assessing children, caregivers, and program.

Message Board Some records are temporary, as is the daily message board for parents. During the time the parent is away, the infant is busily going about the business of growing up. Each new achievement, each practiced skill is an important part of the child's day. These achievements should be shared with parents. Parents want the caregiver's general evaluation: How was Carlyle's day today? And they also want specific information: Phyllis drank from her cup by herself. Provide details rather than simply saying "He was good" or "She was better than yesterday."

Some records are permanent and are kept filed, for example, admission and health records, anecdotal or narrative records, and developmental profiles (see Appendix A for samples of permanent records). You and the other staff will learn from experience what kinds of records are most helpful to you and your parents. If you never use some items of information, it is a waste of time to record them.

Taking the time to write something down seems to be the biggest obstacle to record keeping. Therefore, use records which can be written quickly and easily.

All caregivers should use the same format for recording incidents. Many places use index cards and notebook entries. You can write and file the entries quickly, yet find and use them very easily later. Computers permit a new means of storing information.

MESSAGE BOARD
(wall chart)

CHILD'S NAME:	HOME SCHEDULE: (stays on board)	DATE: (Messages wiped off at end of every day)
E: (Eating) S: (Sleeping) T: (Toilet) O: (Other)		

EXAMPLE:

DAN		FEB. 16
E: 8 oz.–3 hrs. S: 3 naps; fights sleep T: doesn't like soiled diapers O: Upset when sleep is interrupted		8:30–6 oz.; 12:00–7 oz.; 3:00–8 oz. 8:45–11:00; 12:30–3:00 BM 11:00; 3:00

Reporting Sheets Reporting sheets provide the same information in a form which can be filed or taken home. The Infant Welfare Society of Evanston (Illinois), Inc., says this about the "Care Sheets" used by caregivers in its Baby Toddler Center:*

1. Care Sheets: An important source of information, both to parents and to staff. For parents they serve to answer questions and provide feedback in a reliable, concrete manner. For us, they form a detailed, day-to-day record which reflects development, health, and program.

   Each child has a file for his/her care sheets, which passes with the child from group to group. Files are kept in a specific place which is known and accessible to staff. In order to protect the confidentiality of information, staff should give the files to parents, rather than have parents seek them out themselves. Therefore, it is important for "late" staff and substitutes to know the location of files.

   Copies shall be provided to parents, upon request, at the end of the week. Care sheets shall be shown to parents at conferences.

2. Content of Care Sheets:

   a. Routines: As a minimum, some information about each of the "care routines" must be included: a) Naps: times of going to sleep and waking; b) Eating: quality of appetite; c) Elimination: number of bowel movements. In addition, it is important to make note of atypical responses; e.g., restless sleep or nightmares in a child who normally sleeps peacefully or loose stools in a child who normally has firm ones. Relative to children with specific conditions of concern, more data is required. For example, for a child with a milk intolerance, notation should be made of milk products withheld or given. For a child who has a tendency to have intestinal problems, more information should be given regarding stools. For babies, notes about food served are necessary, in order to be alert to allergies.

   b. Activities: Care sheets shall indicate the major activities of each day, as well as whether and how long the child participated. This enables the care sheets, over time, to reflect preferences and abilities of the child.

   c. Special Information: Other pertinent information which shall be recorded includes, but is not limited to, the following: a) injuries which occur at the Nursery, regardless of source; b) injuries which occur outside the Nursery, and the explanation provided by the parent; c) times the child is sent home or not accepted and the reason, including unsuccessful attempts to send a child home; d) developmental milestones reached by the child, e.g., taking a first step or saying a new word. Special instructions from parents should also be noted.

3. Style of Care Sheets: Information must be given clearly (although grammar is unimportant). Therefore, statements must be objective,

---

Care Sheets reprinted by permission of the Infant Welfare Society of Evanston, Inc.

rather than judgmental. For example, say "Tommy cried off and on all morning" or "Joey fought with other children over toys 8 or 10 times today" rather than "John had a terrible day." Say "Jane SEEMED restless (or tired or unhappy) today" rather than "Judy WAS sad." This is important because evaluative or judgmental statements are "emotionally loaded" and often lead to misunderstanding, whereas factual, objective statements cannot be disputed.

In order to be effective, care sheets need to be written daily. In this way information is more easily remembered, and, more importantly, is available to parents and other staff, both late in the day and early the next day.

Care sheets shall be shown to parents at parent-staff conferences.

(Caregivers may use a similar care sheet or devise one which very specifically fits their program.)

Assessing

ASSESSING THE CAREGIVER

Caregivers can assess their own behavior, using the Child Development Associate Competency Standards as criteria. As a part of the Child Development Associate training and assessment program, observations and records are made regularly. The caregiver's behavior is assessed in each of the functional areas (see Appendix B).

Honig and Lally developed checklists to assess caregivers who work with infants and toddlers. The list below shows categories of behaviors for caregivers of infants under 18 months:*

    I. LANGUAGE FACILITATION
      1. Elicits vocalization
      2. Converses with child
      3. Praises, encourages verbally
      4. Offers help or solicitous remarks
      5. Inquires of child or makes requests
      6. Gives information or culture rules
      7. Provides and labels sensory experience
      8. Reads or shows pictures to child
      9. Sings to or plays music for child
   II. SOCIAL-EMOTIONAL: POSITIVE
      1. Smiles at child
      2. Uses raised, loving, or reassuring tones
      3. Provides physical, loving contact
      4. Plays social games with child
      5. Eye contact to draw child's attention
  III. SOCIAL-EMOTIONAL: NEGATIVE
      1. Criticizes verbally; scolds; threatens

*Reprinted by permission from Alice S. Honig and J. Ronald Lally, "How good is your infant program? Use an observational method to find out." *Child Care Quarterly* 4(3): 137-39.

    2. Forbids; negative commands
    3. Frowns, restrains physically
    4. Punishes physically
    5. Isolates child physically—behavior modification
    6. Ignores child when child shows need for attention

IV. PIAGETIAN TASKS
    1. Object permanence
    2. Means and ends
    3. Imitation
    4. Causality
    5. Prehension: small-muscle skills
    6. Space
    7. New schemas

V. CARE-GIVING: CHILD
    1. Feeds
    2. Diapers or toilets
    3. Dresses or undresses
    4. Washes or cleans child
    5. Prepares child for sleep
    6. Physical shepherding
    7. Eye checks on child's well-being

VI. CARE-GIVING: ENVIRONMENT
    1. Prepares food
    2. Tidies up room
    3. Helps other caregiver(s)

VII. PHYSICAL DEVELOPMENT
    1. Provides kinesthetic stimulation
    2. Provides large-muscle play

VIII. DOES NOTHING
(1975, 196–97).

Caregivers who work with toddlers from 18 to 36 months are assessed in the categories of behaviors shown below.

I. FACILITATES LANGUAGE DEVELOPMENT
    1. Converses
    2. Models language
    3. Expands language
    4. Praises, encourages
    5. Offers help, solicitous remarks, or makes verbal promises
    6. Inquires of child or makes request
    7. Gives information
    8. Gives culture rules
    9. Labels sensory experiences
    10. Reads or identifies pictures
    11. Sings or plays music with child
    12. Role-plays with child

II. FACILITATES DEVELOPMENT OF SKILLS
   SOCIAL: PERSONAL
   1. Promotes child-child play (cognitive and sensorimotor)
   2. Gets social games going
   3. Promotes self-help and social responsibility
   4. Helps child recognize his own needs
   5. Helps child delay gratification
   6. Promotes persistence, attention span
   SOCIAL: PHYSICAL
   1. Small muscle, perceptual motor
   2. Large muscle, kinesthesis
III. FACILITATES CONCEPT DEVELOPMENT
   1. Arranges learning of space and time.
   2. Arranges learning of seriation, categorization, and polar concepts
   3. Arranges learning of number
   4. Arranges learning of physical causality
IV. SOCIAL-EMOTIONAL: POSITIVE
   1. Smiles at child
   2. Uses raised, loving, or reassuring tones
   3. Provides physical loving contact
   4. Uses eye contact to draw child's attention
V. SOCIAL-EMOTIONAL: NEGATIVE
   1. Criticizes verbally, scolds, threatens
   2. Forbids, negative commands
   3. Frowns, restrains physically
   4. Isolates child physically—behavior modification
   5. Ignores child when child shows need for attention
   6. Punishes physically
   7. Gives attention to negative behavior which should be ignored
VI. CARE-GIVING: BABY
   1. Diapers, toilets, dresses, washes, cleans
   2. Gives physical help, helps to sleep, shepherds
   3. Eye checks of child's well-being
   4. Carries child
VII. CARE-GIVING: ENVIRONMENT
   1. Prepares/serves food
   2. Tidies up room
   3. Helps other caregiver
   4. Prepares activities, arranges environment to stimulate child
VIII. QUALITATIVE CATEGORIES
   1. Encourages creative expression
   2. Matches "tempo" and/or developmental level of child
   3. Actively engages child's interest in activity or activity choice
   4. Follows through on requests, promises, directions, discipline
IX. DOES NOTHING
(1975, 200–201).

ASSESSING CHILDREN

Caregivers should act as assessor very prudently in this age of testing and making judgments about children. They should determine before making the assessments why the assessments are necessary, which ones are appropriate, and how they will be used.

Developmental assessment is used to determine the child's level of development. It may focus on one area, such as cognition, or the whole child, e.g., physical, emotional, social, and cognitive. Since children are continually developing in all areas, periodic assessment can be useful.

Developmental profiles or checklists can be developed by analyzing past descriptions and selecting categories of behavior or content. You can also develop checklists by listing objectives and competencies for children or caregivers. Checklists, however, only provide information about single incidents, and the information is isolated from the situation in which it occurred.

Developmental profiles or checklists of children's behaviors can be used most effectively by noting a behavior the first time you observe it. One day you may record one new behavior for Jeff, three new behaviors for Deborah, and nothing for Sandra.

We see infants perform many tasks. However, infants cannot tell us in words what they have learned. When you assess infants or toddlers on performance by planning to observe one instance of that activity, you should take care about interpreting the results, for a child may choose not to perform. A child may have learned something but not wish to perform on that occasion.

Few caregivers have received the specialized training required to use standardized assessment techniques and tests. If your program wants to carry out specialized assessment, seek out the necessary training first.

Organizing

PLANS

The caregiver organizes plans. Daily, weekly, and long-term planning are important guides to awareness and continuity of development. The child's developmental profile provides information about the child's strengths and about areas in which development may occur next. Planning specific experiences in advance for each child helps make sure you are considering the needs and development of the whole child, rather than focusing on one or two areas and forgetting other areas.

SCHEDULE

The caregiver organizes the schedule. You decide how to use the major blocks of time and how much flexibility you need in that schedule to meet the child's needs. Consistent patterns of events help children learn order in their lives. This develops in them feelings of security and trust because they know that some parts of their world are predictable.

MATERIALS

The caregiver organizes materials. Good infant programs need a variety of learning materials every day. The caregiver will want to select some materials to set out in the room and store away the rest. The caregiver decides when to change the materials and how to arrange them for the children to get to them.

ENVIRONMENT

The caregiver organizes the environment—the room and the playyard—to meet the developmental needs of the children. Caregivers rely on their knowledge of the individual children in their care as well as on their background in child development. Each caregiver decides how and when to change the environment.

Managing

CDA
Ⅴ . 12

Careful management of time, space, materials, and people is needed to provide meaningful daily experiences for children.

TIME

The caregiver manages and coordinates time within the guidelines of the daily schedule and plans. You give Suzy a five-minute notice before outdoor play time since Suzy takes a long time to put her toys away and start getting ready to go outside. You feed lunch to Jack at 11:00 A.M., because he falls asleep at 11:30. You allow Vanessa to get up after her half-hour sleep, because she usually takes very short naps. You encourage Joshua to stay on his cot, knowing that he usually sleeps two hours.

SPACE

The caregiver manages space. Before the children arrive, you plan and organize the space in your caregiving environment. When the children are actively using that space, you will make suggestions, decisions, and adjustments to help each child have positive experiences. Orrin is piling up blocks near the shelf. Shiwanda is trying to reach a block. For Shiwanda to get the block she wants, she will probably bump into Orrin's pile of blocks. You can walk with Shiwanda around to the other side of Orrin where she can reach the block without getting into Orrin's space.

MATERIALS

The caregiver manages materials. With very young children you make decisions about how many kinds of materials are needed, where they can be stored and where they can be used, what is safe or not safe, and how the materials can or cannot be used. Lois asks for a toy and begins pulling toys out of the toy box. She pulls out blocks, dolls, cars, puzzle pieces, fabric scraps, and assorted other toys. She looks back and forth between the inside of the box and the clutter of toys on the floor. She finally walks away to another part of the room, leaving all the toys behind. Too many materials can be confusing, but too few can bore a child.

PEOPLE

The caregiver manages and coordinates people. When two caregivers work with a group of children, they should coordinate their plans and their actions. While the director can provide guidance, the moment-by-moment actions require dialogue and give and take between the caregivers.

Caregivers coordinate the children's use of time, space, and materials. Willard, a 15-month-old, flings toys. One of the caregivers needs to help him move to a part of the room where he can fling toys safely.

BEHAVIOR

CDA
Ⅲ . 10

The caregiver manages behavior by using external controls and helping children develop internal controls.

External Controls Because young children lack judgment, caregivers must exert external control over the child's life. The kinds of controls you select and ways you implement them can be positive and helpful, providing secure and trust-evoking experiences. Your decisions and actions will provide models for the young children who are trying to develop independence and self-control. For example, Julian is a singing child. When Russell is still sleeping, the caregiver asks Julian to sing quietly in another part of the room.

Different techniques to control an infant's behavior are effective at different ages. In the first few months, if you do not want an infant to play with a toy, you remove it and place it where the child cannot see it. Because infants respond only to objects they can see, the child thinks the toy does not exist anymore.

In the second year you can distract an infant's attention with a different object. Show the child another toy, book, or object.

At some point the young child grows too old to be distracted. Try then to substitute objects. When Viki is using a book to pound everything around her, trade her a block for the book and direct her to the place and materials she can use to pound.

> There are many different positive and negative control procedures. Positive techniques consist of rewarding, praising, and supporting the child in desired activities; negative techniques are reflected in physical punishment, isolation, and withdrawal of love. . . . the use of positive techniques is associated with greater social adequacy and more desirable personality traits, and negative techniques are associated with poorer and less desirable performance and characteristics (Coopersmith 1967, 190–91).

The attitude of the caregiver is evident in the controls used. You can reflect positive attitudes, showing that the rules or decisions are necessary for the child's safety, assistance, or pleasure. A dictatorial "do this because I say so" gives children no information to use in learning to control their own behavior.

Internal Controls Internal controls of behavior are slow to develop in the young child. However, your management techniques can help children begin to exert their own controls on their behavior. You identify which decisions children may be able to make on their own and which ones you need to make.

Allowing children no initiative in controlling their behavior limits their experiences in developing necessary internal controls. Allowing children to make decisions when they do not have the necessary maturity or understanding of the situation places them in situations where they are likely to fail. Only give choices when you actually intend to abide by the child's choice. If you ask, "Do you want to take a nap now?" when you mean "Everyone needs to rest now," you must be prepared to allow the child to stay up.

Facilitating

CDA
Ⅴ . 12

CDA
Ⅲ . 8–9

PROVIDER

As a facilitator the caregiver is involved with the whole child.

Nurturance Caregivers provide nurturance, love, concern, and attention (see Figure 5–5). You provide encouragement for all categories of the child's

Figure 5–5 The caregiver provides nurturing attention to the waking child.

behavior. You respond to the children, helping them learn about themselves and their world. You provide comments which may be evaluative or reinforcing.

Assistance Caregivers provide assistance to infants and toddlers, who need help with many tasks. You help them with tasks they cannot accomplish alone (unbutton) and with tasks they can accomplish if they have a little help from you (you turn on the water when they can wash their own hands).

Information Caregivers provide information which children cannot get on their own. You are their main storehouse of knowledge while they are with you. One of the most difficult tasks as a provider of information is to determine what children can or cannot learn by listening to you. In addition, you can encourage children to use a variety of materials and to learn from first-hand experiences. These facilitate children's self-discovery so they may construct their own knowledge base.

Questioner The caregiver is a questioner. You raise questions to stimulate and clarify a child's thinking. The child answers through words or other activities. Ms. Yearwood points to the apple and asks, "What is this?" Eighteen-month-old Louise answers, "Apple." Eric, 25 months old, waves a twig with leaves on it and asks, "What is it?" Mr. Davis repeats the question, and Cassy answers, "Leaf, tree."

Interpreter The caregiver is an interpreter. Young children are involved in many experiences they do not understand. You interpret facts and feelings to them. "Sit up on your chair" may have several meanings: (1) get up into your chair; (2) sit up; don't lean over your plate; or (3) maybe you mean to get into the chair, sit up, and don't lean over your plate. The tone of your statement gives directives to the child regarding how you expect the statement to be interpreted.

You can select and develop other caregiver behaviors and strategies. Use the following list to stimulate your thinking of ways in which you can facilitate a child's development.

CDA
II . 5-6

accepts	engages	plays
allows	establishes	praises
arranges	exhibits	promotes
assists	explains	protects
attempts	extends	provides
attends	informs	questions
carries	interprets	reinforces
consults	introduces	shares
decides	involves	sings
discusses	listens	suggests
elaborates	modifies	supports
enables	participates	talks
encourages	plans	waits

COMMUNITY RESOURCES

CDA
IV . 11

Every community offers a variety of resources. The caregiver may need help in compiling and maintaining a list of resources.

Community resources serve several purposes. Some can be used in the daily program; some are good to use with children; and some are services which you refer parents to.

There are several sources of information relating to nutrition. The U.S. Dept. of Agriculture through its Food and Nutrition Services (Washington, D.C. 20250) has numerous bulletins and books presenting valuable ideas for lay people. Each state has a Cooperative Extension Service office in every county and a main office usually in the state's land grant university. Pediatricians, public health departments, and home economics nutrition specialists may provide flyers and bulletins. Printed materials are available on such topics as balanced diets, iron-fortified food, child obesity, and nutritious snacks.

CDA
I . 2

Many communities have resources regarding good health. A child's *pediatrician* is a primary source of information concerning the child's health and how to maintain it. A crucial aspect in infant and toddler care is the flow of information among pediatrician, parent, and caregiver. The pediatrician needs the observations of the parent and caregiver in order to provide accurate recommendations and diagnoses.

A pediatrician may serve as a health care consultant to a child care program, providing expertise to the staff, parents, and children. Pediatricians can contribute in a number of ways:

1. They may speak up as informed advocates on the quality of day care services in their community.
2. They may comment on day care educational materials, concepts, and programs.
3. They may provide care to children who are enrolled in day care.
4. They may be regular members of a health committee or board for one or more day care centers.
5. They may be employed full or part time by a large center or several centers as members of the health team. Their responsibilities would include "direct" services as well as health consultation to all staff from director to janitor.
6. They may act in an advisory capacity to state and local health, welfare, or education departments, and others who set standards for health in day care centers (American Academy of Pediatrics 1980, 50–51).

Public health nurses may be on the staff of local or county health departments. They serve several functions which affect families and child care programs. They are involved in health education programs which provide information through meetings, literature, and the media. They assist in communicable disease prevention through immunization programs. They provide information and guidance in setting up and maintaining a healthy and safe environment. Public health nurses may be available for on-site visits to provide information, in-service training, or to help caregivers analyze specific health problems.

Well-child clinics provide services to children and families to foster and maintain health. Developmental examinations, immunizations, and health education information enable the physician and parent to regularly assess the child's development and to determine whether specific changes or assistance are needed to facilitate the child's health. Well-child clinics are provided by a number of facilities: hospitals, pediatric groups, health departments, churches, and nonprofit agencies. Determine whether well-child clinics are needed or available to children in your care.

Child abuse and neglect identification is increasing. Attention to child abuse and neglect is long overdue. In the last few years governmental and professional organizations have become increasingly active in research and public information programs. Caregivers and parents need this information to assess their own situations to ensure that their behavior is neither abusive nor neglectful.

A public information campaign is helping to lessen the public stigma and to enable the adult to seek needed help. County departments of health, mental health, social services, or day care services can provide information and referrals for those who need it. Some communities have a crisis center or a telephone hot line to call for urgent assistance. Nationally, help is also available.

By law many states require that all incidents of child abuse or neglect be reported; social agencies or the police are designated to process these reports. As a caregiver you must obey the law and provide needed information. Wood has provided guidelines for reporting procedures for day care programs:

1. Staff members who observe abuse or neglect
    a. do not discuss it with other staff members
    b. do not question the child
    c. do report it to the director
    d. do make a written report with dates and times and be very specific about what was observed.
2. The director
    a. makes the report
    b. accompanies the investigator if the investigator sees the child at the center (1981, 44).

The caregiver can help to improve conditions for the child and the parent.

When an abused or neglected child is enrolled in a regular child care program, Haugen suggests that some daily individual attention be programmed for the child. Screening tools, followed by assessment and further observation, can help determine the child's needs. Parental involvement should be encouraged too. She suggests if staff can gain the parents' trust, they may be able to refer the parents to appropriate resources for help with family problems (Samples 1981, 47).

Emergency care is sometimes needed. Several organizations have printed posters which provide information on simple first aid procedures you might use with a child. One is the chart prepared by the Committee on Accident Prevention and the Subcommittee on Accidental Poisoning, American Academy of Pediatrics. First aid given at the day care home or center may be all that is needed for Molly's skinned knee. However, more severe cuts, head bumps, or ingestion of harmful substances require immediate referral to other help. At the time a child enrolls in day care, fill out an information card supplying the names of the child's physician and the hospital the parents choose if an emergency room visit is necessary. This card should stay beside the telephone for immediate access in an emergency. The rescue squad or ambulance service number should also be posted near the phone. Telephone numbers for the local hospital poison information center and the state Poison Control Center should be posted by the telephone. The Poison Control Center has a flyer which presents needed information for Poisoning Emergency Action. Refer to Chapter 3 for a listing of agencies which may have information and services to assist you and your child care program.

PROFESSIONAL PREPARATION OF THE CAREGIVER

Both informal and formal educational opportunities are available to caregivers.

Informal experiences may be spontaneous or planned. An article in a magazine may stimulate your thinking by providing new information and raising questions. You may take time to do further thinking and discuss your ideas with other staff, or you may think of the ideas periodically and begin changing your caregiving techniques to incorporate what you have learned.

Formal educational opportunities are those that are planned to meet specific needs. You choose experiences to help you gain desired knowledge and skill. The following types of experiences contribute to your learning either by using your experiences with children, independent study, or a combination of both.

- On-the-job training: You work under a more experienced caregiver, which gives you opportunities to observe, participate, and discuss techniques. It is organized, supervised, and evaluated; isolated work does not count.

- Workshops, seminars: These may be sponsored by adult schools, colleges, universities, and professional organizations. They usually focus on a single topic or skill.

- Speakers: Libraries, colleges, and hospitals may sponsor speakers.
- Short courses provided by local or state groups or agencies.
- Continuing education courses sponsored by local schools and colleges.
- Technical school courses and programs in child care.
- Junior and senior college courses and programs in child care.
- Child Development Associate: "The Child Development Associate, or CDA, is a person who is able to meet the specific needs of children and who, with parents and other adults, works to nurture children's physical, social, emotional, and intellectual growth in a child development framework. The CDA conducts herself or himself in an ethical manner" (CDA 1984).

The Council for Early Childhood Professional Recognition has designed both training and assessment systems, effective in 1990, for persons interested in the CDA credential. In their words, "one is designed for individuals who want only to have their skills evaluated and the other for individuals who wish to be trained" (Council for Early Childhood Professional Recognition 1988). For information contact:

Council for Early Childhood Professional Recognition
1718 Connecticut Avenue, N.W., Suite 500
Washington, D.C. 20009
phone: 202-265-9090 or 1-800-424-4310

The Child Development Associate (CDA) Competency Standards and assessment system for infant/toddler caregivers in center-based programs have been developed to support quality care for our youngest children by providing standards for training, evaluation, and recognition of infant/toddler caregivers based on their ability to meet the unique needs of this age group.

The special developmental characteristics of very young children require that their care in a group setting be different from that of older children for several reasons:

- Physical, social, emotional, and cognitive development are more interbirth and 3 years than during any other period in life.
- The younger child is more dependent on the caregiver—more vulnerable to adversity, less able to cope actively with discomfort or stress from without or within.
- Physical, social, emotional, and cognitive development are more interrelated for this age group than for older children and more dependent on a consistent relationship with an adult caregiver (CDA National Credentialing Program 1987, i).

REFERENCES

American Academy of Pediatrics. 1980. *Recommendations for Day Care Centers for Infants and Children.* Evanston, Illinois: Author.

Child Development Associate National Credentialing Program. 1984. *CDA Competency Standards and Assessment System for Infant/Toddler Caregivers.* Washington, D.C.: Author.

Child Development Associate National Credentialing Program. 1987. *Child Development Associate Assessment System and Competency Standards Infant/Toddler Caregivers in Center-Based Programs.* Washington, D.C.: Author.

Council for Early Childhood Professional Recognition. 1988. *Council Model for CDA Assessment and Training.* Washington, D.C.: Author.

Coopersmith, S. 1967. *The Antecedents of Self-Esteem.* San Francisco: W. H. Freeman.

Honig, A. S. & Lally, J. R. 1975. How good is your infant program? Use an observation method to find out. *Child Care Quarterly.* 4(3), Fall.

Infant Welfare Society of Evanston (Illinois) Inc. *Care Sheets.* Not dated.

Samples, P. 1981. Total family care for abusive families. *Day Care and Early Education.* 8(3): 44–47.

Spradley, J. P. 1980. *Participant Observation.* New York: Holt, Rinehart & Winston.

Wood, P. 1981. Helping maltreated children and their parents. *Day Care and Early Education.* 9(2): 43–45.

STUDENT ACTIVITIES

1. Identify your strengths and weaknesses in the caregiver roles. Write a growth plan for yourself.
2. Observe one infant and one toddler for ten minutes each. Use narrative description to record what you see and hear. Categorize the behaviors of each.
3. Using the record of Leslie in the playyard, list her behaviors using the following categories:
   a. physical
   b. emotional
   c. social
   d. cognitive
   e. language

4. Observe two caregivers, each for ten minutes. Tally a mark in the appropriate category each time you observe the caregiver assume that role.

	CAREGIVER 1	CAREGIVER 2

Observer
   Caregiver
   Self
Recorder
   Message Board
   Sheets, Notes
Assessor
   Caregiver
   Child
Organizer
   Plans
   Schedules
   Materials
   Environment
Manager
   Time
   Space
   Materials
   People
   Behavior
Facilitator
   Provider
      Nurturance
      Assistance
      Information
   Questioner
   Interpreter		

5. List four available community resources and explain how each can serve your child care program.

REVIEW

1. Why do you want to be a caregiver?
2. List four personal characteristics which you can use as a caregiver. Explain why each is important.
3. List three caregiver roles and give an example of each.

	CAREGIVER ROLE	EXAMPLE
1. 2. 3.		

4. How can you use observation in a child care program?
5. Identify who exerts control in the internal and external control of behavior.

6

What Is Development/ Learning?

THE WHOLE CHILD

It is crucial for the caregiver to know about and understand the developing child. You will apply this knowledge and understanding as you plan appropriate experiences for each child and develop your caregiver strategies.

Interrelatedness of the Child's Behaviors

The child is a whole person, a physical, emotional, social, and cognitive being. Sometimes we speak of children as though they are just a collection of little parts: Joey's feet are always moving; Takisha is still drooling; Becky pinches everything. To understand the whole child it is sometimes helpful to look at separate characteristics or areas of development. A part of the learning process is to understand the related effects of experiences on the whole child.

When Kevin falls down and skins his knee, it does more than just break the skin on his knee. His nerves send impulses to his brain which he interprets as pain (**physical** and **emotional**). His brain decides whether the pain is great or small (**physical, emotional,** and **social**). What he has learned about himself and his world influences his response to the pain after the initial surprise; he may scream, cry, whimper, or not say anything (**temperament** and **social**). Kevin decides whether he will stay down to wait for someone's attention or whether he will pick himself up and ask for help for his bleeding knee, or whether he will start playing again (**social** and **temperament**).

Interrelatedness of Interactions with Others

Jeffrey, 4½ months old, just had his diaper changed and is lying on the floor on his back looking around. Miss Vivian, the caregiver, rolls him over, and he sees 14½-month-old Neola sitting close by. He reaches out and touches her and stares at her hand. He kicks his feet. He touches her arm and kisses her hand. He watches her wriggle her fingers and keeps grabbing her arm. Neola watches him and sucks on her fingers. Jeffrey watches her hands. Neola leaves and Jeffrey looks around the room, kicking his feet, flapping his hands, giggling, and babbling. He sucks on his fingers and kicks his feet. When another child comes over and cuddles him, he smiles. Miss Vivian picks him up and rocks him, rubbing his back and talking quietly to him. He kicks his legs and flaps his arms as he babbles. He quiets and falls to sleep. Jeffrey, Neola and Miss Vivian are actively involved with each other, each initiating, responding, and enjoying one another. Looking stimulated touching and talking, touching stimulated kissing and kicking. They shared their enjoyment of each other by looking and touching, giggling, babbling, and talking.

From the moment of birth the child and the people around the child affect each other. This dynamic interaction is sometimes deliberate and controlled and sometimes unconscious behavior. Caregivers working with infants and toddlers plan many experiences for children. Simultaneous with these planned experiences are the literally thousands of actions which are spontaneous, which stimulate new actions and reactions and challenge both the child and the caregiver (see Figure 6–1).

 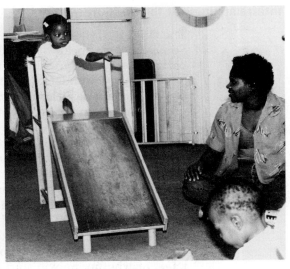

Figure 6-1 The child's need for spontaneous interactions stimulates and challenges the caregiver.

Figure 6-2 Knowing the child's level of development helps the caregiver feel comfortable when allowing the child to climb the stairs alone.

AREAS OF DEVELOPMENT AND LEARNING

CDA
VI . 13

Infants are born developing and learning. They are actively involved with themselves and the world. Development is more general and global; learning is specific. The child is constantly interacting with his world, making adjustments in his actions as he organizes and structures his behaviors.

Children's levels of physical, emotional, social, and cognitive development affect what they are ready to learn. Understanding the interrelationships among development, learning, and experience is the basis for providing high-quality care.

Physical Development

CDA
II . 4

Mary Lynn, 3 months old, sits in Ms. Annette's lap cooing and waving her arms. She smiles, grabs at Ms. Annette's nose, and listens to her talking. Ms. Annette lays Mary Lynn on the floor on her back and goes to another part of the room. Mary Lynn balls up a fist and sucks on it. She takes her fist out of her mouth and wrinkles up her face. Ms. Annette returns and plays with Mary Lynn, jiggling her leg and talking. Mary Lynn smiles, her tongue moving in and out of her mouth.

April, 19 months old, is riding her Big Wheel on the outdoor riding strip. She stands up, turns the bike around, gets on, and rides again. She runs into a trike, stands up, and moves the trike. She rides until she hits an object, and then stands up and turns the bike in different directions. She does not seem to be able to turn corners.

Mary Lynn and April are at different levels of physical development. Nevertheless, there are some similarities in their behaviors. Each is using her senses, muscular coordination, strength, and balance; each is actively moving in her world.

Newborns use all their senses: hearing, seeing, tasting, smelling, touching. During the first year their senses become physically developed; for example, their vision becomes similar to that of adults. Infants and toddlers then become involved in coordinating and controlling the use of their senses with their moving and thinking.

Movement develops in a predetermined order. The direction of the infant's physical development is from head to foot and from mid-body out to the limbs, the fingers, and the toes. This directional development is readily observable in infants as they gain control of their necks, then backs and legs to turn over, then lower backs and legs to crawl, and finally necks, shoulders, backs, legs, feet, and toes to walk.

Infants develop control of their arm movements from erratic waving to accurate reaching. Their hand control develops from bumping and hitting to touching. Their fingers develop from reflexive pinching, grasping, and reflexive releasing to controlled opening and closing to pick up small and large objects.

Movement is essential. Children must move to gain control over some of their movements. Three areas of movement for infants are (1) sitting and standing upright (stability); (2) crawling and walking (locomotion); and (3) reaching, grasping, and releasing (manipulation).

Basic manipulative, nonlocomotor, and locomotor movements provide the basis for skilled movements:

CDA
II . 4

Manipulative motor patterns
    grasping
    releasing
    flinging
    throwing
    rolling and trapping objects
    catching
    striking
    kicking
Nonlocomotor movements
    pushing
    pulling
    stretching
    curling
    swinging
    bending
    twisting

Locomotor movements
    crawling
    sliding
    walking
    running
    jumping
    hopping
    rolling
    climbing

During the first year of life infants grow more rapidly physically than they will for the rest of their lives. At birth the infant's head represents 20 to 25 percent of total body length compared to an adult's head, which represents about 10 percent of total body length (Lamb and Campos 1982, 29). In the first year the average infant triples birth weight. In the first two years the brain triples in bulk, "attaining 80 percent of its adult size" (Lamb and Campos 1982, 6). At birth the baby will have about twenty teeth growing inside the jaws. By 2½ all the baby teeth probably will have emerged (National Institute of Dental Research and the National Association of Community Health Centers, Inc. 1979). These phenomenal physical changes directly influence the curriculum for each child.

The chapters in Part III identify the sequence of physical development. Each child's Developmental Profile (see Appendix A) will show *similarities* in *sequence* and *variances* in the *rate* of physical development.

Emotional Development

Young children develop many feelings and emotions in the first years of life. They experience fear and anxiety, anger and hostility, jealousy, shame, affection and love, pleasure, joy, trust and security, and pride.

Newborns seem to have an unfocused excitement. In the next few years through their active involvement in their environment, they have pleasurable and nonpleasurable experiences. They tend to repeat pleasurable experiences. Their parents and caregivers provide a base of trust and security for them. Children move through emotions rapidly; one minute they may scream, "I hate you," yet the next minute jump into your arms, give you a big hug, and say, "I love you."

SECURITY AND TRUST

Consistent and appropriate behavior from the caregiver is necessary to provide security for the child. Consistent but inappropriate behavior or inconsistent but appropriate behavior in a particular situation may be detrimental. For example, Rose is just learning to wash her own hands. Ms. Miller carefully shows her what to do and patiently waits while Rose washes her own hands. Later, after lunch, Rose is rushed through the bathroom with time only to swish her hands under the faucet. Following the afternoon snack Rose comes out of the bathroom with banana still on her hands, and Ms. Miller scolds her for not taking time to get her hands clean.

Ms. Miller's behavior is neither consistent nor always appropriate. For Rose to learn and use the appropriate handwashing techniques which Ms. Miller has demonstrated, Rose needs consistent opportunities and assistance to use those techniques. Being permitted to just swish her hands after lunch confuses Rose about what proper handwashing is. When Rose is scolded after the snack for handwashing similar to what she did at lunch, when she did not get scolded, Rose is confused as to what is acceptable or unacceptable. In order for Rose to trust Ms. Miller, she needs Ms. Miller to behave consistently.

There need to be reasonable expectations of children. To have these reasonable expectations you need to know (1) normal patterns of development and (2) each child's individual pattern of development. Because the sequence of development is similar among children, you have some guidelines for your expectations. Because there is a range in the timing of development, you need to know where any particular child fits in that range (see Figure 6–2, page 108). If you expect children to accomplish things which are below or above them developmentally, it can produce undue stress. For example, you can expect 30-month-old Mark to be able to hold a spoon in his hand, fill it with food, and usually get it up to his mouth. You should not expect 9-month-old Naomi to have that level of muscular coordination.

Infants and toddlers depend upon their caregivers for many things. Caregivers who provide comfort and assistance help children learn that the caregiver, and thus a part of their world, can provide a secure place and can be trusted. Children who live in a world where their needs are ignored or only occasionally met will have difficulty building security and trust. One reason that caregivers have responsibility for fewer infants and toddlers than caregivers who work with older children is so that the caregivers will be available to respond to the many needs of each dependent infant or toddler.

Young children's temperaments, feelings of self-esteem, and coping skills are important factors in their emotional development.

TEMPERAMENT

Temperament has been defined as "the basic style which characterizes a person's behavior" (Chess, Thomas, and Birch 1965, 32). All children are born with particular temperaments. It will influence what they do, what they learn, what they feel about themselves and others, and what kinds of interactions they have with people and objects.

Chess, Thomas, and Birth worked with 231 children and their parents to investigate several questions. How do babies differ in their styles of behavior, their temperament? How does individual temperament develop? What role does it play in personality development? What part does the environment play in shaping of personality? Is the mother's approach to the baby fixed, or does the baby's temperament affect the mother's handling? What were the specific circumstances in which the child's behavior occurred? (1965).

Their analysis of hundreds of observations and interviews revealed nine patterns of behavior. Within each pattern they found a range of behaviors. The following examples show each end of the ranges. The behavior of most people falls somewhere in between these extremes.

Activity Level Ryan runs into the room, yells "Hi," and goes to the blocks. He stacks them quickly, they fall down, and he stacks again and leaves them as they tumble down. He walks over to stand by Barbara, the caregiver, who is reading a picture book to another child. Ryan listens a few minutes and then moves on to another activity. Ryan has a high activity level. He has always been very active. He kicked and waved and rolled a lot when he was a baby. His body needs to move. He becomes very distressed when he is physically confined with a seat belt in the car or must sit quietly.

Benjamin sits quietly on the floor playing with nesting cans. He stacks the cans and then fits them inside. He accomplishes his task with few movements: his legs remain outstretched; his body is leaning forward slightly but not rocking back and forth; he has the cans close to him so his arms and hands need limited movement. Benjamin has a low activity level. He was a quiet baby, not kicking his blankets off or twisting and turning often. He becomes distressed when he has to rush around to put away toys or quickly get ready to go somewhere.

Regularity Valeria may act like she is hungry for her first bottle at 9:00 one morning, not until 10:00 the next day, and at 8:30 the third morning. Her bowel movements occur at no regular times. Valeria's body is having difficulty establishing its biological time clock for eating, sleeping, and eliminating. She has an unpredictable body schedule.

Sarina has a bowel movement every morning at about 9:00, takes a bottle at about 9:30, and then takes a 1½ hour nap. Sarina has a well-established body schedule.

Approach or Withdrawal as a Characteristic Response to a New Situation David hides behind his mother as he enters the room each morning. He hides behind the caregiver whenever someone strange walks in the door. He stands by the wall and watches others play with the new ball. He leaves food he does not recognize on his plate, refusing to take a bite. David is slow to warm up. He needs time to get used to new situations. David is distressed when he is pushed into new activities. Being told that a new ball will not hurt him or that the strange food is good for him does not convince him. When he feels comfortable, he will play with the new ball. He needs time and space for himself while he becomes familiar with a situation.

Ricky arrives in the morning with a big smile. He looks around the room and notices a new puzzle set out on the table. He rushes over to it, asking the caregiver about it and giggling at the picture. He takes the puzzle pieces out, puts some of the pieces back in and then seeks assistance from the caregiver. Ricky warms up quickly. He is excited about new situations and eager to try new experiences.

Adaptability to Change in Routine Brenda is used to snack time at the table. She knows how to get her hands washed, seat herself, enjoy her snack with her friends, and then wash her hands and go play. Today the caregiver has planned a surprise. She takes the children out into a corner of the play yard and serves a special snack. Brenda is upset because this new place for snack is different from what she is used to. Brenda fusses and will not eat her snack. Brenda follows routines well and finds security in their consistency. She has difficulty making adjustments when a routine is changed.

Nancy is delighted with having a surprise snack outdoors. She also adjusts quickly when the books are changed to a different shelf and the home living center is moved to a different part of the room. Nancy adapts well to changes. She takes them in stride and focuses on the experiences rather than the changes in routine.

Level of Sensory Threshold Greg is bothered by light when he is trying to go to sleep or is sleeping, so the caregiver holds a blanket to shield his eyes as she rocks him to sleep. Greg awakens when a door is quietly closed. Greg is very sensitive to noise, light, and pain. He is easily bothered by what others believe are mild sounds and light.

Allen "sleeps through anything." He can sleep in the same room with children who are playing. He does not need the room darkened. When he falls and bumps himself, he often does not even whimper. Allen has a high tolerance for sound, light, and pain. Sometimes the caregiver has to check his injuries to see if he needs help, since he may not realize his needs.

Positive or Negative Mood Angela looks at the toy shelf and says she does not like toys. She plays with a toy dog and complains about his tail. Angela's negative mood characterizes the way she views familiar experiences.

Gayle looks at the toy shelf and sees many toys she likes. She plays with a cat which has lost one eye and is limp from children's pinching fingers. Gayle loves the cat; she croons to it and cuddles it. Gayle tends to look on life positively. She is positive until something happens to hurt or anger her.

Intensity of Response Arturo has just put a lock block together and turning to the caregiver he excitedly screams in her face, "Look! Look!" His response to his achievement shows up in his loud voice and his wriggling body. When Arturo cries, he cries loudly. When he talks, he talks loudly. Arturo uses a high level of energy to express himself. He puts himself fully into his response.

Carlos has just put some people into his lock-blocks car and is pushing the car around. He has a smile on his face and is humming. He stops by the caregiver, points to the people, and excitedly says, "Daddy!" Carlos uses a low level of energy in expressing his excitement. His smiling, humming, and words show he is happy and excited, but his responses are quiet. He talks quietly and he cries quietly.

Distractibility Tamela is dropping blocks into a plastic jar. She sees Sheri go by, pushing a buggy. Tamela stops putting in blocks and walks over to push another buggy. She walks by the caregiver, who is reading a book to Stacy. Tamela stops to listen for a few minutes and then, noticing Carolyn sliding, she goes to the slide and slides. Tamela is very distractible. She plays with something or does something she is interested in until another activity catches her attention. Then she leaves her activity to move on to the activity that has attracted her attention.

Geraldine is building a block structure. Two other children are building their own block structures. Geraldine reaches for and places the blocks she wants, occasionally looking at the others playing with blocks or glancing around the room. She notices other activities, but she concentrates her attention on her own activity with blocks. Geraldine can maintain a high level of concentration. She can continue a task even when other activities are occurring around her.

Persistence and Attention Span Gene takes the three puzzle pieces out of the puzzle. He successfully puts in the banana. He picks up the apple piece and tries to fit it into a space. When it does not fit, he drops the piece and leaves the table. Gene gives up when he is not immediately successful. He does not keep trying.

Clayton takes the three puzzle pieces out of the puzzle. He then turns and pushes and turns and pushes each piece until he has returned all three pieces to their proper places. Clayton persists with an activity even when it may be challenging or frustrating or takes a long time. When he completes his task, he expresses his pleasure with smiles and words.

All people have temperament traits. Temperament behaviors can be modified but not changed drastically. Very physically active people will never become very physically quiet. As they develop, they can make adjustments and modifications to reduce and control their outer actions, but internally they still have a high need for movement.

Caregivers must identify each child's temperament as well as their own. For example, Olaf is playing with blocks. The tall stack he built falls over, one block hitting hard on his hand. He yells loudly. Ray is playing nearby and also is hit by a falling block. He looks up in surprise but does not say anything. What will you do? What will you say? What is "loud" to you? What is acceptable to you? Why is a behavior acceptable or not acceptable to you? Do you think Ray is "better" than Olaf because he did not react loudly? What you do and what you say to Olaf reflects your acceptance or rejection of him as a person, reflects whether you are able to help him adapt to his environment, and reflects your ability to adapt to the child.

Caregivers can help infants and toddlers make small adjustments in their temperament behaviors. And caregivers should consciously make some adjustments for their own temperaments. For example, since Benjamin has a low activity level, you can advise him to begin putting toys away several minutes before you expect him to complete the task. You adjust a little by giving him extra time, and he adjusts a little by working slightly faster than he might have.

SELF-ESTEEM

Self-esteem has been defined as "the evaluation which the individual makes and customarily maintains with regard to himself: it expresses an attitude of approval or disapproval, and indicates the extent to which the individual believes himself to be capable, significant, successful, and worthy. In short, self-esteem is a *personal* judgment of worthiness that is expressed in the attitudes the individual holds toward himself" (Coopersmith 1967, 4–5).

Summarizing his data on childhood experiences which contribute to the development of self-esteem, Coopersmith related, "The most general statement about the antecedent of self-esteem can be given in terms of three conditions: total or near total *acceptance* of the children by their parents, clearly defined and enforced *limits;* and the *respect* and latitude for individual actions that exist within the defined limits" (1967, 236). It is important that children think they are worthy people. Coopersmith's three conditions for fostering self-esteem—acceptance, limits, respect—provide guidelines for caregivers.

Acceptance Each child needs to feel accepted for who he or she is right now. Children need to feel worthy and appreciated. For adults to focus on what children ought to be or what they may become can give children the impression that they are not all right. What children build on for the future is their sense of being all right now. Caregivers can encourage the children to demonstrate acceptance of the other children.

Limits Adults set boundaries on behavior to help infants and toddlers learn to live safely and acceptably in their world. Society has rules. Some are physical: play in the yard, not in the street (to keep from physical harm). Some are interpersonal: you play with your doll and Greta will play with hers (possession, ownership—temporary in this case).

The boundaries set for children must fit their developmental level and be observed consistently. For example, both Yolanda and Theresa have difficulty sharing, so the caregiver does not force one to share her airplane with the other. All the children have been told, however, that when someone is playing with a toy, no one else is to take it. Therefore, when Yolanda grabs the airplane Theresa is playing with, the caregiver reaches in to hold the airplane still while she reminds Yolanda about taking a toy someone else is playing with.

Respect Ralph is playing with a tractor. He must play with it in the space away from children building with blocks. Miss Jana watches him push his tractor around in a circle, push it under a chair and bring it out the other side, lift it to climb the side and seat of the chair and down the other side. Miss Jana allows Ralph to explore with his tractor. He is not hurting the tractor or the chair as he moves the tractor under and over the chair. Miss Jana does not force Ralph to be realistic, that is, to recognize that tractors don't really drive over chairs. She allows him to use his fantasies and his explorations.

STRESS

Many situations may distress the child in child care. Some of these are

- separation from the parent
- adjustment to another caregiver
- adjustment to different surroundings (room, children, materials)
- developmental changes, e.g., later naptime (such changes should change caregiver's behavior)
- adjustment to developmental changes, e.g., walking allows child to move into areas which may be dangerous
- conflicts and anxieties from home, e.g., illness, divorce, death, abuse
- over- or under-stimulation

Everyone encounters stress. Caregivers can plan ways to reduce stressful situations and to assist infants and toddlers and parents in coping with stress.

COPING

Coping means learning how to make adjustments and adaptations and causing others to do so. Infants from birth make adjustments to their life situations. They adjust themselves to heat, cold, wetness, and hunger. They express their pleasure or displeasure by smiling, cooing, squirming, and crying. They learn that their behavior—cooing, crying—can affect their wetness and hunger. What started as unplanned reactions become planned and controlled actions to get assistance. The infant is adjusting to a situation —wetness—by tolerating wetness for longer periods of time and by calling attention to his or her displeasure at being wet.

Through her research with young children, Murphy identified the coping tasks of infancy. In infancy and the early years the following major tasks face the child:*

1. Managing the various basic bodily functions, breathing, feeding, eliminating, sleeping, etc., and the drives which evolve from them.
2. Persistent day-by-day dealing with the stimulation from the environment, especially that associated with newness, pain, and over-stimulation;

*Reprinted by permission from Lois Barclay Murphy, *The Widening World of Childhood* (New York: Basic Books, 1962).

as part of this, strong stimuli; developing ways of using the environment, dealing with the opportunities and frustrations it offers, and developing a capacity for deriving and contributing pleasure.

3. Coping with periodic challenges rising from "developmental crises" or "critical phases" at times of maturation of new functions, or major shifts in the relation of the child to the environment (such as weaning) as he gets older.

4. Mastering special impacts, traumata, or threats to integration from illness, accidents, and the like.

5. Learning to use all of his resources to move, both autonomously and with help, toward his goals and toward mutually gratifying exchanges with the environment.

6. Becoming a member of his culture who can deal with the deepest feelings and conflicts involved in relationships with the parent of each sex and with siblings and peers and can communicate and participate in play and work (1962, 293).

Social Development

SELF AND NOT SELF

Infants and toddlers are egocentric. They understand the world only from their own perspective. They think that when they hurt a finger, everyone feels the hurt the way they do. They think that when they say "Dink," everyone knows exactly what they mean. They do not understand that there are other points of view.

Infants are learning about themselves. In the process of learning about self, they learn about "not self." During the first year one major development is that children construct knowledge about themselves.

Recognition of one's physical self develops gradually during the first eighteen months. For example, Brian is touching the face on the mirror. Mrs. Larsen points to the child in the mirror and says, "Who is that?" Brian smiles and says, "Brian." Brian was able to match his mental image of when he looked at himself in the mirror before with what he now sees in the mirror. In the first year infants relate to their mirror image as though it is someone else. By 18 months of age toddlers identify themselves in the mirror.

The continuing development of the concept of self is evident in the child's language. The pronouns *I, me, my, mine* represent one's own point of view. *You* refers to someone else. Young children must learn that when they use the words *I, me, my, mine*, each means that particular child, and *you* is someone else. When children hear someone saying, "I want you to sit down in your chair," they must learn that the "I" is the person who spoke and the "you" means that particular child. In other words, each child is "someone else" to the other person. As children construct the concept of self and others, they generalize these language usage rules even though they could not state the rules. Their language reflects their level of understanding about themselves and others. Many 2-year-olds have difficulty with personal pronouns.

INTERACTIONS WITH OTHERS

The children in Lynn's day care home are playing on the floor of the den. Andy, 16 months old, walks up to Cameron, almost 4, who is lying on the floor. Andy smiles, pats Cameron's back, and lies on top of him, humming. Andy rolls off Cameron and holds his legs in the air. He pulls on Cameron's belt loops and rolls up beside Cameron. Cameron is giggling and gives Andy a big hug. Andy is showing affection for Cameron, and Cameron is showing affection for Andy. Each is constructing a value of himself by feeling the affection of the other person toward him. The young child's sense of self is related to his experiences with others (see Figure 6–3).

Attachment Fourteen-month-old Louise is walking in the yard carrying a small truck in her hand. She sees Randy, the caregiver, and squeals and giggles. She walks rapidly to Randy with arms up and a big smile on her face. Attachment is the special, close relationship that develops between the infant and an adult. The attachment relationship provides security for infants as they encounter new experiences in their world.

A strong attachment develops out of lots of looking into each other's eyes, touching, stroking, and cuddling; it comes from rapid and consistent response to the infant's cries, and by the infant's picking up cues from the adult that the adult feels the infant has worth and is someone special. When the adult, whether parent or caregiver, responds quickly and appropriately to the infant's needs, e.g., for food, for touching, for comforting, the infant builds up trust in that adult.

Attachment to the mother and caregiver affects what the infant does later on. Strong attachment has a positive influence on infants' confidence and effectiveness in relating to their world.

Most research regarding attachment has examined infants and their mothers. This research has produced several ideas which relate also to the infant-caregiver relationships.

1. Each infant needs to establish an emotional attachment with one caregiver. This attachment can be developed through regular care activities like feeding and changing diapers as well as in special times of cuddling, crooning, looking, touching.

   The primary caregiver should provide much of the physical contact, should learn a particular infant's needs, schedule, likes and dislikes, temperament, and should act in ways which comfort that particular infant when distressed, which stimulate the infant, and which respond to the infant's preferences.

   When more than one caregiver is responsible for a group of infants, the infant's care may be shared with other caregivers. The primary

Figure 6-3 Young children value themselves when they know other children like them.

caregiver can share her knowledge about the infant's needs and preferences so other caregivers may match their care to the infant. These caregivers should report observations of the infant's behavior to the primary caregiver. The primary caregiver thus has two unique responsibilities: (a) establishing special attachment with the infant, and (b) gathering, coordinating, and sharing information with other caregivers and the infant's parents.

2. Each infant needs to have a caregiver respond quickly and consistently to his or her cries or cues of distress. The infant learns to trust the caregiver. When crying infants are left alone for several minutes before a caregiver checks to see what they need, or when the caregiver responds to their cries sometimes and leaves them alone sometimes, infants may have difficulty establishing a strong attachment to the caregiver because it may be difficult for them to develop a strong sense of trust. Responding to infants does not spoil them. The most important task an infant has now is to develop trust in and attachment with the caregiver. For this to happen, the caregiver must respond quickly and consistently to the infant's needs.

3. The infant and the primary caregiver need special time to be together. This "getting to know you" time and "let's enjoy each other" time is a calm, playful time to relax, look, touch, smile, giggle, cuddle, stroke, talk, whisper, sing, make faces, and carry out all the other special activities infants use. Sometimes this may be a very active time, e.g., holding the infant up in the air at arm's length and talking and giggling and then bringing the infant almost face-to-face and talking and giggling. Other times it may be very quiet, e.g., rocking the infant, cuddling, and softly stroking the infant's arms, legs, back while not talking at all (see Figure 6–4).

4. The caregiver must like the infant as a special, important person. Infants pick up cues which show that you like or dislike them. They can pick up cues which reflect that you think they either have or do not have worth as a person. Infants are not objects to be taken care of; they are individuals of worth with whom you establish an emotional relationship as well as provide for their physical, emotional, social, and intellectual needs.

LOCUS OF CONTROL

CDA

III . 10

The culture in which we live expects us to behave in appropriate ways. These expectations are passed on to infants by their families, their caregivers, and their peers. In order to live in a world of other people, young children's behavior must be controlled. Some of the control is external and some is internal.

External Controls Adults control the infant's feeding. Infants give cues to indicate when they are hungry. At one time adults set the feeding time in a rigid schedule. If infants were hungry before the scheduled time, they were left to cry until the clock said it was time to eat. Pediatricians now recommend that adults follow the infant's internal clock for feeding time. When the infant gives adults hunger cues, adults supply the food.

Each infant has individual sleep needs. In a day care home or day care center, sleep needs must be coordinated with the sleeping and awake times of other children. Caregivers should focus control on providing sufficient space and time for some infants to sleep while others may be awake. Blankets around cribs, dividers, and area lighting can help separate the sleepers. A misuse of control is to arbitrarily change the infant's sleeping time to fit into the caregiver's schedule. The 12-month-old has increasing hours of wakefulness but may still need a morning nap. Keeping one child awake all morning because no one else in the infant room takes a morning nap creates stress in that infant.

Early external controls also focus on the infant's movement. Restrictive clothing, cribs, playpens, and walkers keep children from moving how and where they want to. Some restrictions may be for the child's benefit (safety), and some may be for the benefit of the adult (to keep the child and toys in a playpen instead of scattered all over the floor). Adults may be tempted to use controls which benefit themselves, but sometimes these are too re-

Figure 6-4 The caregiver spends special time with each child to look, touch, cuddle, and talk.

strictive and harmful for the child. It may be handy for the adult to have four playpens, one for each infant and that child's toys. But infants need **space** to move in for their muscular development and coordination, and they need **stimulation** from the novelty and variety made possible by moving around a room touching, pulling, tasting, and throwing different objects in different positions and locations.

Internal Controls Two-year-old Sara asks for a glass of orange juice. When Ms. Brewer, the caregiver, says, "Yes, here's a glass of orange juice," and turns to the counter to get it, Sara starts screaming. Sara needs her desires met immediately—the instant she has stopped talking. Even though the caregiver's words say "Yes," it still takes her a few seconds to get the glass to where Sara can see it. Sara has not learned to "wait." After Sara has expressed her desire, she must control her feelings and actions. Instead of instant gratification, she now has to "hold" for those few seconds. Waiting

CDA
III . 10

or delaying gratification is a very frustrating process. In the early childhood years the child slowly increases his "wait" time, but each desire is tested in each new situation.

During the first two years of life the infant gradually identifies causality, that an action causes something to happen. As infants construct this cause-and-effect relationship, they also must learn to distinguish between what they cause and what others cause. When infants learn that they can cause actions, they gain some power to control what they will do and when they will do it. They can use this newly developed power both positively and negatively to control themselves and their environment.

The struggle to control one's behavior is a continuing process. Young children see a world full of objects they want and places they want to go. They think everyone should agree with their desires, and these desires direct much of their behavior.

Fraiberg tells a story showing the struggle the young child has in putting controlling words into self-controlling behavior.

> Thirty-month-old Julia finds herself alone in the kitchen while her mother is on the telephone. A bowl of eggs is on the table. An urge is experienced by Julia to make scrambled eggs. She reaches for the eggs, but now the claims of reality are experienced with equal strength. Her mother would not approve. The resulting conflict within the ego is experienced as "I want" and "No, you mustn't" and the case for both sides is presented and a decision arrived at within the moment. When Julia's mother returns to the kitchen, she finds her daughter cheerfully plopping eggs on the linoleum and scolding herself sharply for each plop, "NoNoNo. Mustn't dood it. NoNoNo. MUSTN'T dood it!" (1959, 135).

Independence After the first months of dependence infants become competent to do some tasks by themselves. The 1- and 2-year-old child also **wants** to do things independently. This assertion of independence is an important step.

Young children are happy accomplishing tasks by themselves. However, the desire for independence also causes frustration. Children sometimes want to do something that is unsafe or for which they are not physically able. Their judgment may not match the difficulty or danger of the task. Their internal desires and controls help them decide what they want to do and help them achieve their tasks. However, they also need assistance from others who exert external control for the children's safety and to help them achieve their intentions.

Control of one's own or others' behavior is an area requiring continuing adjustments. The dependent infant soon becomes a toddler vigorously asserting his or her independence. The caregiver must seek a balance of doing some things for the child, assisting the child to do other things, and in allowing the child to do yet other things all by him- or herself. The child's assertion of independence is healthy, but the child is not always knowledgeable and wise. The caregiver must therefore decide what is best to help the child accomplish tasks which reinforce the child's feelings of worth and competence.

CDA
III . 9

Knowing that the infant will gain competence in walking by trying to walk, the caregiver can provide space and allow the infant to try to walk unassisted. The caregiver must give the infant opportunities to stand up, fall down, stand up, step, and fall down. That way the infant takes control of learning to walk. The caregiver helps by providing space where the infant will not get hurt when falling and by encouraging and comforting the infant in his or her persistent efforts.

Caregivers must guard against allowing their own desires for neatness and order to unduly limit the child's experiences. For example, toddlers want to feed themselves. In the process of developing the necessary muscular control and concentration on the task of feeding, toddlers may drop much food on the floor, table, and self; they may spill their milk, juice, etc., many times; they may get food in their hair, in the caregiver's hair, and in anybody else's hair when they flip the food out of their spoons. You can help children feed themselves by helping them focus on their task, by providing food which is easily transportable in a spoon, and by providing a small yet adequate amount of food for them to eat so they can successfully accomplish their task. It delays development and limits toddlers' feelings of independence, worth, and competence if you do not allow them to feed themselves just so you will have no mess at mealtime.

Cognitive Development

Young children think differently from adults. Adults are *logical* thinkers; they consider facts, analyze relationships, and draw conclusions. Young children are *pre-logical* thinkers; their conclusions may be based on incomplete or inaccurate understandings of their experiences. For example, 2½-year-old Ivan has made a tilting stack of blocks. When he places a small car on top of the blocks, the stack tumbles down. Ivan tells Mrs. Young that the car broke the blocks. Ivan does not understand about gravity, about the need to stack blocks straight up rather than at a tilt, and about why the car's rolling wheels may have started the car's movement downhill. The object Ivan put on the stack just before it fell was the car, so as far as Ivan is concerned, the car broke the blocks.

Jean Piaget's research contributed significantly to the knowledge of cognitive development in young children. A brilliant young scientist, Piaget began his studies as a biologist. Later, listening to children respond to questions on an intelligence test, he became intrigued by their incorrect responses and the patterns of the children's verbal reasoning. Combining his scientific orientation, his knowledge of biology, and his experiences with the children's incorrect response patterns, Piaget began to study children's cognitive development. Piaget's clinical observation method included close observations of his own three young children as well as many other children in his extensive subsequent research. He observed what the children did and wrote narrative descriptions, including the date, the participants, and the actions. Later, analyzing these detailed observations, he developed his theories of cognitive development.

STAGES OF COGNITIVE DEVELOPMENT

Central to Piaget's theory is that there are stages of cognitive development. That is, 4-month-olds are cognitively different from 24-month-olds.

Piaget contended that the sequence of development is the same for all children. However, the age and rate at which it occurs differs from child to child.

Piaget's first two stages of cognitive development involve children between birth and three years of age. These stages, the sensorimotor stage and the beginning of the preoperational stage, are those aspects of cognitive development relevant to an infant and toddler curriculum. Part III of this book includes detailed information about and suggested experiences to match with the child's level of cognitive development.

Sensorimotor Stage The sensorimotor stage of cognitive development occurs from birth to about age two. Piaget identified six substages.

CDA
II . 5

Substage 1: Reflex
Reflex actions become more organized.
Directed behavior emerges.
Birth to approximately 1 month.

Substage 2: Differentiation
Repeats own actions.
Begins to coordinate actions, for example, hearing and looking.
Approximately 1–4 months.

Substage 3: Reproduction
Intentionally repeats interesting actions.
Approximately 4–8 months.

Substage 4: Coordination
Intentionally acts as a means to an end.
Develops concept of object permanence (an object exists even when the infant cannot see it).
Approximately 8–12 months.

Substage 5: Experimentation
Experiments through trial and error.
Searches for new experiences.
Approximately 12–18 months.

Substage 6: Representation
Carries out mental trial and error.
Develops symbols.
Approximately 18–24 months.

Preoperational Stage The early part of the preoperational stage is called the **preconceptual** stage. The preconceptual substage occurs from about 2 to 4 years of age.

The child can now mentally sort events and objects. With the development of object permanence the child is moving toward representing objects and actions in his thinking without having to have actual sensorimotor experiences. The development and structuring of these mental representations are the tasks during the preoperational stage of cognitive development.

Preconceptual substage: Mentally sort objects and actions

Mental symbols partly detached from experience

Nonverbal classification
  graphic collections
    focus on figurative properties
    own interpretations
  no consistent classes of objects
  no hierarchy of classes
Seriation
  no consistent ordering of series of objects
Verbal preconcepts
  meanings of words fluctuate, are not always the same for child
  meanings of words are private, based on own experience
  word names and labels tied to one class
  focus on one attribute at a time—not class inclusion
Verbal reasoning
  transductive reasoning—from particular to particular
  if one action is in some way like another action, both actions are alike
    in all ways
  generalizes one situation to all situations
  reasoning sometimes backward—from effects to causes
  reasoning focuses on one dimension
Quantity
  How much?
  some, more, gone, big
Number
  How many?
  more, less
Space
  Where?
  use guess and visual comparison
  up, down, behind, under, over
Time
  remember sequence of life events
  now, soon, before, after (Cowen 1978).

CDA
II . 5

DEVELOPMENT AND LEARNING

Piaget studied the interrelatedness of intelligence, development, and learning, and he made a distinction between development and learning.

Cognitive Functions Piaget identified processes and functions in thinking. When you solve a problem, you have that feeling, "I understand it!" Piaget calls this **equilibration,** a cognitive balance. This cognitive balance may be only momentary. Soon you may see, hear, touch, taste, smell, or mentally think of something which presents additional information which your mind seeks to process; this is called **disequilibrium.** If the additional information fits something you already know, you **assimilate** it into your concepts. If it does not quite fit, you must make **accommodations.** All people use these processes and functions.

For example, Shane is looking around and notices a ball on the floor. As he crawls to it, he bumps the ball so the ball rolls. He crawls to it again, picks up the ball, looks at it, licks it, and puts it down on the floor (see Figure 6–5).

Figure 6–5 The child touches and moves the toy and watches to see what happens.

Shane started out in seeming equilibrium; that is, he seemed settled and quiet. Something caused disequilibrium; that is, something stimulated him. Shane responded to seeing the ball. What he saw may match in some way with what he has seen before in previous play with a ball. He may have assimilated some idea about the ball. When he bumped the ball and it rolled, he was presented with additional information about the ball which did not fit into his present concept. Therefore, through accommodation he makes adjustments in his concept of "ball" to now include the rolling movement. His disequilibrium is over, and he once again for an instant has attained equilibration, a sense of balance, of understanding his world. These processes or functions—assimilation, accommodation, and equilibration— occur continually through life.

Cognitive Structures Shane's actions also show one of the **structures** of intelligence. Shane constructs concepts or **schema** as his mind organizes or structures its experiences. The schema or concept of ball is constructed as Shane sees, touches, holds, and tastes a ball. When he sees the ball roll, that does not fit into his schema or structure of ball-ness. He continues to construct his knowledge of ball-ness by reorganizing his schema so that now rolling is included in ball-ness. Shane's schema of ball today is different from his schema yesterday, when he had never seen a rolling ball. Individual experiences and behavior bring about changes in schema.

KNOWLEDGE

Constructing Knowledge Young children construct knowledge about themselves and their world. They cannot copy knowledge. They must act on their own and construct their own meaning. Each of their actions and interpretations is unique to them. They see an object and construct thoughts about that object. Young children's thinking organizes information about their experiences so they can construct their own understanding.

Types of Knowledge Piaget identified three types of knowledge: physical knowledge, logico-mathematical knowledge, and social-arbitrary knowledge.

Physical knowledge is knowledge children discover in the world around them. Twenty-five-month-old Tommy kicks a piece of pinestraw as he walks in the play yard. He picks up the pinestraw, throws it, and picks it up again. He drops it in the water tray, picks it up, and pulls it through the water. Tommy has discovered something about pinestraw from the pinestraw itself. Tommy uses actions and observations of the effects of his actions on the pinestraw to construct his physical knowledge of pinestraw.

Kamii and DeVries have identified two kinds of activities involving physical knowledge: movement of objects and changes in objects. **Actions to move objects** include "pulling, pushing, rolling, kicking, jumping, blowing, sucking, throwing, swinging, twirling, balancing, and dropping" (1978, 6). The child causes the object to move and observes it rolling, bouncing, crack-

(CDA II.5)

ing, etc.   The authors suggest four criteria for selecting activities to move objects:

1. The child must be able to produce the movement by his or her own action.
2. The child must be able to vary his or her action.
3. The reaction of the object must be observable.
4. The reaction of the object must be immediate (1978, 9).

A second kind of activity involves **changes in objects.** As compared to a ball which, when kicked, will move but still remain a ball, some objects **change.** When Kool-Aid is put in water, it changes. Ann sees the dry Kool-Aid and observes that something happens when it is added to water. She can no longer see anything that looks like the dry Kool-Aid. She sees the water change color and can taste the difference between water without Kool-Aid and water with Kool-Aid in it. Her observation skills (seeing and tasting) are most important to provide her feedback of the changes that occur.

Logico-mathematical knowledge is invented by the child and involves relationships of objects.

Figure 6-6 The caregiver shares books which provide pictures, language, and stories.

Andrea is in the sandbox playing with two spoons, a teaspoon and a serving spoon. She notices the spoons are "different." Though they fit into her schema of "spoon," she notices some difference in **size**. Thus, in relationship to size, they are different. At some time someone will label these differences for her as different or bigger or smaller than the other, but these words are not necessary for her to construct her concepts of sizes.

Social-arbitrary knowledge is knowledge a child cannot learn by him- or herself. It comes from "actions on or interactions with other people. Language, values, rules, morality, and symbol systems are examples of social-arbitrary knowledge" (Wadsworth 1978, 52) (see Figure 6–6).

Chad is eating a banana. He bites it, sucks on it, swallows it, looks at the remaining banana, and squeezes it. All of these are concrete actions which help him construct his physical knowledge of this object. Then someone tells him this object is a banana. The name, **banana**, is social-arbitrary knowledge. It could have been called "ningina" or "lalisa," but everyone using the English language uses "banana" to name that object.

Here is another example of social-arbitrary knowledge. Kurt follows Mrs. Wesley into the storage room. She sees him and says, "Kurt, go back into our room right now. You are not supposed to be in this room." Kurt did not make the decision that it is not permissible for him to be in the storage room; someone else decided and told him the rule.

REFERENCES

Chess, S., Thomas, Al., and Birch, H. G. 1965. *Your Child is a Person.* New York: Parallex.

Coopersmith, S. 1967. *The Antecedents of Self-Esteem.* San Francisco: W. H. Freeman.

Cowen, P. A. 1978. *Piaget with Feeling.* New York: Holt, Rinehart & Winston.

Fraiberg, S. H. 1959. *The Magic Years.* New York: Charles Scribner's Sons.

Kamii, C. and Devries, R. 1978. *Physical Knowledge in Preschool Education: Implications of Piaget's Theory.* Englewood Cliffs, New Jersey: Prentice-Hall.

Lamb, M. E. and Campos, J. J. 1982. *Development in Infancy.* New York: Random House.

Murphy, L. B. 1962. *The Widening World of Childhood.* New York: Basic Books.

National Institute of Dental Research and the National Association of Community Health Centers, Inc. 1979. *Good Teeth for You and Your Baby.* (NIH Publication No. 79-1255). Bethesda, Maryland: Authors.

Wadsworth, B. J. 1978. *Piaget for the Classroom Teacher.* New York: Longman.

STUDENT ACTIVITIES

1. During the children's alert play time observe two children of different ages between birth and 3 years, focusing on one area (physical, emotional, social, cognitive). Write down everything each child does and says for five minutes. Make a chart to compare the behaviors.

CHILD:	AGE:	CHILD:	AGE:
AREA:		AREA:	
Behaviors		Behaviors	

2. Observe one child between birth and 3 years interacting with one adult. List the behaviors each uses to get the other's attention.

	INITIATE	RESPONSE
Child		
Adult		
Child		
Adult		
Child		
Adult		

3. Use the developmental profile in Appendix A while observing one child between birth and 3 years for ten minutes. (If you do not have access to a day care center or day care home for observations, try the park, playground, laundromat, supermarket, etc.).

REVIEW

1. List four areas of development and learning.
2. What is the direction of the infant's physical development?
3. List four temperament patterns.
4. Define attachment as it relates to the child in a child care program.
5. List the stages of cognitive development of children from birth to 3 years of age.
6. Write one example of a child's behavior while constructing each of these kinds of knowledge:
   a. physical knowledge
   b. logico-mathematical knowledge
   c. social-arbitrary knowledge

7
The Indoor and Outdoor Environment

The environment for infants and toddlers must be planned carefully. As Olds has said, "it is the environment, in all its manifestations, that is the curriculum" (1982, 16). This chapter focuses on the tangible objects and space within the child care setting.

ROOM ARRANGEMENT

Designing the Setting

Jones and Prescott emphasized that "planning space is a problem-stating as well as a problem-solving process" (1982, 18). They offered the following suggestions to the child care staff for analyzing the setting:

1. Articulate program goals in a general fashion. What kinds of experiences and feelings do we wish to provide? What are the special needs of the children we serve?
2. Look critically and closely at how existing arrangements work or fail to work.
3. Be willing to experiment with alternative arrangements. Design does not mean fixing ideas in concrete. Rather, it is a process of devising ad hoc solutions, informally monitoring how they work, and remaining open to change if the results warrant it (1982, 18).

Arranging the room is not a one-time task. There are several reasons for rearranging your room(s):

1. Activity areas are changed to offer a new and novel area.
2. Materials in the activity areas are changed to maintain challenge.
3. Modifications need to be made in equipment and placement when the age of the children changes.
4. Room arrangement is changed when the children's behavior shows that the room arrangement causes management problems.

Licensing regulations state minimum requirements for activity floor space per child; 30–50 square feet are often required. The arrangement of equipment, materials, activities, and people in this space is the responsibility of the child care staff. Though the arrangement of inside space may differ between day care homes and day care centers, some basic principles apply to all settings.

Creating Activity Areas

The room arrangement will reflect program goals. In describing a developmentally optimal day care center Olds stated, ". . . a child's successful interaction with the physical environment must satisfy three basic needs: the need to move, the need to feel comfortable, and the need to feel competent" (1982, 16). Olds emphasized the need for movement, stating, "Sensorial and motoric experiences are the bedrock upon which all intellectual functions are built" (1982, 16). She identified the following benefits in meeting the need for comfort: "Comfortable surroundings foster playful attitudes that help lower anxiety, promote understanding, and enable children to be more open in divulging their personal responses to events and materials" (1982, 16). Olds also suggested that variations in architecture "provide pleasing changes in sensory stimulation":

- scale—small spaces and furniture for children, larger ones for adults; areas for privacy, semiprivacy, and whole group participation; materials at child-eye level and at adult height.
- floor height—raised and lowered levels, platforms, lofts, pits, climbing structures.
- ceiling height—mobiles, canopies, eaves, skylights.
- boundary height—walls, half-height dividers, low bookcases.
- visual interest—wall murals, classical art, children's paintings, views to trees and sky.
- lighting—natural, fluorescent, incandescent, local, indirect.
- auditory interest—hum of voices, mechanical gadgets, music, gerbils scratching, children laughing.
- olfactory interest—cookies baking, fresh flowers in a vase, plants in earth.
- textural interest—wood, fabric, fur, carpeting, plastic, formica, glass.
- kinesthetic interest—things to touch with different body parts; things to crawl in, under, and upon; opportunities to see the environment from different vantage points (1982, 17).

CDA I.3

The environment can be organized to provide for a variety of activities. Olds identified five categories of activity which the setting should make possible:

1. quiet, calm activities
2. structured activities
3. craft and discovery activities
4. dramatic play activities
5. large motor activities (1982, 18).

Dalziel took the categories of wet and dry and quiet and active and related them to the arrangement of materials and space:

1. "wet-quiet" area—cooking, eating, messy media (paste, paper maché, etc.)
2. "wet-active" area—coats, toilet, sand, water, painting, some science materials
3. "quiet-dry" area—learning games and materials, writing, library, listening
4. "active-dry" area—large motor activities, construction (woodworking, blocks, building), dress-up, housekeeping (n.d., 2).

To provide for these activities adequately, you must design the areas carefully (see Figure 7–1).

Figure 7–1 The library area provides quiet space to enjoy books and stories.

An activity area has five defining attributes: a physical location with visible boundaries indicating where it begins and ends, within which are placed work and sitting surfaces along with the storage and display of materials which are to be used on the surfaces in performing the activities for which the area is intended (Olds 1982, 19).

To help the child develop feelings of competence, Olds asserted, "A teacher needs to provide a room which allows children to fulfill their own personal needs, execute tasks successfully, readily control their own tools and materials, make easy transitions, and control their own movements from place to place" (1982, 18).

PLAY YARD ARRANGEMENTS

Integrating into the Program

The play yard serves many functions as an integral part of a child care program. Just as caregivers evaluate and carefully design the indoor space to provide challenging and satisfying experiences, the outdoor space requires that same attention to program goals and design of space, equipment, and materials (see Figure 7–2).

Figure 7–2 Wooden logs can be used for climbing and sitting.

Designing Areas

Caregivers must know the needs and interests of their children in order to design appropriate and appealing outdoor environments. Essa recommended that "more thought should go into organizing the yard into interest areas—as indoors—to include quiet and noisy spaces, social areas, places to be alone, materials to manipulate, etc." (1981, 41).

Nature provides readily available and adaptable materials in many play-yards. Grass, leaves, seeds, flowers, trees, bushes, dirt, sand, and water present intriguing exploring and manipulating opportunities. Caregivers should help children gain access to these areas and should allow and encourage their creative uses of the materials.

Sharing Space

The playyard needs to be able to accommodate the children in the program. If infants and toddlers share playyard space with older children, equipment and materials especially designed for the younger children should be arranged into a section in the areas of the playyard. Day care homes must utilize their yards or a nearby park. With the multi-aged group of children usually present in day care homes, the caregiver must make adaptations.

Plan carefully to design shared space for use by several age groups. Establish rules which identify the way each age group can safely share the space, or have the children use the space at different times. For example, toddlers, who like to start and stop often and whose balance is sometimes unstable, may use tyke bikes on their own riding strip, and 5-year-olds may have a different riding strip, where they can ride faster and ride through more complex patterns and lanes. If there is not enough space, each group may use the same strip at different times.

Safety Considerations

Playyard arrangements should contribute to safe play conditions. Playgrounds and equipment should be arranged with an eye toward the traffic patterns which will result (Gordon 1981, 47). The playyard must be safe to get to and to use. Licensing often requires that the playyard be fenced. Grass provides the best surface covering for infants and toddlers and should cover most of the playyard. Concrete and asphalt surfaces hold the heat on hot summer days and cannot be used then by infants who are sitting and crawling.

Figure 7-3 The refrigerator door becomes a bulletin board in a family day care home.

BASIC EQUIPMENT AND MATERIALS

Matching Program Goals

What are your program goals?   The equipment and materials you select should help the children in your program develop to their fullest potential physically, emotionally, socially, and cognitively. This requires a variety of high-quality equipment and materials (see Table 7–1, page 139).

Equipment

The child care setting includes equipment necessary for providing basic care. Day care homes often include some special equipment or they adapt available home furnishings (see Figure 7–3).

Equipment is needed to facilitate all areas of development and for all ages of children in the setting. One piece of equipment may aid development in more than one area. For example, a child using a very low slide is moving physically and is also usually having an emotional response which may be pleasure, excitement, fear, or pride in accomplishment. Children of various ages may be able to enjoy the same piece of equipment. Two-year-olds may use the low slide competently, while a 1-year-old may use it with caregiver assistance, and a 9-month-old may use it as a low structure to crawl on and to stand up to with caregiver assistance.

Materials

Materials include toys, books, paper, paint, clay, sand, glue, water, boxes, tires, and other items children use in the room and playyard. Like equipment, materials help children attain program goals relating to physical, emotional, social, and cognitive development.

Jones divided the environment into several dimensions: soft or hard, open or closed, simple or complex, intrusion or seclusion, and high mobility or low mobility (1973, 1). These dimensions can be applied in the child care setting to the materials, equipment, and arrangement of space as well as to the behavior of people.

Lists of materials in a child care setting help identify materials which meet children's needs. Kate may need a toy which is intrusive, which puts her into contact with others. Another time she may need a toy which encourages seclusion so she can be by herself (see Table 7-2, page 140).

Catalog age-designations do not fit all children. Caregivers must determine whether or when the item is appropriate for a particular child. Materials may have merit for some children but not for others. For example, a colorful mobile hanging above the crib may attract the attention of 3-month-old Sam. It would go unnoticed by 1-month-old Fred because (1) the tonic neck reflex keeps Fred's head turned to the side rather than looking up, and (2) his

TABLE 7–1
BASIC EQUIPMENT FOR INFANTS AND TODDLERS

DAY CARE CENTER CLASSROOM	DAY CARE HOME
Indoor	**Indoor**
EATING	*EATING*
High chairs	High chairs
	Booster seats for kitchen and dining room chairs
Low chairs and tables	Kitchen and dining room table
SLEEPING	*SLEEPING*
Rocking chair	Rocking chair
Cribs	Cribs
Cots	Family beds and sofa covered with the child's sheet and blanket for naps
TOILETING	*TOILETING*
Changing table	Changing table or counter space in the bathroom for changing diapers and storing supplies
Supply storage	
Toilet seat adapter	Toilet seat adapter
Steps (if needed at sink)	Steps (if needed at sink)
STORAGE	*STORAGE*
Coat rack	Coat rack near door
Cubbies	
Shelves: toys, books	Especially designated shelves in the family room, living room, and/or bedroom where books and toys are kept for the day care children
RECORD KEEPING	*RECORD KEEPING*
Bulletin boards	Wall and refrigerator door space to exhibit art treasures
Record-keeping table, counter	Table, counter, drawer
Outdoor	**Outdoor**
CLIMBING STRUCTURES	*CLIMBING STRUCTURES*
Wood, tile, rubber tires, steps, tied ropes	Rubber tires, steps, tied ropes
CONTAINERS	*CONTAINERS*
Sand table or box	Large plastic trays, pools for sand and water
Water table or pool	

TABLE 7–2
TYPES OF EQUIPMENT AND MATERIALS

SOFT	HARD
Cloth puppets	Blocks
Cloth and soft plastic dolls	Hard plastic dolls
Dress-up clothes	Cars, trucks
Fur	Plastic curtains
Pillows	Sand
Mats	Paper
Rugs	Cardboard
Cloth curtains	Books
Water	Posters
Clay	Plastic, wood mobile
Paint	Wood
Cloth wall hangings	Linoleum
Glue	Baseball
Ribbon	Plastic bottles
Cushions	Catalogs
Cloth mobile	Magazines
Rubber balls	Buttons
Sponge balls	Metal cans
Cloth scraps	Sandpaper
Foam scraps	
Yarn	

OPEN	CLOSED
Puppet	Puzzle
Doll	Zipper
Water	Button/buttonhole
Sand	Snaps
Clay	Stacking rings
Blocks	Wind-up doll
	Wind-up mobile

SIMPLE	COMPLEX
1-piece puzzle	4-piece puzzle
Doll	Doll clothes
Clay	Clothes fasteners

INTRUSION	SECLUSION
Bike	Large box to hide in

HIGH MOBILITY	LOW MOBILITY
Bike	Sit and Spin
Toy cars, trucks	Slide
Stroller, buggy	Books
Balls	Blocks
	Clay
	Painting
	Puzzles
	Water
	Sand

eyes focus best at about 7–9 inches and if the crib mattress is set low, the mobile will be beyond his focusing range.

Sand and water can be used both inside and outside. Their characteristics stimulate varied and satisfying experiences for children of all ages. Most children love sand.

Water and water play also fascinate children. Johnson offered these ideas:

> "But why provide water play?" The reasons are numerous. Children discover the qualities of water: water flows, things float on it, it conforms to the shape of a container, it mixes with other substances, it will evaporate. Children gain skills and concepts through water play: coordination, concepts of volume and measurement, language practice and extension, competence and mastery. Finally, children perceive water as pleasurable and satisfying, and the teacher can too if plans and precautions are made to make it a wet and wonderful experience (1981, 14).

Analyzing Equipment and Materials

(CDA
V . 12)

Selection of appropriate equipment and materials involves the caregiver's knowledge of the program goals, the children's needs and interests, the time and space for use, and the budget. The following guide may help caregivers decide what to get (see Table 7–3).

With program goals emphasizing holistic development, a variety of items facilitating physical, emotional, social, and cognitive development are needed. Use Table 7–3 to help you see graphically whether there are items in each category. Some materials attract interest at particular ages. The age groupings in the Guide are approximations; an 11-month-old and a 13-month-old may use the same item. Therefore, an item may overlap more than one age grouping. The Guide will help you see which items a wide age range can use and which ones only a limited age range can use. Each age group needs a variety of items.

Using program goals which focus on holistic development, consider some equipment not included in Table 7–3.

1. Playpen: The purpose of the playpen is to contain the child in a small space. There may be a variety of reasons to do this. You may wish to keep the infant or toddler away from unsafe situations. You may wish to keep a child and his or her toys together. Some caregivers believe it is easier if every child has a separate playpen. Whatever the reason, the caregiver must evaluate the use of the playpen.

   (CDA
   II . 4)

   Physically infants and toddlers need gross motor movement, which includes crawling, pushing, pulling, walking. The playpen limits the amount and types of gross motor movement. Children who spend much of their waking time in a playpen (or the crib used as a playpen) have limited opportunities for gross motor movement.

   Socially and emotionally the playpen isolates rather than facilitates interactions with others. Visual and verbal exchanges must take place through the bars of the playpen across a certain distance to the other

TABLE 7–3
GUIDE FOR ANALYZING EQUIPMENT AND MATERIALS

ANALYSIS	ITEMS (Example)
Facilitated Development	*Telephone*
Physical	
Emotional	
Social	X
Cognitive	X
Age Group	
0–6 months	
6–12 months	
12–18 months	X
18–24 months	X
24–30 months	X
30–36 months	X
Senses Appealed To	
Seeing	
Hearing	X
Touching	
Tasting	
Smelling	
Number of Uses	
Single	X
Flexible	
Safety Factors	
Nontoxic	X
Sturdy	X
No sharp edges	X
Construction	
MATERIAL	
Fabric	
Paper	
Cardboard	
Rubber	
Plastic	
Wood	X
Metal	
QUALITY	
Fair	
Good	
Excellent	X
DURABILITY	
Fair	
Good	
Excellent	X
Cost—$	
Commercial	$15.00
Homemade	
Comments	

people. Approaching others, touching, and selecting social experiences are severely limited or sometimes eliminated when children stay in play-pens. The caregiver maintains strong control, while the children have almost no control over when to get in and out of the playpen and what materials to play with. These children have little opportunity to learn to exert control over themselves and over their world.

Cognitively children find very quickly that the materials put in the playpen lose one of their fundamental elements, novelty. Since there are only so many ways to use the same toys, after spending hours and days and weeks in the same space, children become bored. They are not challenged. These same materials used in different places in the room in combination with other materials and space and in interaction with other children may continue to stimulate cognitive constructions.

2. Wheeled walker: Infants are seated in wheeled walkers supposedly to help them learn how to walk. In walkers infants are upright with their weight on their backs and seats. If their feet reach the floor, some weight is on the legs and feet. Often infants can reach the floor only with their toes, so the toes bear the body weight.

If you examine the physical development which precedes walking, you see that development and muscular control start with control of the head and neck, then chest, arms, back, lower back, legs, feet, and toes. Innumerable opportunities and hours are needed to roll, reach, push, pull, step, creep, and crawl to develop the muscular strength and control necessary for standing alone and for walking. The wheeled walker restricts these opportunities for upper body, lower back, and lower body movements. Undue stress is placed on the lower back, legs, and toes before they are developed adequately.

Infants and toddlers interact with their environment through their senses and therefore need items which stimulate these senses. At different ages children can make use of their senses in different ways. In the first few months of life infants see many things and need items to stimulate their interest in and use of seeing. They do not have much control of their hands and fingers, so touching is limited to bumping and banging and finally grasp-ing. A limited number and kind of items are needed to stimulate touching. However, 2-year-olds actively use all their senses, and so they need a number of items to stimulate them to use each of their senses.

Some equipment and materials can be used in only one way; others have flexible uses. Children and caregivers can adjust and adapt them in a variety of ways to facilitate development. Single-use materials are in themselves neither good nor bad, but they may be costly.

The caregiver must select items which are safe and will remain safe. Be-cause infants mouth objects, all materials which can be licked, sucked, or bitten must be nontoxic. Toys and toy parts should be too large to swallow; food should not cause problems in swallowing, e.g., hard candies.

It is important to analyze how materials and equipment are constructed. What they are made of and how they are put together will determine their durability for the varied ways children will use them. This in turn will determine whether the item can serve the purposes for which it was intended in the program. Poorly constructed items which fall apart are frustrating, often unsafe for the children, and costly for the program.

All child care programs must consider costs. To determine whether an item is cost effective, analyze the following factors for each item:

1. the importance for program goal attainment
2. the areas of development facilitated
3. the durability of construction
4. the number of ways it can be used
5. the number of children who can use it
6. the ages of children who can use it

A $45 wooden truck which is well constructed may be used for years and years by hundreds of children. In contrast, five $9 plastic trucks will probably be damaged and have to be thrown away within a year or so. Thus, for the same amount of money, the wooden truck is more cost effective.

The cost of equipment and materials can become astronomical. Therefore, most child care programs must decide which commercially made items they can purchase and which items they can make themselves. Some purists maintain that only commercially made equipment and materials have the quality young children require. But because some child care programs cannot afford to purchase all these items, they must make sure that the quality is built into their homemade items or else get along without the item.

Homemade Materials

Homemade items should meet high standards for construction, durability, and safety. Some things can be more individualized than commercially prepared items to stimulate the interest and development of children in the program, e.g., a cardboard-mounted colored photograph of each child in your room or home.

Diligent scrounging of free and inexpensive materials from parents, friends, and community businesses and industries can greatly reduce the cost of homemade items. One group which has developed a very creative and beneficial support system to child care programs for locating and using scrounged materials is the Maryland Committee for Children. In Baltimore, Maryland, it operates reSTORE, a recycling center for discarded or excess industrial materials which can be used by child care providers and parents to provide learning activities for children at a fraction of the usual cost.

Pat Clar, reSTORE Coordinator of the Maryland Committee for Children, compiled the following list of types of businesses which may have recyclable discards (see Figure 7–4).

Billboard-advertising Companies
- billboard posters: These are large pieces of paper which are very heavy, white on one side and printed on the other side

Container and Packaging Companies
- a variety of unique materials: Some often make large donations of items that do not meet their quality control standards—posters, specialty boxes, etc.; cardboard cut outs of circles, squares, large cardboard tubes, etc.

Contractors and Builders
- lumber, linoleum, wood shavings, formica table top cut outs (discarded portions from a kitchen counter top, the area where the sink is installed; they make wonderful table tops)

Country Clubs and Tennis Clubs
- golf balls and tees, tennis balls and cans

Department Stores
- contact display departments for fabrics, felt, etc., rug samples, large packing boxes from appliances
- contact wrapping desks for ribbon scraps, paper scraps and cardboard tubes

Doctors' Offices, U.S. Post Office
- magazines

Electronics Manufacturers
- circuit boards, components, metal parts, etc.

Foam Manufacturers
- foam scraps

Frame Shops
- mat board scraps, frame scraps

Furriers and Fur Storage
- fur scraps

Garment Manufacturers
- a wide variety of materials: Fur, silk, yarn, buttons, buckles, thread, thread spools

Gasket Manufacturers
- rubber rings and rubber gaskets

Grocery Stores and Liquor Stores
- sturdy cardboard boxes, posters of fruits, etc.

Leather Manufacturers and Shoemakers
- leather scraps, shoe soles, fur lining material from slippers

Paint Companies
- paint sample cards and books

Photo Shops—Film Developers
- film cannisters, metal spools from movie film

Plastics Manufacturers—Sign Makers
- plexiglass scraps, plastic tubing, plastic materials

Printers and Stationery Stores
- old card samples and sample books

Newspapers
- newsprint rolls of paper

Rug Companies
- rug samples and swatches

Seed Companies
- seed catalogs

Shade Companies
- dowels and wooden slats, vinyl shade material, cardboard tubes

Tile and Ceramic Companies
- tile scraps

Tire Stores
- inner tubes and old tires

Tobacco Stores and Cheese Shops
- unique wooden and cardboard boxes

Travel Agencies
- travel brochures, displays and posters

Wallpaper Companies
- wallpaper sample books

Figure 7–4 Community resources for recyclable materials.

Salkever has used some of these materials to suggest applications in child care programs. A few ideas adapted from her *Recycle Dictionary* (1980, 56–57) are included here (see Figure 7–5).

Some books and articles are available which specifically identify home-made materials. Burtt and Kalkstein present "77 easy-to-make toys to stimulate your baby's mind" in their book, *Smart Toys* (1981), for babies from birth to two. Wilson identifies age-appropriate materials in filmstrips and a text, *Caregiver Training for Child Care*. Zeller and McFarland matched

	EX-THROW-AWAY	USES
A	aluminum foil	a mobile for an infant
B	bleach bottle	sand play; planting seeds; water play; crayon holder
	bottle caps	counters for games
		to make tambourines
	boxes	(large ones)—to play in
		(small ones)—car garages
		(boxes food comes in)—to play store or build a city
		building; doll beds; doll houses; tiny scenes
	broomstick	a wash tub bass
	buttons	counting, sorting
C	calendars	cutting and pasting
	cans	drums
	carpet samples	to sit on; jumping, walking games
	catalogs	sorting
	Christmas cards	cut and paste; mobiles; books; scrap books; illustrating stories
	cloth	doll clothes; doll covers; baby books
	clothespins	small dolls
	coat hangers	mobiles
	coffee cans	stacking games; nesting toys; a feely can; pull toys
	corks	water play; science experiments
D	dowels	drumsticks; marionettes
E	egg cartons	scissor holder; a sock sorter
	elastic	dangle (crib) toys
F	fishing line	musical instruments
G	gears from clocks, radios	for fiddling with
	greeting cards	book markers; puppet stage props
H	hooks	gadget boards
I	ice cream cartons	storage
	inner tubes	for the ends of drums
J	jars	to hold paint
K	kitchen pots and pans	drums

Figure 7–5 Recycle dictionary.

	EX-THROW-AWAY	USES
L	linoleum tiles	clay activities
M	magazines	cut and paste; language games
	mesh (turkey) bags	storage of clothing
	milk cartons	storage; trains; planters; piggy banks; object sorting box
N	nuts and bolts	feeling; sorting
O	oatmeal boxes	doll cradle; drum
P	paper bags	pictures; wrapping paper; puppets; masks
	paper plates	pictures; holders; hats; tambourines
	plastic containers	stacking toys; to grow plants
	popsicle sticks	God's eyes
Q	quilting materials	use scraps for collages
R	ribbons	collages
S	sandpaper	sand blocks; sandpaper letters
	socks	puppets; a feely can
	spools (from thread)	pull toys; necklaces
	string	string paintings
T	tissue paper	tearing; collages; puppet hair
	tongue depressors	weaving; puppets
	travel brochures	pictures for language development
	tubing (inside paper towels)	musical instruments; smokestacks; art
U	utensils (kitchen)	use with playdough or clay
V	velvet	finger puppets
W	wrapping paper	collages; drawing; hats
Y	yarn	weaving; God's eyes
Z	zippers	for practicing zipping

Figure 7-5 Recycle dictionary. (continued)

materials, ages, and skill development in their article, "Selecting Appropriate Materials for Very Young Children," (1981). In this text each of the chapters in Part III, Matching Caregiver Strategies and Infant Development, includes ideas for homemade materials (see Figure 7–6).

Conditions Fostering Safety and Health

Materials and equipment must be selected with special care for use with infants and toddlers. Young children put everything they touch to a hard test: they bite, pinch, hit, fling, bang, pound, and tear at whatever they can. In their explorations of what they can do with the materials and equipment, young children focus on actions and do not think in terms of cause and effect so far as use is concerned. Therefore, the caregiver must take care to provide only materials and equipment which can safely withstand the child's use.

Figure 7–6 Scrap computer paper can be used to define a child's personal play space.

Safety is a matter to consider when analyzing the sturdiness of construction, the materials of construction, the size, the weight, the flexibility of use, and the effect the item will have on the child.

> Look for wood that doesn't splinter, wheels that won't pinch, corners and edges carefully rounded. Design, too, must be safety-conscious, stable and secure without small openings to catch fingers or limbs (Community Playthings 1981, 10) (see Figure 7–7).

The developmental capabilities of the child affect safety. A tyke bike may be safe for a 30-month-old but unsafe for a 9-month-old. Some equipment is safe if it is used with assistance but may be unsafe if it is used independently, e.g., for some children a record player.

Aronson analyzed insurance claims for injuries in child care. She found that the following were associated with the most frequent or more severe injuries: climbers; slides; hand toys, blocks; other playground equipment; doors; indoor floor surfaces; motor vehicles; swings; pebbles or rocks; and pencils (1983, 19). Aronson recommended the following:*

---

*Courtesy of Susan Aronson, Ph.D., Associate Clinical Professor Pediatrics and of Community and Preventive Medicine.

Figure 7-7 Children of varying ages enjoy playing in the sand within safe plastic piping.

1. Unsafe climbers, slides, and other playground equipment should be modified or eliminated. The U.S. Consumer Product Safety Commission suggests these modifications to make safer playgrounds: place climbing structures closer to the ground, mount them over 8–12 inches loose fill material such as pea gravel, pine bark, or shredded tires; space all equipment far enough away from other structures and child traffic patterns to prevent collisions; cover sharp edges and exposed bolts; limit the number of children using equipment at one time; and teach children to play safely.

2. Hazardous activities require closer adult supervision than activities with a lower injury rating.

3. Architectural features such as doors and indoor floor surfaces require special attention. Doors should have beveled edges and mechanisms which prevent slamming or rapid closure. Full-length-view vision panels will help assure that small children are seen before the door is opened. Changes in floor surfaces and edges which might cause tripping should be modified. Long open spaces should be interrupted to discourage running in areas where running is dangerous.

4. Children must always travel in seat restraints in cars or vans and must follow school bus safety rules in larger vehicles.

5. Training and resources to change hazardous conditions should be made available to all staff. Injury reports should be routinely examined by trained personnel to identify and correct trouble spots. A systematic study of injury in child care centers and in home child care is needed to

assist adults in making provision for the safe care of children (1983, 19-20).

The Massachusetts Department of Public Health developed a Site Safety Checklist and a Playground Safety Checklist that can be used and/or adapted for assessing and providing safe and healthy indoor and outdoor environments for infants and toddlers (Tables 7-4 and 7-5).

Traffic safety involves safety near traffic and auto safety. Toddlers are excitable and change interests suddenly. Therefore, when walking with toddlers, one adult should be responsible for only a few children. You must be able to reach out and touch the children with whom you are walking. Many toddlers will not keep holding onto a rope or onto a child's hand five children away from you.

When traveling with children in a car or van, be sure all children are in child restraints. A crash at 30 miles per hour can produce a force on impact similar to falling from a three-story building (Transportation Hazards Commission 1984). Check the infant seats to make sure they are securely attached to the seat belt or floor. Strap the child securely into the infant seat. Some children do not like to ride with restraints and will wriggle around until they are twisted in the straps. Be available to help settle the children and to keep their seat restraints on correctly so they will not be injured from improper use of the restraints. Check with your local or state traffic safety department or local hospital for specific details on approved infant seats and restraints.

In the child care home or room it is essential to be able to go out of and come into the room immediately. Evaluate the setting for fire safety, looking not only at what everything is made out of (will it burn?) but also at its location in the room. Children and adults need to be able to get out rapidly, and firemen need to come in. Therefore, doors and windows should open easily, and the space in front of them should be kept free from clutter.

Regular fire drills are necessary. Determine the closest exit route and post on the wall a room diagram marked with your fire exit route. Talk with the children about times when all of you might need to get out of the building quickly; be careful, however, not to scare them. If you have nonwalkers, select one crib which will fit through doorways, put heavy-duty wheels on it, and put a special symbol on it. In case of fire, put your nonwalkers in this special crib and wheel the crib outside. Holding hands and talking calmly, walk the toddlers as quickly as possible out of the building. Continue to hold hands and talk calmly as you stand outside the building.

Equipment must be disinfected regularly. Food containers and utensils must be washed regularly and thoroughly. Since infants put toys in their mouths, these toys should be washed daily in a solution of 1/4 cup chlorine bleach to 1 gallon water, or 1 tablespoon bleach per quart of water, and left to air-dry. Toys for older children should be washed regularly. Large equipment should be sprayed and cleaned. During the cold and flu season, disinfect toys and equipment more often than at other times of the year.

TABLE 7–4
SITE SAFETY CHECKLIST

ITEM	YES/NO	CORRECTIONS/ COMMENTS	DATE MADE CORRECTION
General Environment			
Floors are smooth and have a non-skid surface			
Pipes and radiators are inaccessible to children or are covered to prevent contact			
Hot tap water temperature for handwashing is 110°–115° F or less			
Electrical cords are out of children's reach and are kept out of doorways and traffic paths			
Unused electrical outlets are covered by furniture or shock stops			
Medicines, cleansers, and aerosols are kept in a locked place where children are unable to see and reach them			
All windows have screens that stay in place when used; expandable screens are not used			
Windows can be opened 6″ or less from the bottom			
Drawers are kept closed to prevent tripping or bumps			
Trash is covered at all times			
Walls and ceilings are free of peeling paint and cracked or falling plaster; center has been inspected for lead paint			
There are no disease-bearing animals, such as turtles, parrots, or cats			
Children are always supervised			
There is no friable (crumbly) asbestos releasing into the air			
Equipment and Toys			
Toys and play equipment are checked often for sharp edges, small parts, and sharp points			

TABLE 7–4 (continued)

ITEM	YES/NO	CORRECTIONS/ COMMENTS	DATE MADE CORRECTION
All toys are painted with lead-free paint			
Toys are put away when not in use			
Toy chests have lightweight lids or no lids			
Art materials are non-toxic, and have either the AP or the CP label			
Art materials are stored in their original containers in a locked place			
Teaching aids (e.g., projectors) are put away when not in use			
Curtains, pillows, blankets, and soft toys are made of flame-resistant material			
Hallways and Stairs Stairs and stairways are free of boxes, toys, and other clutter			
Stairways are well-lit			
The right-hand railing on the stairs is at child height and does not wobble when held; there is a railing or wall on both sides of stairways			
Stairway gates are in place when appropriate			
Closed doorways to unsupervised or unsafe areas are always locked unless this prevents emergency evacuation			
Staff are able to watch for strangers entering the building			
Kitchen Trash is kept away from areas where food is prepared or stored			
Trash is stored away from the furnace and hot water heater			
Pest strips are NOT used; pesticides for crawling insects are applied by a certified pest control operator			

TABLE 7-4 (continued)

ITEM	YES/NO	CORRECTIONS/ COMMENTS	DATE MADE CORRECTION
Cleansers and other poisonous products are stored in their original containers away from food and out of children's reach			
Food preparation surfaces are clean and free of cracks and chips			
Electrical cords are placed where people will not trip over them or pull them			
There are no sharp or hazardous cooking utensils within children's reach (e.g., knives, glass)			
Pot handles are always turned in toward the back of the stove during cooking			
The fire extinguisher can be reached easily in an emergency			
All staff know how to use the fire extinguisher correctly			
Bathrooms			
Stable step stools are available when needed			
Electrical outlets are covered with shock stops or outlet covers			
Cleaning products, soap, and disinfectant are stored in a locked place, out of children's reach			
Floors are smooth and have a non-skid surface			
The trash container is emptied daily and kept clean			
Hot water for handwashing is $110°-115°$ F			
Emergency Preparation			
All staff understand their roles and responsibilities in case of emergency			
At least one staff person is always present who is certified in first aid and CPR for infants and children			

TABLE 7–4 (continued)

ITEM	YES/NO	CORRECTIONS/ COMMENTS	DATE MADE CORRECTION
The first aid kit is checked regularly for supplies and is kept where it can be reached easily by staff in an emergency			
Smoke detectors and other alarms are covered regularly to make sure they are working			
Each room and hallway has a fire escape route posted in clear view			
Emergency procedures and telephone numbers are posted near each phone in clear view			
Children's emergency phone numbers are kept near the phone, where they can be reached quickly			
All exits are clearly marked and are free of clutter			
Doors open in the direction of all exit travel			
Cots are placed so that walkways are clear for evacuation in an emergency			

Source: Statewide Comprehensive Injury Prevention Program (SCIPP), Department of Public Health, 150 Tremont Street, Boston, Massachusetts 02111.

TABLE 7–5
PLAYGROUND SAFETY CHECKLIST

ITEM	YES/NO	CORRECTIONS/ COMMENTS	DATE MADE CORRECTION
All Equipment Nuts, bolts, or screws that stick out are covered with masking tape or sanded down			
Metal equipment is free from rust or chipping paint			
Wood equipment is free from splinters or rough surfaces, sharp edges, and pinch/crush parts			
Nuts and bolts are tight			

TABLE 7–5 (continued)

ITEM	YES/NO	CORRECTIONS/ COMMENTS	DATE MADE CORRECTION
Anchors for equipment are stable and buried below ground level			
Equipment is in its proper place and is not bent with use			
Children who use equipment are of the age/developmental level for which the equipment was designed			
Ground Surface			
All play equipment has 8″–12″ of shock absorbing material underneath (e.g., pea gravel or wood chips)			
Surfaces are raked weekly to prevent them from becoming packed down and to find hidden hazards (e.g., litter, sharp objects, animal feces)			
Stagnant pools of water are not present on the surface			
There is no exposed concrete where equipment is anchored			
Spacing			
Swing sets are at least 9 feet from other equipment			
Swings are at least 1 1/2 feet from each other			
Slides have a 2 1/2– to 3-yard run-off space			
There is at least 8 feet between all equipment			
Boundaries between equipment are visible to children (for instance, painted lines or low bushes)			
Play areas for bike-riding, games, and boxes are separate from other equipment			
Swing sets are at least 6 feet from walls and fences, walkways, and other play areas; there is a barrier to prevent children from getting into traffic (e.g., when chasing a ball)			

TABLE 7-5 (continued)

ITEM	YES/NO	CORRECTIONS/ COMMENTS	DATE MADE CORRECTION
Slides			
Slides are 6 feet in height or less			
Side rims are at least 2 1/2 inches high			
Slides have an enclosed platform at the top for children to rest and get into position for sliding			
Slide ladders have handrails on both sides and flat steps			
There is a flat surface at the bottom of the slide for slowing down			
Metal slides are shaded to prevent burns			
Wood slides are waxed, or oiled with linseed oil			
The slide incline is equal or less than a 30° angle			
Steps and rungs are 7″ to 11″ apart to accommodate children's leg and arm reach			
Climbing Equipment			
Ladders of different heights are available for children of different ages and sizes			
Bars stay in place when grasped			
The maximum height from which a child can fall is 7 1/2 feet			
Climbers have regularly spaced footholds from top to bottom			
There is an easy, safe "way out" for children when they reach the top			
Equipment is dry before children are allowed to use it			
Rungs are painted in bright or contrasting colors so children will see them			
Swings			
Chair swings are available for children under age 5			

TABLE 7–5 (continued)

ITEM	YES/NO	CORRECTIONS/ COMMENTS	DATE MADE CORRECTION
Canvas sling and saddle seats are available for older children			
"S" or open-ended hooks have been removed			
Hanging rings are less than 5" or more than 10" diameter (smaller or larger than child's head)			
The point at which seat and chain meet is exposed			
Seesaws The fulcrum is enclosed or designed to prevent pinching			
Handholds stay in place when grasped, without turning or wobbling			
Wooden blocks or part of a rubber tire are placed below the seat to prevent feet from getting caught			
Sandboxes Sandboxes are located in a shaded spot			
The frame is sanded and smooth, without splinters or rough surfaces			
The sand is raked at least every two weeks to check for debris and to provide exposure to air and sun			
The box is covered at night to protect from moisture and animal excrement			
The sandbox has proper drainage			
Poisonous plants and berries are removed from play area			
There is a source of clean drinking water available in the play area			
There is shade			
The entire play area can be seen easily for good supervision			

Source: Statewide Comprehensive Injury Prevention Program (SCIPP), Department of Public Health, 150 Tremont Street, Boston, Massachusetts 02111.

The floor should be cleaned daily, with spills and spots cleaned up immediately. Vinyl flooring should be swept or vacuumed and then sponge-mopped with detergent and disinfectant. Carpeting should be vacuumed daily, with periodic shampooing of the whole area. The eating area needs to be swept or vacuumed after each meal.

The sleeping equipment should be cleaned and disinfected regularly. Every child should have an individual sheet and blanket. These should be washed at least weekly and changed immediately if soiled. Diapers should not be changed on the sheet. The crib mattress and sides and the cots should be cleaned regularly with a disinfectant spray of 1 ounce chlorine bleach to 1 gallon water, or 1 teaspoon bleach to 1 quart water.

Toilet seats should be kept as clean as possible. Toddlers just learning to take care of their own toilet procedures often get urine and feces on the seats. Allow toddlers to be as independent as possible, and assist them when necessary with wiping, handwashing, and clothes. Wipe the seat and spray with disinfectant afterwards. Some pediatricians recommend using an adapter seat on the toilet rather than using a potty chair.

Remember that the quality of human relationships is one of your primary focuses. Your attention to cleanliness and sanitation should be an automatic procedure rather than a major obstacle to relationships. Find a balance so that the children experience a normal life. Conditions which are either dirty or overemphasize disinfecting and not touching children or materials focus undue attention on physical health while hampering emotional, social, and cognitive growth.

REFERENCES

Aronson, S. S. 1983. Injuries in child care. *Young Children.* 38(6): 19-20.

Burtt, K. G. and Kalkstein, K. 1981. *Smart Toys.* New York: Harper & Row.

Clar, P. 1981. Industrial scraps go to school. *Day Care and Early Education.* 8(3): 34-35.

Community Playthings. 1981. *Criteria for Selecting Play Equipment.* Rifton, New York: Author.

Dalziel, S. No date. *Spaces in Open Places.* Cortland, New York: SUNY. Project Change. Unpublished manuscript.

Essa, E. L. 1981. An outdoor play area designed for learning. *Day Care and Early Education.* 9(2): 37-42.

Gordon, D. M. 1981. Toward a safer playground. *Day Care and Early Education.* 9(1): 46-53.

Johnson, E. 1981. Water. Wet and wonderful. *Day Care and Early Education.* 8(3): 12–14.

Jones, E. 1973. *Dimensions of Teaching-Learning Environments.* Pasadena, California: Pacific Oaks.

Jones, E. and Prescott, E. 1982. Planning the physical environment in day care. *Day Care and Early Education.* 9(3): 18-25.

Massachusetts Department of Public Health. *Statewide Comprehensive Injury Prevention Program.* Boston, Massachusetts: Author.

Olds, A. R. 1983. Planning a developmentally optimal day care center. *Day Care Journal.* 1(1): 16-24.

Salkever, M. 1980. Don't throw it away. *Day Care and Early Education.* 8(1): 55-57.

Transportation Hazards Commission, American Academy of Pediatrics. 1984. *The Perfect Gift.*

Wilson, L. 1977. *Caregiver Training for Child Care.* Columbus, Ohio: Charles E. Merrill.

Zeller, J. M. and McFarland, S. L. 1981. Selecting appropriate materials for very young children. *Day Care and Early Education.* 8(4): 7-13.

STUDENT ACTIVITIES

1. Identify one item in your child care setting for each category of Jones's dimensions of the environment.
2. Use the Guide for Analyzing Equipment and Materials (Table 7–3) to analyze five pieces of equipment and five materials used indoors and five pieces of equipment and five materials used outdoors in your child care setting.
3. Observe two children playing with materials. Write down the actions of each child as he or she manipulates the object(s).
4. Draw a diagram of the child care room or home showing the placement of basic equipment and activity areas.
5. Draw a detailed diagram of one activity area. Compare it to the specifications identified by Olds.
6. Draw a diagram of the playyard arrangement. Identify activity areas. List equipment and materials in each area.
7. Interview a caregiver in a child care program where age groups share the outdoor space. Describe how that program facilitates playyard use and insures safety.

REVIEW

1. How can caregivers determine whether a piece of equipment or material is useful in the program?
2. When planning room arrangements, why do we distinguish between soft and hard, wet and dry, quiet and active?
3. What does it mean that the playyard is "an integral part of the program"?
4. List four safety factors which caregivers must consider in selecting toys and equipment for infants and toddlers.
5. Describe how a toy or equipment may be safe for one child and unsafe for another child.
6. List two adaptations which caregivers can make when young infants, crawlers, and toddlers share space.

Part III

Matching Caregiver Strategies and Child Development

The chapters in Part III discuss how the caregiver works with infants and toddlers in specific age ranges. Each chapter refers to the developmental profile and characteristics of many children in a specific age range, lists materials, and presents examples of caregiver strategies which may be used with individual children. Most caregivers care for wider age ranges of children than the four-to-six-month intervals in these chapters. Therefore, refer to each chapter which contains information relevant to the children with whom you work. As your children develop, refer back to these chapters for additional information to help you meet the changes.

The *sequence* of development is common to all infants and toddlers. The *time* the behavior occurs or the *rate* at which it develops differs. Two eleven-month-olds may be at different levels of development. You should concentrate on each child as an individual rather than comparing them and deciding that one is faster than another, better than another, etc. Compare infants and toddlers to themselves. Look at their individual records to see whether they are making progress; that is, gradually developing new, more complex skills and behaviors, or whether they seem to be stuck at one level. Check to see whether this progress or slowdown of development is appropriate.

Remember that infants and toddlers seem to make spurts of growth. When one area of an individual child's development is in a spurt, the other areas seem to slow down. For example, an infant's talking may increase dramatically for several weeks. Then you notice repetition of old sounds but nothing new for a while. But you also see that during this lull in language the infant is beginning to creep. His or her energies seem to have turned away from language and toward creeping. This is a common pattern for infants: They seem to have one major development at a time.

Appendix A contains a complete Developmental Profile. Begin using this with each child in your program. It is cumulative, with information added regularly. Refer also to Chapter 6, What is Development/Learning? The more complete picture may help you understand where a phase of development fits into a child's ongoing total development.

Use the Developmental Profile to discover what the child *can* do. Concentrate on the child's accomplishments. Reflect back to the child your enthusiasm about his or her development and report to the parent how the child is developing. Your enthusiasm helps all of you feel good about the child.

You need information from the Developmental Profile to plan appropriately for the child. Total program planning of curriculum, schedule, routines, and space must be based on the information from the Developmental Profile of each child in your program. The Developmental Profile is divided into areas of development: physical, emotional, social, cognitive, and language. These are listed separately to help you in your observations and planning. You should remember that in the child's life these five areas are integrated.

Age designations are included in the Developmental Profile. These are approximations, since all children develop at their own rates. Use the age designations to examine the chapters in Part III which present suggestions of possible materials and caregiver strategies to use.

Many caregiver strategies enhance development. In order to understand better the importance of what the child is doing and what the caregiver is doing, several areas of child development will be examined. It is extremely necessary to remember, however, that the purpose for looking at the parts of the picture is to understand the whole picture better. Areas of development are *interrelated* and *interdependent.*

The crucial issue in looking at Developmental Profiles is to become familiar with the *sequence,* the *pattern* of development. The age at which a particular behavior appears and the time it takes to develop varies from child to child. Examples of possible materials and caregiver strategies which may facilitate the infant's or toddler's development are included in each chapter in Part III. The caregiver must look again at the goals and objectives of the program; there is no one curriculum or teaching strategy for all infants and toddlers everywhere. There are, however, some situations which have in general been very effective in helping individual children reach their potential.

Infants and toddlers are growing and developing rapidly. As their alert time and playtime lengthen, they become ready for more involvement with people and materials. Selection of materials is determined by the interest and development of each child. You can use the materials identified in each chapter with many children in that age range. Let the child's developmental profile help you determine which materials will be appropriate for that child. The materials listed are suggestions. All need not be used with all children. You can also add other materials to fit the particular child's development.

Day care homes and centers plan to use part of their budget for the purchase of high-quality toys and equipment. However, the wide range of ages of children in the program often means that each year only a few sturdy toys can be purchased for different developmental levels of children. Each chapter in Part III includes a list of homemade materials so that a variety of materials can be available for limited cost.

There is no one best way to care for children. Therefore, the caregiver must constantly make choices. The child's development, the society, and the setting place expectations, possibilities, and limits on the caregiver. All of these become a part of the reasoning for the caregiver's decisions and actions.

It is important to realize that caregiving is first of all a relationship between caregiver and child. Everything in the infant's and toddler's curriculum occurs in a context which interrelates physical, emotional, social, and cognitive development. Even though each of the outlines in this section focuses on one area of development, the other areas are necessarily involved.

8

The Child from Birth to Four Months of Age

Review Chapter 6. Use Appendix A, The Developmental Profile, with each infant. Children follow a **sequence** of development. There can be ranges in **rate** of development.

Myron, 2½ months old, has just arrived at the day care home. He sits in his infant seat which is on the floor beside the sofa. Myron's fists are closed and his arms and legs make jerky movements. As each of the other children arrive, they come over to touch him and smile and "talk" to him, with the caregiver watching nearby. Myron looks at each child who kneels in front of him. After several minutes his face twists and he starts to whimper, then cry. Paul, the caregiver, picks him up, cuddles him, and says, "Are you getting sleepy? Do you want your nap?" Paul takes Myron into the bedroom and puts him in his crib where Myron promptly falls asleep (see Figure 8–1).

MATERIALS AND ACTIVITIES

Materials used with infants of this age must be safe and challenging. Every object these infants can grasp and lift will go into their mouths. *Before* you allow an infant to touch a toy, determine if it is safe. Each toy should pass **all** the following criteria:

Figure 8–1 The caregiver anticipates and provides for the young infant's needs.

1. It is too big to swallow.
2. It has no sharp points or edges to cut or puncture the skin or eyes.
3. It is edible, not poisonous, if parts of it are chewed on or swallowed.
4. It can be cleaned.
5. It has no movable parts which can pinch.
6. Painted surfaces have nontoxic paint.
7. It is sturdy enough to withstand biting, banging, and throwing.

To be challenging for the young infant, materials should do the following:

1. catch the infant's attention so the infant will want to interact with it in some way, e.g., reach, push, grasp, look, taste, turn, and practice these movements over and over again.
2. be movable enough so the infant can use arms, legs, hands, eyes, ears, or mouth to successfully manipulate the object and respond to it.
3. be able to be used at several levels of complexity so that the infant can use it with progressively more skill.

Look for toys and materials which the infant can use in several different ways. These provide greater opportunities for the infant to practice and develop new skills. Change the toys often so they seem new and interesting. An infant seems to get bored using the same toy for months.

Types of Materials

Crib gyms
Mobiles
Rattles
Yarn or texture balls

Small toys to grasp
Sound toys
Pictures, designs
Mirrors

Examples of Homemade Materials

Materials may be homemade or commercially made. The following are suggestions for making some of your own materials:

CRIB GYM

Tie a sturdy cotton rope from one side of the crib to the other. Tie on three different objects (these can be changed regularly) so they hang just at the end of the infant's reach. Poke a small hole in the bottom of a small colored plastic margarine tub; thread and knot it on one rope. It will swing when the infant hits it.

RATTLES

Film cannister (plastic or metal):   Put in one teaspoon uncooked cereal.   Replace the cap and tape it on with colored tape.

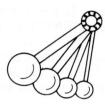

Plastic tablespoons: tie together on a circle of strong yarn.

YARN BALLS

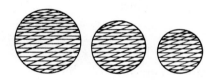

Roll up balls of washable yarn.   Tuck the loose end inside.   Make the balls different sizes and different colors.

Wrap yarn around the palm of your hand until you have a thick mitt.   Carefully slide it off your hand and tie a short piece of yarn tightly around the middle of the "mitt."   Cut the ends apart.   Pull the loose ends around to shape a ball.

FABRIC TWIRLS

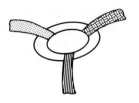

Cut out the center of a lid from a margarine tub. Cut carefully, leaving a clean, smooth edge.   Use the remaining rim ring.   Sew on three strips of printed washable fabric 3 inches long by 2 inches wide.   Hang from the crib gym or put on the infant's wrist.

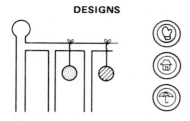

DESIGNS

Cut faces, wallpaper, pictures, fabric to fit inside the lids of margarine tubs. Glue one piece in each lid. Hang some from the sides of the crib or give several to the infant to play with.

CAREGIVER STRATEGIES TO ENHANCE INFANT DEVELOPMENT

Physical Development

CDA
II.4

Infants from birth to 4 months of age show a very rapid rate of physical development. Starting at birth with reflexive movements, infants rapidly gain an increasing level of muscular control over much of their bodies.

The control moves from their heads and necks to their shoulders, backs, waists, and legs. Muscular control also develops from mid-body out to the hands and feet. Gradually infants are able to control to some degree their arm and leg movements. They develop control of their hands and fingers and can grasp some objects.

Infants also increase their ability to notice differences in their seeing, hearing, touching, smelling, and tasting.

VISUAL PERCEPTION

Research in the 1970s and 1980s found that vision is acute though limited from birth and that visual perception gradually expands during the first year. Lamb and Campos stated

perceptual processes undergo a sequence of developmental changes in the first few months of life. The infant at birth has far more complicated visual capabilities than had once been believed, but these competencies serve to isolate for the infant's vision only *features* of forms, such as edges and contours. Only after two months of age or so does the infant begin to notice the simple relationship among elements of figures, such as whether figures have internal details or not. Subsequently, perhaps by three months, the infant can notice whole forms, but even after the infant has the capacity to organize a *gestalt* visually, further improvement in whole-form perception takes place, so that by seven months the infant is capable of perceiving whole form when the physical stimulus only suggests the outline of such a figure (1982, 66).

HEARING

Newborns can hear sounds. By moving their heads they show they can identify the direction of the sound. They do better locating sound coming from either side than from above or below or in front or behind them. In the first few months they can discriminate between speech sounds.

TASTE

Newborns can distinguish between water and sugar water. They prefer sugar water to plain water. They can distinguish between sweet, salty, and bitter solutions and prefer the sweet ones.

SMELL

Newborns can distinguish odors and respond positively or negatively to them.

MOVEMENTS

Newborns' movements are reflexive; they occur without the infants' control or direction. Through growth and learning infants begin to control their movements.

In the first few months infants learn to use many movements well but they have not yet coordinated the movements. Bruner and his colleagues at Harvard's Center for Cognitive Studies observed, recorded, and analyzed infant behavior in 1968. They found that infants learn to control their sucking in the first month of life and that sucking is used for relieving distress, holding attention, and exploration as well as for feeding. In their studies they found that infants used looking, or visual focusing, to stimulate sucking. Infants apparently separate the two behaviors:

> One can summarize the relation between sucking and looking by noting that it goes through three phases in its growth. The first is *suppression* of one by the other—and mostly it is looking that suppresses sucking. The second phase is simple *succession* of sucking and looking, organization by alteration. The third phase is *place holding*, in which the two acts can go on, with one in reduced form that is sufficient for easy resumption, while the other goes into full operation (1968, 21–22).

Reflexive hand and arm movements develop into a grasping-groping action which can be independent of vision. Within the first four months "this slow reaching has the mouth as its inevitable terminus. There is an invariant sequence: activation, reach, capture, retrieval to the mouth, and mouthing" (Bruner 1968, 38) (see Figure 8–2). In the next year these hand and arm movements will become directed voluntary activity, which may be visually controlled.

STABILITY

The newborn's head moves reflexively from side to side. When upright, the neck cannot yet support the head. Within the first month infants can lift their heads when lying on their stomachs. By the third month they are

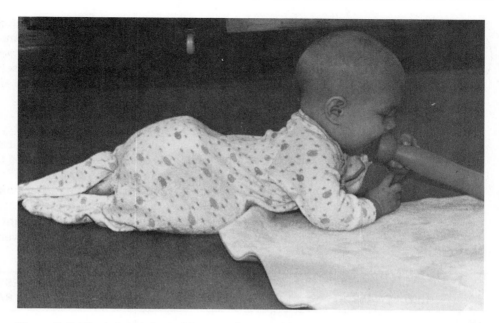

Figure 8–2 The infant brings objects to the mouth.

using their arms to push against the floor or bed to raise their head and chest.

During these first three months infants are also busy with their legs. The legs have been kicking and pushing in the air and against anything within range. The infants roll and kick their legs from side to side. Their upper and lower back muscles are developing so that one day when they kick and roll to one side, they keep going right onto their backs or their stomachs. The baby has rolled over!

SLEEP

Newborns sleep about sixteen to seventeen hours a day. Gradually they spend less time asleep and more time alert and attentive.

Many caregiving strategies at this time involve providing appropriate space so infants can move as they want to. The caregiver does not tell the infants to arch their backs, kick their legs, or wave their arms wildly. Infants do this naturally. The caregiver facilitates infant movement by making sure their clothes do not limit movement, by providing a safe environment, and by offering infants materials and toys which are safe and appropriate.

SUGGESTIONS FOR IMPLEMENTING CURRICULUM

The caregiver can employ several strategies to enhance the infant's **muscular control**.

1. Place infants in positions where they can practice developing muscular control. For example, when you lay them on their stomachs, they can keep trying to lift their heads, shoulders, and trunks.
2. Until infants can roll over, sit up, and stand by themselves, they will need to be moved into those different positions several times each day during their waking hours.
3. Interact with the infant using yourself as a stimulator. Grasp the infant's hands and slowly lift the child upright. Hold your hands in different places so the infant will look around and reach for you. Gently snap your fingers behind, beside, and in front of the infant and watch the child turn his or her head to locate the sound.
4. Use toys and materials to play with the infant; offer some for the infant to use independently.

     Place objects within the vision and reach of the infant. Select toys the infant can grasp. First there is a gross, grabbing movement. Later a more refined finger-thumb or pincer grasp is used.

CHILD BEHAVIOR	MATERIALS	EXAMPLES OF CAREGIVER STRATEGIES
Reflex*		
Grasp reflex (hand closes).	Finger, rattle.	Lift infant's body slightly. Place object in palm of infant's hand.
Startle reflex.		Touch, hold infant to calm him.
Tonic neck reflex (head facing one side or other, not facing up).	Mirror, mobile, toys, designs.	Place objects at side of crib, not above middle of crib.
Muscular Control (Develops from head to feet.)		
HEAD AND NECK		
Turns head.	Stuffed toy.	Place infant on back or stomach. Place toy to one side.
Holds head upright with support.		Support infant's head when holding infant upright.
Lifts head slightly when on stomach.		Place infant on stomach.
Holds head to sides and middle.		Place infant on stomach.
Holds up head when on back and on stomach.		Place infant on stomach or back.
Holds head without support.		Set and hold infant upright.
TRUNK		
Holds up chest.		Place infant on stomach.

*Reflexes are automatic. Caregiver uses materials and strategies to respond to a reflex rather than to direct the reflex.

CHILD BEHAVIOR	MATERIALS	EXAMPLES OF CAREGIVER STRATEGIES
Sits with support. May attempt to raise self. May fuss if left lying down with little chance to sit up.		Place infant in sitting position. Support head and back with arm or pillow. Lengthen sitting time as infant is able.
Holds up chest and shoulders.		Place infant on stomach.
LEG Rolls from stomach to back.		Place infant on flat surface where infant can not roll off.
Muscular Control (Develops from mid-body to limbs.) *ARM* Moves randomly.	Toys.	Place objects within reach of infant.
Reaches.	Bright toys which make noise.	Place objects slightly beyond reach of infant; give to infant when child reaches for it.
HAND Opens and closes.	Toys with handles, bumps which fit in fist.	Place handle in fist; help infant close fist around object.
Keeps hands open.		
Plays with hands.	Colorful plastic bracelet.	Place colorful objects which attract infant's attention on infant's hands, fingers (must be safe to go in mouth).
Uses hand to grasp object. Whole hand and fingers against thumb.	Toys with bumps to hold onto.	Place object within reach of infant.
Thumb and forefinger.	Toys which can be grasped with one hand.	Place object within reach of infant.
Holds and moves object.	Toys which can be pushed, pulled, or lifted with hands; toys which make noise.	Place toy on flat surface free from obstructions.
EYE-HAND COORDINATION Moves arm toward object; may miss it.	Toy, bottle.	Place within reach of infant.
Reaches hand to object; may grab or miss it.	Toy, bottle.	Place within reach of infant.

The caregiver can use several strategies to enhance the infant's **seeing**.

1. Place the infant or objects the correct distance so the infant can focus to see people or objects. The newborn focuses at about 4 to 8 inches. When infants are about 4 months old, they can adjust focal distance as adults do. The caregiver can place materials at the proper focusing distance. These should attract the infant's attention (see Figure 8–3).
2. Select eye-catching materials. Contrasts seem to interest infants: designs, patterns, shapes, colors. Faces also attract their attention.

Figure 8–3 The caregiver moves a toy where the infant can see and reach for it.

CHILD BEHAVIOR	MATERIALS	EXAMPLES OF CAREGIVER STRATEGIES
Seeing Focuses 8 inches from eyes.	Mirror, mobile, toys, pictures, designs (e.g., patterns, faces).	Place object 8 inches from infant's face.
Follows with eyes.	Mobile, toys, hand.	Move object slowly after infant focuses on object.
Stares. Sees objects beyond 8 inches.	People, pictures, toys.	Attract attention by shape, color, movement.
Looks from object to object.	Toys, mobile, designs, pictures.	Provide two or more objects of interest to infant.
Looks around; stops to focus on object which has caught attention; then looks at something else; continual visual searching.		Provide eye-catching items in room: faces, patterned designs, contrasting colors in objects, and pictures.

The caregiver can use several strategies to enhance the infant's **hearing.**

1. Newborns respond to sound. The caregiver can produce and select sounds which help infants differentiate between voices as well as among other sounds.
2. Provide a variety of sounds. Tie a bell to the infant's wrist to catch the child's listening attention as the child moves his or her arm. Music can calm or excite infants. Clicking, clucking, snapping, humming, or singing all can provide opportunities for listening. Infants gradually learn to search for and identify the source of the sound. Later they also may try to reproduce the sound (see Figure 8–4).

CHILD BEHAVIOR	MATERIALS	EXAMPLES OF CAREGIVER STRATEGIES
Hearing Responds to voice.		Talk to infant.
Hears range of sounds.	Music, singing, caregiver movements.	Talk, sing to infant. Enter and leave room.
Calms while hearing low-pitched sounds.	Humming, singing, records.	Select quiet, gentle music to calm infant.
Becomes agitated while hearing high-pitched sounds.	Singing, records.	Select songs to sing to calm infant.
Locates sound	Mechanical sounds, voices, music, musical toys.	Move sound around so infant searches for source.

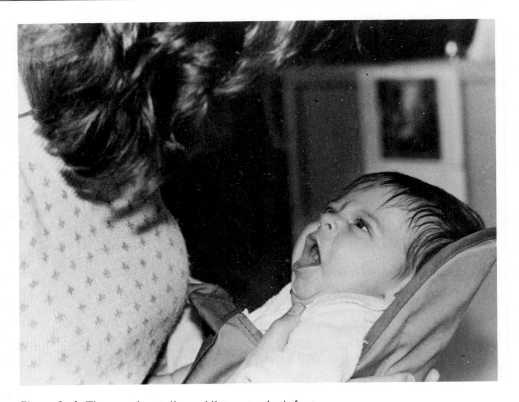

Figure 8-4 The caregiver talks and listens to the infant.

The caregiver can use several strategies to enhance the infant's **sleeping.** Anticipate when the infant probably will take a nap. Plan very calming time and activities for the infant just before naptime so the infant can get in a mood to sleep. Sitting with the infant in a rocking chair and humming a lullaby often prove very effective.

CHILD BEHAVIOR	MATERIALS	EXAMPLES OF CAREGIVER STRATEGIES
Sleeping Sleeps much of the day and night.	Flat, firm mattress.	Provide restful environment, moderate temperature, free from sudden loud noises.
Takes a long morning nap and a long afternoon nap.		Adjust routines to fit infant's changing sleep schedule.
May have irregular sleep habits.		Shorten or lengthen activities with infant to assist establishing some pattern for sleeping.

The caregiver can use several strategies to enhance the infant's **eating**. Parents and pediatricians determine what and how much infants are fed during their first four months. The caregiver is responsible for making eating a happy, successful time for the infant. Organize your time so you can hold each infant when bottle feeding. Eye focusing, eye-hand coordination, as well as emotional bonding, language, and communication all occur while holding the infant for feeding.

CHILD BEHAVIOR	MATERIALS	EXAMPLES OF CAREGIVER STRATEGIES
Eating Takes bottle on demand.	Formula and bottle.	Determine formula with parent. Determine schedule with parent. Hold infant when bottle feeding. Tilt bottle so milk fills the nipple to prevent infant's swallowing excess air. Burp the infant.

The caregiver can use several strategies for **elimination**. Two important caregiver responsibilities are to change the infant's diaper frequently and to record the time and any abnormalities of bowel movements. Eating schedules affect the time infants have bowel movements. As they establish eating schedules, some infants develop predictable elimination patterns. Cleanliness is critical for the infant and the caregiver.

The infant's bowel movement reflects the child's health. Ask the parent what color, texture, and frequency are normal for the infant. Record the frequency daily. Record any differences in color and texture and inform the parent.

CHILD BEHAVIOR	MATERIALS	EXAMPLES OF CAREGIVER STRATEGIES
Elimination Begins to establish predictable eating and elimination schedules.	Diapers, cleansing supplies.	Remove soiled diaper and dispose of it. Wipe infant's bottom with warm, soapy washcloth. Rinse. Dry. Put on dry diaper. Disinfect the changing surface. **Wash your hands with soap.**
Establishes regular time for bowel movement.		Record time of bowel movement. Note changes in times of bowel movements.
May suffer from diarrhea or constipation (both problems call for attention).		Record type of bowel movement. Record changes in type of bowel movement. Discuss with parent. If diarrhea, notify parent immediately. Do not wait until the end of the day; the baby can dehydrate rapidly and may need medical care.

Emotional Development

During the first months of life infants develop their basic feelings of security. There seems to be little "catch-up" time for emotional security. If the infant does not develop these feelings of security now, it is difficult to develop them as adequately later. Along with the parents the caregiver plays a key role in providing the kinds of relationships and experiences which enable the infant to develop this basic security.

Feelings of security and trust develop out of relations with others. Infants cannot develop these on their own. They develop these feelings from the way other people treat them. Parents and the primary caregiver are probably the most influential people in the lives of young infants in child care. Therefore, the caregiver is very directly responsible and involved in helping the infant feel secure.

Two caregiver behaviors of special importance are responding immediately to the infant's distress signals and responding constantly to the infant's signals of distress, need, or pleasure.

Temperament, the infant's basic style of behavior, gradually emerges in the first four months. Some styles are easily recognized, whereas others may be more difficult to observe.

The activity level of infants is obvious. They may kick and wriggle and squirm a great deal or they may lie quietly in both sleep and wakefulness. Highly active infants may kick their covers off consistently and get tangled in their clothes. Their bodies get plenty of activity. They may need to be checked frequently to be sure they can move freely. A blanket may be more bother than it is worth, since it seldom covers the infant. Infant suits or long smocks and socks may keep the active infant just as warm. Very quiet infants may seem easy to care for. They seldom kick off their covers or need their clothes adjusted. They may, however, need to be picked up and moved around to stimulate their physical movement.

Infants' living patterns usually take on regularity in the first months of life. The infant who establishes a regular, though slowly changing, schedule for eating and sleeping creates a predictable world into which the caregiver can easily fit. Infants whose feeding and sleeping times remain erratic create stress for themselves and their caregiver.

Differing levels of sensory threshold are apparent in young infants. One infant will awaken when a light is turned on or a person steps into the room. Another infant will sleep in a brightly lit room with the record player on. When several children are in one room, special adjustments need to be made for the sleeping infant who reacts negatively to light and sound.

Infants characteristically use differing levels of energy when responding to stimuli. One infant will cry loudly whenever he or she cries. Another infant will whimper and fuss and occasionally cry more loudly when very distressed. The caregiver, when responding to the infant's cries, will need to learn cues other than loudness to determine the type and severity of stress. The caregiver may need to check infants who fuss and cry quietly to make sure their needs are being met.

The caregiver can use several strategies to enhance the infant's **emotional development.** Whereas physical development can be enhanced by moving the infant, toys, and oneself around, emotional development demands more than manipulation.

Something special occurs in eye-to-eye contact. The infant and caregiver communicate with each other and reinforce good feelings about one another. There are hundreds of opportunities for this eye contact. Some occur during the routine physical care of the infant. Some are planned especially by the caregiver. Some are initiated by the infant.

Touching also communicates feelings. Young infants cannot understand words, but they respond to touch. Touch can be exciting, threatening, accepting, or calming. The manner in which the caregiver touches, strokes, holds, picks up, places, or moves the infant conveys the feelings of the caregiver to the infant. Touching sends a strong nonverbal message to the infant (see Figure 8–5).

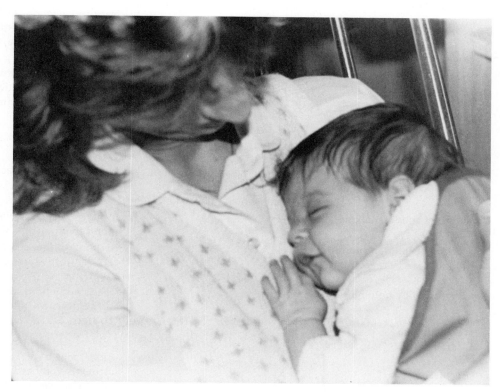

Figure 8–5 Gentle touching and cuddling comfort the infant.

SUGGESTIONS FOR IMPLEMENTING CURRICULUM

CHILD BEHAVIOR	MATERIALS	EXAMPLES OF CAREGIVER STRATEGIES
Types of Emotions-Feelings Shows excitement.	Attention-catching objects.	Use voice and facial expression to reflect back excitement.
Shows stress.	Calming touch, talk, music, singing.	Determine cause. Change situation to reduce stress, e.g., change diaper; change position; talk to infant (child may be bored).
Shows enjoyment.	Interesting, challenging toys, objects.	Provide pleasant experiences, e.g., give infant a bath; snuggle; converse; smile.
Shows anger.		Determine cause. Remove or reduce cause. Divert infant's attention, e.g., turn infant around to look at something else.
Shows fear.		Hold, comfort infant. Remove fear-producing object or change situation, e.g., hold infant startled by sudden loud noise, remove source of pain.
Protests.		Determine what infant is protesting about. Eliminate activity or do it a different way, e.g., change how you wash infant's face.
Control of Emotions-Feelings Seems to occur automatically. Decreases crying.	Activities, toys which catch infant's attention and which infant likes.	Involve infant in an activity.
Increases sounds (talking).		Initiate "conversations" and respond to infant's talking.
Reflects feelings in sounds (talking).		Respond to the feelings expressed, e.g., comfort whining child; change situation.
Comforted by holding.		Consistently hold, caress, cuddle, and comfort when infant needs it.
Temperament Activity level.		Observe and identify where infant is in a range of behaviors. List adjustments you need to make to fit infant's temperament.
Regularity.		

CDA
III . 8

CHILD BEHAVIOR	MATERIALS	EXAMPLES OF CAREGIVER STRATEGIES
Approach or withdrawal as a characteristic response to a new situation. Adaptability to change in routine. Level of sensory threshold. Positive or negative mood. Intensity of response. Distractibility. Persistence and attention span.		

Social Development

The caregiver must become emotionally involved with the infant. Just as infants develop a unique attachment to their mothers, they can develop an additional attachment to their own primary caregivers. Many of the caregiver strategies which build this emotional relationship involve frequent use of looking and touching.

Attachment theory and research have identified phases in the development of attachment. Ainsworth identified infants' social behaviors during the first few months of life which relate to developing attachment.

Phase 1: Undiscriminating Social Responsiveness
first two-to-three months
orienting behaviors: visual fixation, visual tracking, listening, rooting, postural adjustment when held
sucking and grasping to gain or maintain contact
signaling behaviors: smiling, crying, and other vocalizations to bring caregiver into proximity or contact (1982, 139).

Infants from birth to 4 months are egocentric; they have only their point of view. They use their senses to begin to develop a global concept of self. They need to see, hear, smell, touch, and taste themselves. People and objects are familiar insofar as they interact with the infant's sense experiences. For infants at this level people and objects do not exist as separate objects.

The caregiver can use several strategies to enhance **social development**. The caregiver can respond quickly to the infant's needs and can initiate interactions by looking, holding, stroking, talking, playing, carrying, and rocking the infant.

The caregiver arranges time and selects materials which help infants learn about themselves. Mirrors fascinate infants. Dots on bare feet and hands extend the infant's interest in his or her body. The caregiver arranges for the infant to interact with other people and with playthings.

SUGGESTIONS FOR IMPLEMENTING CURRICULUM

CHILD BEHAVIOR	MATERIALS	EXAMPLES OF CAREGIVER STRATEGIES
Attachment Shows special closeness to parent; differentiates response to parent—voice, touch, presence, absence.		Accept that the infant will respond differently to you than to parent.
Develops familiarity with one primary caregiver (significant other).		Same caregiver provides most of infant's care, although other caregivers may share responsibility occasionally.
		Provide consistent care of infant: feed; comfort; change diapers and clothes; talk and sing and play with infant; rock and hold; put to bed; pick up when awake; respond to infant's special needs, likes, and dislikes. Touch, hold, caress, cuddle the infant.
Self Becomes aware of hands and feet.	Bright clothes, materials for hands, feet; bare feet sometimes.	Provide clothes which allow freedom of movement. Occasionally put bright colors, dots on hands, feet, to attract infant's attention.
Smiles spontaneously. Smiles at self in mirror.	Mirror	Smile with infant.
Others Establishes eye contact with another person.		Hold infant so the caregiver is in infant's range of vision. Engage infant in eye contact.
Recognizes voice of parent. Smiles at people (social smile). Watches people.		Hold infant. Smile, talk with infant. Place infant where you can be seen moving about. Carry infant around to see others.

CHILD BEHAVIOR	MATERIALS	EXAMPLES OF CAREGIVER STRATEGIES
Talks (coos) to people.		Respond and initiate talking, singing with infant.
Shows longer attentiveness when involved with people.		Spend time during infant's alert times interacting with infant.
Recognizes parent visually.		
Recognizes individual people.		Provide daily care, interactions with a few persons other than parent.
Behaves differently with parent than with others.		Accept different responses.
Interacts with people.		Initiate interactions, respond; place, carry infant where infant can meet people.
Laughs.		Play with infant; laugh with infant; respond to infant's laugh.
Differentiates self from parent.		
Initiates talking to others.		Answer infant's talk.
Plays with toys.	Toys which attract infant's attention, challenge infant.	Provide toys; change toys to renew interest.

Cognitive Development

CDA
II.5

Piaget's theory of cognitive development categorizes the first four months of life as a part of the sensorimotor stage. Infants get information in this stage through their senses and motor activity. When infants interact with their environment, they are **doing** something. Infants use all their senses. With experience they refine their capacities for seeing, hearing, smelling, tasting, and touching. Moving themselves, moving others, and handling objects become coordinated with their senses. For example, when hearing a sound, infants turn their heads in the direction of the sound.

> Sensorimotor intelligence is primarily focused on action, not on classification and organization. . . . the knowledge that young infants have of objects is in terms of the sensorimotor impressions the objects leave on them and the sensory and motor adjustments the objects require. For young infants objects do not have an existence independent of their reactions to them (Anisfeld 1984, 15).*

The sensorimotor stage has been divided into six substages; the first two are evident in the first four months. In each stage the infant develops new behaviors.

In Stage One the newborn's behavior is reflexive. Infants quickly start to change their behavior from passive reactions to active searching. Each of the senses operates independently.

*From *Language development from birth to three*, (15) by Moshe Anisfeld 1984, Hillsdale, New Jersey: Lawrence Erlbaum. Copyright by Lawrence Erlbaum. Reprinted by permission.

During Stage Two infants begin to coordinate their senses. They begin to develop hand-mouth coordination, eye coordination, and eye-ear coordination. One behavior can stimulate another; for example, a reflexively waving arm may attract the infant's attention so that the child visually focuses on his or her hand.

The caregiver uses several strategies to enhance cognitive development. Selecting items for and arranging an attention-catching environment stimulates the infant to respond in any way possible at his or her particular stage. Repeating and reinforcing the infant's behaviors pleases and stimulates the infant.

SUGGESTIONS FOR IMPLEMENTING CURRICULUM

CHILD BEHAVIOR	MATERIALS	EXAMPLES OF CAREGIVER STRATEGIES
Piaget's Stages of Sensorimotor Development *STAGE 1 (Reflex)* Carries out reflexive actions—sucking, eye movements, hand and body movements.		Provide nonrestricting clothes, uncluttered crib, which allow freedom of movement.
Moves from passive to active search.	Visually attractive crib, walls next to crib, objects; occasional music, singing, talking, chimes.	Provide environment which commands attention during infant's period of alertness.
STAGE 2 (Differentiation) Makes small, gradual changes which come from repetition.		Provide change for infant; carry infant around, hold infant, place infant in crib. Observe, discuss, record changes.
Coordinates behaviors, e.g., a sound stimulates looking.	Face and voice, musical toy, musical mobile, rattle.	Turn on musical toy; place where infant can see it.
Puts hand, object in mouth and sucks on it.	Objects infant can grasp and which are safe to go in mouth.	Place objects in hand or within reach. Infants attempt to put **everything** in their mouths. Make sure they get only safe objects.
Moves hand, object where can see it.	Objects which infant can grasp and lift.	Provide clothes which allow freedom of movement. Place objects in hand or within reach.
Produces a pleasurable motor activity and repeats activity.		Provide time, space for repetition.

CHILD BEHAVIOR	MATERIALS	EXAMPLES OF CAREGIVER STRATEGIES
Piaget's Concept of Object Permanence* *SENSORIMOTOR STAGES 1 AND 2* Follows moving objects with eyes until object disappears. Looks where object has disappeared. Loses interest and turns away. Does not search for it.	Toys, objects which attract visual attention.	Place object in range of infant's vision. Allow time for infant to focus on object. Move object slowly back and forth within child's field of vision. Move object where infant cannot see it, e.g., ball which rolls behind infant.

*Object or person exists when out of sight or touch.

Language Development

CDA
II.6

Language is a tool one uses to communicate with oneself and with others. Crying is one way infants communicate with others. Even newborns cry in different ways depending on whether they are startled or uncomfortable.

Prelinguistic vocalizations contribute to the infant's developing ability to speak. In the first 8 weeks vocalizations are of two kinds: One category consists of vegetative sounds and includes burping, swallowing, spitting up, and the like. The other category consists of discomfort sounds and includes reflexive crying and fussing (Anisfeld 1984, 221).

Infants produce sounds as they use their mouths and throats. These sounds are the infants' "talk." At first they seem unaware of their sounds, and then gradually they begin to repeat their own sounds. Infants will talk to themselves for the pleasure of making the sounds and hearing themselves talk.

Infants use several kinds of sounds as part of their language. They produce sounds as they eat and as they play with their tongues and mouths. They use their throats, saliva, tongues, mouths, and lips to produce gurgling, squealing, smacking, and spitting noises. Gradually they produce sounds which can be classified as "cooing," which resemble vowellike sounds. A second stage of vocalization occurs between 9 and 20 weeks. "It is characterized by *cooing* and laughter; sustained laughter occurs at 16 weeks" (Anisfeld 1984, 222).

When infants hear someone talk to them, it stimulates them to talk. This dialogue is very important. Effective dialogue can occur when the caregiver looks at the infant while alternately listening to and answering the child's talk. The one-to-one dialogue is what stimulates the infant. Talking not directed to the infant personally is not as effective a stimulator. Adults conversing with

CDA
II . 6

each other in the presence of the child, or a radio or television program turned on do not involve the child in language dialogue.

SUGGESTIONS FOR IMPLEMENTING CURRICULUM
The caregiver can use several strategies to enhance the infant's **language.**

1. Talk: Sounds, words, sentences, nursery rhymes, reading stories and books.
2. Sing: Humming; original songs or talking set to your own music; nursery rhymes; lullabies; songs.
3. Listen and respond: Infants will make sounds by themselves for a few months. This talk will decrease if the infants do not have someone to listen to them and to "answer" them.
4. Initiate conversation: Almost every encounter with an infant is an opportunity for conversation. Routine physical care like feeding, changing diapers, and rocking all present the necessary one-to-one situations where you and the infant are interacting. It is not necessary nor helpful to talk all the time or to be quiet all the time. The infant needs times for language and conversation and times for quiet.

CHILD BEHAVIOR	MATERIALS	EXAMPLES OF CAREGIVER STRATEGIES
Physical Components Involved in Language Communication Back of throat.		Observe, record infant's use of sound.
Nose.		
Mouth cavity.		Record repetitions, changes, new sounds.
Front of mouth.		Record mood of infant when infant is making longer repetitions of sounds.
Tongue.		
Lips.		
Saliva.		
Actions Involved in Language Communication Changes air flow: through nose; through mouth.		
Uses tongue to manipulate air flow, saliva.		
Plays with tongue—twists, turns, sticks it out, sucks on it.		

CHILD BEHAVIOR	MATERIALS	EXAMPLES OF CAREGIVER STRATEGIES
Uses saliva in various places and changes sounds: gurgle in back of throat; bubbling in center of mouth; hissing, spitting with partially closed lips and tongue.		
Initiating-Responding	Rattle, objects which make sounds or noises, music box, music, talking, singing.	Talk, sing to infant while feeding, changing diapers and clothes, holding, carrying around, rocking. Carry on normal conversation with infant—talking, listening, silence.
Initiates making sounds.		"Answer" infant with sounds or words.
Responds vocally to another person.		Hold infant: look at infant eye-to-eye; make sounds, talk, sing to infant; listen to infant's response; talk, sing again; listen, etc.
Makes sound, repeats sound, continues practicing sound a few minutes and lengthening to longer blocks of time.		Talk with infant, show interest, look at infant.
Imitates sounds already knows.		Repeat sound infant has just made; listen to infant make sound; repeat it again, etc.
Experiments with sounds.		
Crying Cries apparently automatically in distress, frustration.		Respond to infant's crying immediately and consistently.
Cries differently to express hunger, discomfort, anger.		Attend to the need infant expressed by crying.
Cries to gain attention.		Find out what infant wants.
Cries less as vocalizing increases.		
Cooing Coos in vowellike sounds.		Imitate, respond, talk to infant.
Adds pitch.		

REFERENCES

Ainsworth, Mary D. 1982. The development of infant-mother attachment. In Jay Belsky, ed. *In the Beginning: Readings on Infancy.* New York: Columbia University Press.

Anisfeld, Moshe. 1984. *Language Development from Birth to Three.* Hillsdale, New Jersey: Lawrence Erlbaum.

Bruner, Jerome S. 1968. *Processes of Cognitive Growth: Infancy.* Clark University Press.

Lamb, Michael E. and Campos, Joseph J. 1982. *Development in Infancy.* New York: Random House.

STUDENT ACTIVITIES

1. List the child's behaviors you see in a picture of an infant under 4 months of age (see pp. 176 and 179).
2. Observe one infant under 4 months of age. Record the infant's behavior in two five-minute sequences using narrative description. Transfer the descriptions to the Developmental Profile.
3. Select toys from catalogs and newspaper ads which are stated to be appropriate for an infant under 4 months of age. Read the toy description. Match it to the category and level of development of a specific infant.
4. Select one category of the Developmental Profiles (for example, physical development). Observe a caregiver and classify the strategies (see Chapter 4) the caregiver used in that category (for example, physical support: holds hand behind infant's head and neck).
5. List five strategies which you competently use with infants from birth to 4 months.
6. List strategies you need to develop and list ways you intend to develop them.

REVIEW

1. In each area state a purpose for using the Developmental Profiles with infants from birth to 4 months of age.

AREA	PURPOSE
a. Physical b. Emotional c. Social d. Cognitive e. Language	

2. Describe how you get information about the infant's developmental levels.

3. List three toys or materials which can be used with infants from birth to 4 months of age. List the area(s) of development which each can enhance.

TOY/MATERIAL	AREA(S) OF DEVELOPMENT
a.	
b.	
c.	

4. State two reasons why it is helpful to the infant to have the caregiver talk to him or her.

9

The Child from Four to Eight Months of Age

OBJECTIVES

After completing this chapter, the caregiver shall

Identify and record sequences of change in the physical, emotional, social, cognitive, and language development of infants from 4 to 8 months of age.

Select materials appropriate to that age-level infant's development.

Devise strategies appropriate to that age-level infant's development.

CHAPTER OUTLINE

I. Materials and Activities
   A. Types of materials
   B. Examples of homemade materials
II. Caregiver Strategies to Enhance Infant Development
   A. Physical development

B. Emotional development
C. Social development
D. Cognitive development
E. Language development

CHILD DEVELOPMENT ASSOCIATE FUNCTIONAL AREAS

All CDA functional areas are integrated into the caregiver decisions and behaviors.

Review Chapter 6. Use Appendix A, the Developmental Profile, with each infant. Children follow a **sequence** of development. There can be ranges in **rate** of development.

Theresa, 6 months old, is lying on her stomach on the floor, kicking her legs and waving her arms. She looks at a toy radio and drools. She fingers the toy radio. She chews and drools. She "sings" with the music. Ellie, the caregiver, winds up the toy radio. Theresa kicks her feet and smiles. She watches the radio and kicks her feet. Ellie smiles at Theresa and Theresa smiles back. She kicks her feet rapidly. Theresa looks at Wayne, another infant. Ellie speaks to Theresa. Theresa tries to lift herself by pushing on the floor with her arms. She turns herself around, still on her tummy. She kicks her feet and keeps trying to lift herself up onto her knees to a crawling position. She presses her feet against furniture. During this time she has turned about 180 degrees.

MATERIALS AND ACTIVITIES

 CDA I.3

Materials for this age group must be safe for the infants to mouth and hit and bang on themselves. These infants have developed some manual skills but their limited control of their arm and hand muscles causes them to be rather rough on their toys and themselves. Attention-catching toys stimulate the interest of these infants and lengthen their playtime.

Types of Materials

Foam toys
Small toys and objects to grasp
Soft balls
Sound toys
Toys safe to throw

Toys safe to bang and hit
Low material and equipment to climb on and over
Mirror
Teething toys

Examples of Homemade Materials

BLOCKS

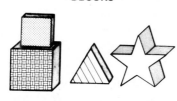

Cut foam rubber into squares, circles, rectangles, triangles, and other shapes. Cover the foam with printed fabric sewn to fit the shapes. Large shapes can be stacked as blocks.

Cut 1-inch-thick sponges into shapes. Make sure the finished pieces are a good size to handle but too big to swallow.

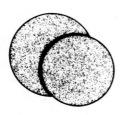

Cover foam ball with washable patterned fabric.

CRIB GYM

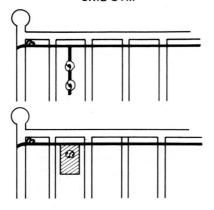

Knot a sturdy cotton rope two times near the end and connect it at the other end to a second rope. The infant can grasp the knots and pull the rope down a little or pull him or herself up a little.

Tie a colorful 3-inch-wide strip of fabric onto the top rope. Cut the length so the infant can just reach it. Use pinking shears to reduce fabric ravelling. Sew on a jingle bell near the top of the strip. It will jingle when the infant pulls and shakes it.

RATTLES

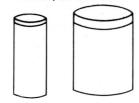

Empty and wash childproof clear plastic medicine bottles. Put in uncooked cereal—one teaspoon white, one teaspoon red (dyed in food coloring). Use sturdy glue to fasten cap tightly.

MUSIC, SOUND TOYS

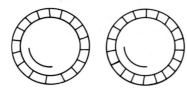

Use empty round cans with lids (oatmeal, potato chip). Put jingle bells or loose items like blocks inside. Glue the lid on securely and tape around the edges. When the infant pushes and rolls it, the bells or blocks will make a noise.

POT PIE FOIL PANS

Place pans near infant to use for mirror, for grasping and for banging. Check frequently. If sharp edge or tear develops, discard.

BEAN BAG

Sew together along three sides two double layers of 3-inch-square colorful terrycloth fabric. Turn right side out. Fill the pouch half-full with aquarium rocks which have boiled to sanitize them. Sew the fourth side shut.

BRACELET

Sew a 4-inch length of elastic together to make a circle. Sew on several yarn pompoms. Place on wrist or ankle for infant to watch while waving arms, kicking feet.

SOCK DOLL

Use a child's sock. Make eyes, nose, and mouth with permanent nontoxic marker or sew features with embroidery thread. Sew on short yarn hair. Stuff with foam or nylon scraps. Sew closed at bottom (top of sock).

TOSS AND PULL

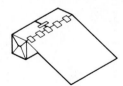

Cut a 1-inch-wide piece of fabric 24 inches long. Use pinking shears to reduce ravelling. Tie one end around a toy (block, ball, doll) and use a velcro fastener to attach the other end around the infant's wrist. Demonstrate dropping or throwing the toy and pulling it back.

CLIMBING INCLINE

Cut off the thick bottom of a large cardboard box. Tape one end to two plastic milk cartons placed end-to-end. Use this for creeping up and down.

CAREGIVER STRATEGIES TO ENHANCE INFANT DEVELOPMENT

Physical Development

CDA
II . 4

Infants develop rapidly during this four-month period. They are awake and alert longer. They are becoming more coordinated. They can sit when propped and are developing the ability to sit alone and can sit in a highchair. They can roll over and may creep. They can grasp objects intentionally and move and bang them purposefully.

The head, neck, arm, chest and back muscles are used to maintain a sitting position. These are developing from the pushing and pulling and kicking and rolling the infant does. Even when the infant can sit when propped or can sit alone, these muscles tire easily, so care must be taken to allow the infant to change positions.

By the middle of the first year infants can stand on their legs. The muscles in their heads, necks, arms, chests, backs, and legs are all functioning but are not yet coordinated. With the aid of people and furniture infants can stay standing and begin to take steps. Their ankle, foot, and toe muscles develop strength and coordination with the rest of their bodies (see Figure 9–1).

LOCOMOTION

While infants are developing some stability in relation to the force of gravity (sitting, standing), they are also attempting to move forward (locomotion).

Figure 9–1 The caregiver smiles, talks, and encourages the infant's movements.

Creeping is the first locomotor movement. Regan is lying on her stomach, reaching for a toy. She twists her body, pulls with her arms, and pushes with her legs. Slowly she moves forward to the toy. To accomplish this major task Regan used her head, neck, back, arm, and leg muscles to move and to lift the top part of her body up and down without tipping over.

MANIPULATION

Manipulation involves reaching, grasping, and releasing. In the first year infants move from reflexive to voluntarily controlled manipulation. During the first six months infants develop from erratic waving to carefully controlled reaching. They use shoulder, elbow, wrist, and hand movements to coordinate with what they see in order to reach purposefully and successfully to an object. Control of reaching is necessary to accompany the task of grasping.

Newborns grasp reflexively. For the next few months their hands will close on anything that touches them. Gradually infants begin to open their hands and use the whole hand to "palm" a toy. By the end of the first year infants use thumb and forefinger to assist in grasping objects.

SEEING

Infants are visually attracted by colorful objects and by faces, shapes, and designs. Hang pictures and objects near the floor or at crib level, where infants can observe them. Put up new pictures and mobiles frequently to stimulate new interest.

HEARING

Infants enjoy making sounds and playing with sounds. Imitate infants' sounds back to them. Hearing and seeing and hearing and reaching are becoming more coordinated.

EATING

Many pediatricians recommend that infants begin solid foods at about 6 months of age. Mouthing and swallowing solid foods involves a coordination of muscles different from those used for sucking. Begin solid foods when the parents request it. Use the same kind of spoon the parents use so the infants do not have to adjust to different sizes and shapes of spoons while they learn to retrieve food from a spoon and swallow the food without spitting it out or choking.

TEETHING

Infants will usually begin teething at this age. Infants react differently to teething. Sometimes an emerging tooth will cause an infant to be very fussy and irritable, while other times a new tooth just seems to appear with the infant behaving no differently at all. Teething infants often like to bite on something. They use teething rings as well as anything else they can put into their mouths. If an infant seems to be hurting, a cold teething ring or crushed ice in a clean cloth provides coldness as well as hardness for the child's gums. Teething infants may drool profusely. They may need to wear a bib all day, and it may need to be changed frequently to keep their clothes dry.

SUGGESTIONS FOR IMPLEMENTING CURRICULUM

CHILD BEHAVIOR	MATERIALS	EXAMPLES OF CAREGIVER STRATEGIES
Muscular Control *HEAD AND NECK*		
Holds head up independently.		Allow infant to lift head. Keep hand near to provide support.
Holds head in midline position.	Mobiles, crib gyms.	Put some objects above center of crib.
Holds head up when on back, stomach, and sitting.		Place infant where child can safely look around.
TRUNK		
Holds up chest, shoulders; arches back, hips.		Provide clothes which allow freedom for pushing up, kicking, and wriggling. Check area for safety.
Sits with support. May attempt to raise self; may fuss if left lying down with little chance to sit up.		Provide pillows, firm items to prop infant against. Hold infant in sitting position.
Leans back and forth.	Place toys within reach.	Keep area around infant free of sharp objects. Infant topples over easily.
Sits in a chair.	Chair with back.	Use chair strap for safety. Let infant sit in chair, but for a short time, for infant's muscles tire quickly.
Sits unsupported for short time.	Safe, flat sitting space.	Place in safe area where infant can sit and play or watch. Infant will tire soon and will lie down. Do not force sitting up again.
Pushes self to sitting position.	Flat sitting space	Provide uncluttered space where infant can roll around and push with arms and legs to sit up alone.
LEG		
Lifts legs when on back and stomach.		Provide clothes which allow free kicking.
Rolls from stomach to back.		Place where infant can move freely and safely. Keep crib sides up. Keep hand on infant while changing diapers.

CHILD BEHAVIOR	MATERIALS	EXAMPLES OF CAREGIVER STRATEGIES
Straightens legs when standing.		Hold infant in standing position for short periods. Hold infant's sides firmly when child bounces.
Stamps feet when standing.		Firmly hold infant upright and provide flat surface for infant to push and move feet against.
Rolls from back to stomach.		Place where infant can move freely and safely. Keep crib sides up. Keep hand on infant while changing diapers.
Raises to hands and knees.		Place on flat, firm surface.
Stands with support.		Hold infant's sides or hands while infant is standing on flat surface.
Pulls self to standing position.		Hold infant's hands and allow infant to use own muscles to pull self up. Check furniture and shelving to make sure neither will tip over when infant pulls on them to stand up.
LOCOMOTION Kicks against surface to move.	Floor space, sturdy furniture.	Provide area where there is safe resistance, e.g., carpeting which helps traction, bare feet on vinyl, furniture to push against.
Rocks on hands and knees.	Blanket on floor.	Provide clear, safe area where infant safely can raise self up and rock, then lurch forward and fall on face. Praise infant for success in getting to hands and knees.
Creeps on stomach.	Blanket on floor.	Provide clear, safe area where infant can creep. Place toy slightly out of reach to motivate creeping. Encourage and praise creeping.
Uses legs to pull, push self when sitting.	Floor space.	Sit a short distance from infant. Call child's name. Encourage infant to come to you. Show excitement and praise.
ARM Visually directs reaching, hitting.	Crib toys, movable toys.	Provide toys which infant can reach and hit. Provide large toys infant accurately can hit against.

CHILD BEHAVIOR	MATERIALS	EXAMPLES OF CAREGIVER STRATEGIES
Throws objects.	Soft, light toys; objects.	Select toys which are light and will not go far and hit other children. Place infant in an area where child can safely throw objects.
HAND Grasps objects with whole hand and fingers against thumb.	Clutch ball.	Provide toys which infant can wrap hand around some part. Flat surfaces slip out of grasp.
Uses thumb and forefinger.	Small toys of any shape.	Make sure toys are too big to be swallowed. Infant will pick up anything, even mouth it.
Picks up object with one hand; passes it to the other hand.	Small toys of any shape.	Place toys around infant so child will use both hands. Ask for toy from one hand. Give toy to each hand.
Uses objects in both hands.	Banging toys.	Play banging game with blocks, bells, balls.
Grasps and releases objects.	Toys which fit in hand or have handles.	Play game, "Put it here." You put one toy in a pile. Infant picks up and puts down a toy in the same place.
Drops objects.	Unbreakable toys and objects, pail.	Provide space for dropping. Play game, "Drop it." Stand up and drop toy into pail. Infant stands against chair and drops toys into pail.
Seeing Focuses on objects near and far.	Designs, pictures, wall space.	Regularly change pictures, floor-to-ceiling projects, and bulletin boards to stimulate new looking.
Distinguishes color, distance; depth perception.	Colorful objects.	Provide colorful items. Put materials within reach so infant can succeed. Respect infant's resistance to moving where child does not feel safe.
Distinguishes visually attractive objects.	Faces, designs, shapes, color in room's materials and space.	Note preferences for faces, designs, shapes. Make frequent changes.
Has visual preferences.	Favorite faces, pictures, objects.	Observe infant's reactions to pictures, objects. Provide access to favorites by displaying them again later.

CHILD BEHAVIOR	MATERIALS	EXAMPLES OF CAREGIVER STRATEGIES
Hearing Listens to own voice.		Provide quiet space where infant can enjoy hearing own voice.
Listens to others' voices.		Place near other infants and care-givers. Direct your talking to the infant.
Looks around to locate sound.	Sounding toys, cans, bells.	Play game: shake can beside infant. Wait for child to turn around and find you shaking the can. Shake bells beside you. Wait for infant to locate the ringing bells. Talk and sing with the infant.
Sleeping Takes a long morning nap and a long afternoon nap.		Adjust routines to fit infant's changing sleep schedule.
Eating 6 months begins solid foods.		
Eats baby food (new tongue and swallowing technique).	Mashed foods, baby spoon, heated dish, plastic-lined bib, washcloth.	Clean up infant and self for feeding time. Check with parent about de-sired food. Feed patiently while in-fant learns to eat from a spoon. Talk calmly. Praise infant's accom-plishments. Clean up.
Drinks from cup (new tongue and swallowing technique).	Cup with special cover to control flow of milk, juice.	Hold cup for infant. Tilt up and back to give infant time to swallow before next drink. Allow infant to help hold cup.
Eats at "mealtimes" with solid foods, milk, juice.		Provide milk or juice in cup and solid foods at regular mealtimes to fit into the infant's sleep and play schedule.
Feeds self finger foods.	Bite-size food.	Clean up infant, self, and eating area. Provide food and time to eat it. Minimize distractions. Talk with infant, encourage infant, label food and actions. Clean up.

Teeth
First teeth emerge.
    2 middle lower.
    2 middle upper.
	Hard teething rings; firm, safe objects to bite, cold objects to bite.	Provide objects safe for infant to bite on hard. May occasionally put ice in sterile cheesecloth for infant to bite on.

CHILD BEHAVIOR	MATERIALS	EXAMPLES OF CAREGIVER STRATEGIES
Elimination Decreases number of times of urination and bowel movements.	Daily report form.	Check diapers frequently; may be dry longer. Record bowel movements.

Emotional Development

Infants now express a wider range of emotions. Pleasure, happiness, fear, and frustration are displayed in a variety of sounds, such as gurgles, coos, wails, cries, along with physical movements like kicking rapidly, waving arms, bouncing, rocking self, and smiling.

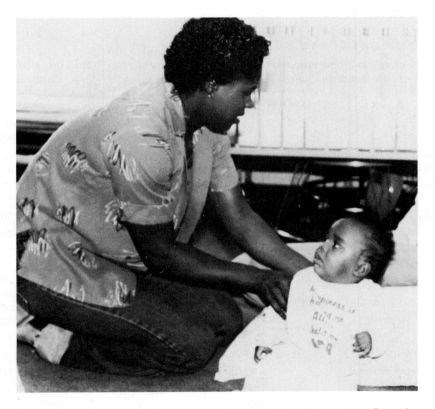

Figure 9–2 The caregiver props the infant into a sitting position for only short periods of time.

FEAR

Many infants experience what is called stranger anxiety, especially between 5 and 7 months of age. People whom the infant does not know and sometimes people the infant does know but does not often see may find the infant acts afraid of them. The infant may cry, cringe, hide, or move away. This very normal infant behavior occurs at a time when the infant is beginning to construct the idea of self as separate from others. It is important that "strangers" not feel something is "wrong" with them. A substitute caregiver may experience this infant withdrawal because the infant has established familiarity and attachment to the primary caregiver, whereas the substitute is different.

TEMPERAMENT

Activity Level The "high active" infant may kick and wriggle and jerk, and therefore tip over when sitting propped more often than the "low active" infant. High active infants need sitting times even though they need more caregiver assistance. On the other hand, low active children are easy to leave in a sitting position longer than may be good for their muscles because they may not fuss and move enough to tip over. These children need to be moved from sitting to lying on their stomachs, to holding, to sitting (see Figure 9–2).

Approach or Withdrawal as a Characteristic Response to a New Situation Infants from 4 to 8 months of age are experiencing many new situations. They are introduced to solid foods and probably will be encouraged to try various vegetables, fruits, and meats. They are beginning to creep and move into room areas on their own, sometimes into areas not meant for them. Those infants who characteristically encounter newness easily may take in stride new foods and new spaces. They will have food preferences, but the act of trying something new usually will not distress them. Those infants who characteristically hesitate or withdraw in new situations will need new experiences presented slowly. Allow time for the infant to become familiar with one kind of food before introducing a new one. Allow the infant to seek new floor spaces and gain familiarity with them; do not move the infant around from new space to new space.

SUGGESTIONS FOR IMPLEMENTING CURRICULUM

CHILD BEHAVIOR	MATERIALS	EXAMPLES OF CAREGIVER STRATEGIES
Types of Emotions-Feelings Shows pleasure in watching others.		Place infant where child can see others playing.
Shows pleasure in repetitive play.	Favorite toys.	Provide favorite toys. Share pleasure in repetitive actions, e.g., clapping hands.

CHILD BEHAVIOR	MATERIALS	EXAMPLES OF CAREGIVER STRATEGIES
Shows depression.		Discuss possible causes with parent. Provide consistent loving, touching, holding, playing whenever possible.
Shows fear of strangers.		Introduce strangers carefully. Do not let stranger hover closely. Give the infant time to become accustomed to the stranger at a distance.
of falling down.		When infant is standing and falling, keep area safe. Comfort when needed and then encourage infant and praise infant's standing.
Shows frustration with stimulation overload.		Provide quiet space and time for the infant. Constant visual and auditory stimulation is nerve-racking. Comfort, hold, talk softly to frustrated infant.
Shows happiness, delight, joy; humor expressed with laughs, giggles, grins.		Share laughing, giggling. Play funny games, e.g., "Touch your nose"—hold your finger by your head and slowly move it to touch the infant's nose while you say excitedly, "I'm going to touch your nose."
Shows rage.		Allow infant to kick legs, flail arms, scream and cry for a short time. Determine the cause of the rage. Reduce or eliminate the cause if possible. Use touching, rubbing back and legs, holding, rocking, soothing talk to help the infant calm down.
Control of Emotions-Feelings Sometimes stops crying when talked to, sung to.		Talk calmly, soothingly to crying infant.
Temperament Activity level. Regularity. Approach or withdrawal as a characteristic response to a new situation. Adaptability to change in routine. Level of sensory threshold. Positive or negative mood.		List two of the infant's behaviors in each category which indicate the infant's basic style. List adjustments you need to make to help the infant cope with daily situations.

CHILD BEHAVIOR	MATERIALS	EXAMPLES OF CAREGIVER STRATEGIES
Intensity of response. Distractibility. Persistence and attention span.		

Social Development

Infants are now developing definite and strong attachments to parents and the primary caregiver. The primary caregiver's presence, consistent care, and emotional involvement with the infant reinforce the attachment.

Infants are engaged in several new social experiences. Their developing physical skills of manipulating objects and moving themselves around contribute to their cognitive development of constructing a concept of self and not-self. During this time from 4 to 8 months of age many infants relate more frequently with other adults and children. Their interest and mobility

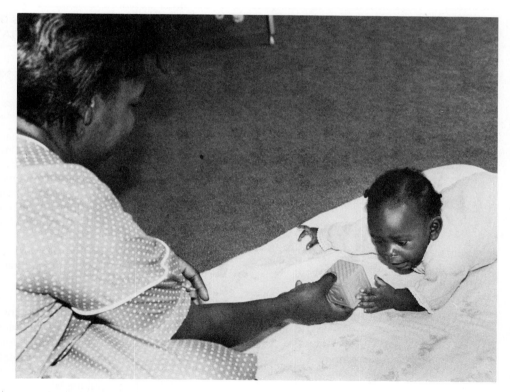

Figure 9–3 The caregiver encourages the infant to play.

contribute to their initiating and responding in interactions with others (see Figure 9–3, page 203).

Ainsworth identified several social behaviors during this age range.

Phase 2: Discriminating Social Responsiveness
6 months or more.
discriminates between familiar and unfamiliar persons. Responds differently to them.
differential smiling, vocalization, crying.

Phase 3: Active Initiative in Seeking Proximity and Contact
around 7 months.
signals intended to evoke response from mother or attachment figure.
locomotion facilitates proximity seeking.
voluntary movements of hands and arms.
following, approaching, clinging—active contact behaviors (1982, 139–41).

SUGGESTIONS FOR IMPLEMENTING CURRICULUM

CHILD BEHAVIOR	MATERIALS	EXAMPLES OF CAREGIVER STRATEGIES
Attachment Shows strong attachment to parent.		Reinforce attachment to parent.
Differentiates response to parent.		
Shows familiarity with one specific caregiver.		Assign a specific, primary caregiver to a specific infant. One caregiver can be a primary person (significant other) to several infants. Primary caregiver assumes responsibility for emotional involvement with the infant while providing care for the whole child.
Shows intense pleasure and frustration with person to whom attached.		Accept, share pleasure; calm, soothe, stroke, sing during infant's frustration periods.
Self Recognizes self in mirror.	Foil, metal or plastic shatterproof mirrors.	Provide hand mirror for the infant to see self. Provide full-size mirror for infant to see self and others.
Seeks independence in actions.		Allow infant to accomplish tasks by self when possible, e.g., creeping to toy, pulling self up.

CHILD BEHAVIOR	MATERIALS	EXAMPLES OF CAREGIVER STRATEGIES
Plays self-designed games.		Allow infant to play own game. Do not distract infant or make infant change and play your game.
Others Observes others.		Place the infant where child can observe other's activities.
Imitates others.		Play games with the infant. Imitate each other, e.g., open mouth wide, stick out tongue.
Recognizes children.		Allow infant to touch, "talk to" other children. Stay close so each is safe from pinching, hitting.
Plays with people.		Let older children and other adults play looking, hearing, touching games with the infant.
Seeks parent's and caregiver's attention by movement, sounds, smiles, cries.		Respond immediately and consistently to happy, sad, angry pleas for attention.
Follows parent and caregiver to be in the same room.		Arrange room so infant can see you from any place the infant is within the room.
Resists pressures from others regarding feeding, eating.		Encourage but do not force the infant to eat. Adjust the time to stop and start according to the infant's rhythm.
Acts shy with some strangers.		Hold, provide security to the infant when meeting a stranger. Allow the infant time to hear and see the stranger before the stranger touches the infant or even gets too close.

Cognitive Development

Infants in sensorimotor substage 3 are constructing the beginnings of the concept of objects separate from themselves. When an object they are watching disappears, they will visually search for it, but they will not manually search for it. When an object they are holding disappears, they will search manually for it. Their senses still strongly control their actions (see Figure 9–4).

Figure 9–4 The caregiver holds the block near the infant so the infant can focus on it and reach for it.

SUGGESTIONS FOR IMPLEMENTING CURRICULUM

CHILD BEHAVIOR	MATERIALS	EXAMPLES OF CAREGIVER STRATEGIES
Piaget's Stages of Sensorimotor Development *STAGE 3* (Reproduction) Produces a motor activity, catches interest, and intentionally repeats the activity over and over.	Objects which attract attention: contrasting colors, changes in sounds, variety of textures, designs.	Watch movements the infant repeats. Waving arm may hit the crib gym; the infant may wave arm more to hit the crib gym again. Watch which movements the infant repeats. Provide materials which facilitate, e.g., new items on the crib gym.
Repeats interesting action.		The infant may pound fists on legs. Watch to see that child's actions are safe.

CHILD BEHAVIOR	MATERIALS	EXAMPLES OF CAREGIVER STRATEGIES
Develops hand-eye coordination further. Looks for object, reaches for it, and accurately touches it.	Toys	Place blocks, dolls, balls, other toys near the infant where child can reach them.
Imitates behavior can see or hear.	Toy, food, body.	Initiate action; wait for infant to imitate it; repeat action, e.g., smile, open mouth.
Piaget's Concept of Object Permanence *SENSORIMOTOR STAGE 3* Visually follows object. Searches visually for short time when object disappears. Does not search manually.	Toys, bottle, objects which attract visual attention.	Show infant a toy. Play with it a minute and then hide the toy. Bring it out and play with it again. (You will not "teach" the infant to look for the toy. Enjoy playing with infant and toy.)
Sees part of object; looks for whole object.	Familiar toy, bottle, rattle, teething ring, ball, doll.	Cover up part of object with a blanket or paper. Infant will pull object out or push off blanket, e.g., with person: play peek-a-boo.

Language Development

CDA
II.6

The crying, cooing, and babbling of the infant help develop the physical mechanisms which produce speech (see Figure 9–5).

> Following the cooing period there is an extended period in which infants engage in babbling. Babbling continues the diversification of sounds begun in cooing. The main difference between the two is in function. Whereas cooing seems to have the function of expressing feelings of comfort, babbling is primarily sound play (Anisfeld 1984, 221–22).

Infants seem to produce sounds first and then "discover" them to reproduce over and over again. They experiment with these sounds and begin to make changes in them. The difference may consist of the same sound made from a different part of the mouth. For instance, when infants play with a voiced sound and the tongue and saliva at the back of their mouths, they produce a gurgle. With the same sound, tongue, and saliva at the front of the mouth they produce a hissing or spitting sound. Infants listen to themselves and seem to enjoy their vocal play.

Babbling is playing with speech sounds. It is spontaneously produced rather than intentionally planned. Infants in their babbling use and learn to control their physical speech mechanisms. They babble different speech sounds, combine them into two- and three-syllablelike sounds. They control

Figure 9–5 The caregiver and children talk and listen to the infant's new sounds.

CDA
II.6

air flow to produce wordlike sounds and change the intensity, volume, pitch, and rhythm of their babbling sound play.

Infants also listen to the sounds around them. When you repeat the sound infants have just made, they may imitate your sound. This stimulation and repetition encourages their practice and the result is increased control over their language. This stimulation also helps infants begin the two-way communication process of talking-listening-talking. They are finding that when they talk, you will listen; infants make you talk to them. Cooing and babbling sounds are used to provide pleasure as well as to convey feelings. Conversations include pitch and volume added to strings of sounds which seem like syllables or words. Infants imitate and initiate private and social talking.

SUGGESTIONS FOR IMPLEMENTING CURRICULUM

CHILD BEHAVIOR	MATERIALS	EXAMPLES OF CAREGIVER STRATEGIES
Coos vowellike sounds for many minutes.		Respond with talk.
Babbles syllablelike sounds.		Respond with talk.
Responds to talking by cooing, babbling, smiling.		Talk directly to infant.
Imitates sounds.		Make sounds, talk, sing to infant.

CHILD BEHAVIOR	MATERIALS	EXAMPLES OF CAREGIVER STRATEGIES
Initiates sounds.		Listen and respond.
Makes vowel sounds.		
Looks for person speaking.		Place self so that infant can see you when you converse together.
Looks when name is called.		Call the infant by name and talk with child.
Makes consonant sounds.		
Babbles conversation with others.		Respond with talking.
Reflects happiness, unhappiness in sounds made.		Let your voice reflect response to mood.
Babbles 2- and 3-syllable sounds.		Respond with talking.
Uses intensity, volume, pitch, rhythm.		Use normal speaking patterns and tones when talking to the infant.

REFERENCES

Ainsworth, Mary D. 1982. The development of infant-mother attachment. In Jay Belsky, ed. *In the Beginning: Readings on Infancy.* New York: Columbia University Press.

Anisfeld, Moshe. 1984. *Language Development from Birth to Three.* Hillsdale, New Jersey: Lawrence Erlbaum.

STUDENT ACTIVITIES

1. Listen to the "talk" of one infant between 4 and 8 months of age. Write down the sounds you hear (they may be strings of vowels or syllables, e.g., aaaa; babababa).
2. Observe a caregiver talking to an infant this age. Write down what the caregiver says and what the infant says.
3. Observe one infant from 4 to 8 months of age. Record the infant's behavior in two five-minute sequences, using narrative description. Transfer the descriptions to the Developmental Profile.
4. Examine the written records of one infant from 4 to 8 months of age. List the Wednesday naptimes for eight weeks. Identify any changes in naptimes.
5. Observe one infant who is creeping. Write a description of the infant's physical movements.

6. List five strategies which you competently use with infants from 4 to 8 months of age.
7. List strategies you need to develop and list ways you intend to develop them.

REVIEW

1. When an infant can roll from stomach to back and from back to stomach, what additional caregiver strategies are needed? Explain three.
2. Deborah, a 5-month-old, is sitting up against a pillow on the floor. She is looking at the toy she has just thrown out of her reach. She leans forward, tips over, and cries. Describe what you would do next. Explain why you would do it.
3. List three caregiver strategies which facilitate the emotional development of the infant between 4 and 8 months.
4. Describe the changes in eye-hand coordination of an infant between 4 and 8 months.

10

The Child from Eight to Twelve Months of Age

OBJECTIVES

After completing this chapter, the caregiver shall

Identify and record sequences of change in the physical, emotional, social, cognitive, and language development of infants from 8 to 12 months of age.

Select materials appropriate to that age-level infant's development.

Devise strategies appropriate to that age-level infant's development.

CHAPTER OUTLINE

I. Materials and Activities
   A. Types of materials
   B. Examples of homemade materials
II. Caregiver Strategies to Enhance Infant Development
   A. Physical development

B. Emotional development
C. Social development
D. Cognitive development
E. Language development

CHILD DEVELOPMENT ASSOCIATE FUNCTIONAL AREAS

All CDA functional areas are integrated into the caregiver decisions and behaviors.

Review Chapter 6. Use Appendix A, The Developmental Profile, with each infant. Children follow a **sequence** of development. There can be ranges in **rate** of development.

Henry, 8 months old, is sitting on the floor with several toys in front of him that Miss Virginia, the caregiver, has just placed there. He picks up a pink toy elephant, lifts it up and down in his right hand and says, "Ahh. Ah, Ah, Yah, Ahya." He picks up lock blocks, saying, "Eee, Ahh, Ahh." He throws down the blocks and then picks up blocks and twirls one in his left hand. He puts down the blocks and crawls away to another part of the room and sits up to watch a child run cars. He crawls to Miss Virginia, who pulls him up to her knees. He stares at her and says, "Ayy." He crawls to the toys, sits back, and then pulls to the train. He pulls up on his knees to the toys and pats the ball. He starts to stand up and goes back to his knees. He pushes the train and it goes forward; his eyes get big. Miss Virginia pulls him up. Henry stands and goes up on his toes as he holds her hands. Miss Virginia picks him up and holds him in her lap a minute.

MATERIALS AND ACTIVITIES

CDA
I.3

Infants in this age range are mobile and will encounter an expanded world. All objects within reach must be safe to taste and touch and move. These

Figure 10–1 Sounds and objects attract the infant's attention.

infants need space as they continue to develop control of gross motor movements like crawling, standing, pulling, and throwing objects. Materials to manipulate must be small enough to grasp with the palm and fingers as well as some items small enough for infants to pick up using their thumbs and forefingers. Attention-catching materials stimulate infants to select and use those materials (see Figure 10–1).

Types of Materials

Very low materials to climb over	Stroking, textured objects
Sturdy furniture to pull self up next to and walk around	Sound toys
	Mirrors
Balls to clutch	Crayons
Stacking objects	Puppets
Nesting objects	Pictures
Pail and small objects to drop into it	1-piece puzzle

Examples of Homemade Materials

CLUTCH BALL

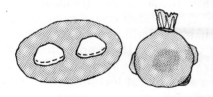

Cut a circle of colorful, washable fabric. Put polyester filling on one part of the fabric and sew around it creating a lump. Repeat, making a second lump. Baste stitch around the edge of the circle and pull the circle almost closed. Stuff in polyester filling to pad the ball. Sew through the fabric and wind thread around the gathered end creating a tuft of fabric.

NESTING TOYS

Select 3 containers of different sizes: plastic margarine tubs; cardboard tubes.

PUZZLE

Glue a picture of one simple object on a piece of thick cardboard (use white glue and water mixture to cover the whole picture and cardboard). Cut out the object, making a simple shape. Place the object into the matching frame.

PUPPET

On child-sized white sock, use nontoxic water-proof marker to draw face on one side, hair on other side.

CAREGIVER STRATEGIES TO ENHANCE INFANT DEVELOPMENT

Physical Development

Infants of this age are rapidly developing muscular control. They learn to sit alone. They crawl, stand with support, and walk with help. Creeping evolves into crawling, where the arms and legs are used in opposition. On hands and knees the infant first slowly moves one limb and then another. With increased control, crawling can become a very fast and efficient means of locomotion, providing the infant with a new world of possible experiences.

When infants have gained stability in standing upright, they can turn their efforts toward moving forward (walking). Ryan is standing next to a chair watching a bright toy on the floor sparkle in the sunshine. He leans toward it and reaches for it, but he cannot reach it. He takes one step away from the chair while still holding on to the chair. He still cannot reach it. He takes another step, and his hand slips off the chair. He is now on his own. He takes another step, stops, weaves, takes another step, and then falls down. Ryan is beginning to walk. His first attempts at locomotion are filled with standing, stepping, weaving, sitting or falling down, pushing himself back up to standing, and trying again. Ryan will repeat this cycle thousands of times, a process which strengthens his muscles and develops his coordination. To accomplish this task Ryan needs open floor space where he can walk without bumping into furniture or having to step on or over toys on the floor.

Many months of movement precede the actual accomplishment of walking. Shirley identified four stages:

1. an early period of stepping, in which slight forward progress is made (3–6 months)
2. a period of standing with help (6–10 months)
3. a period of walking when led (9–12 months)
4. a period of walking alone (12–15 months) (1931).

All infants proceed through these levels of locomotion, though the age will vary among infants.

The accomplishment of unassisted walking is the product of both maturation and appropriate experiences. No one can hasten a child's walking if the child is not ready. We can, however, facilitate a child's movements. Infants need adequate floor space where they can roll, crawl, climb, reach, stand, and walk. Caregivers should be cautious in the equipment they use. Playpens can very easily become prisons for restricting movement. Wheeled walkers can put undue strain on the infant's back, restricting the development and coordination of head, neck, arm, chest, back, leg, and foot muscles, while putting too much emphasis on leg movement.

Infants of this age use their thumb and fingers to grasp objects. Using this skill often, they continue to develop their finger muscles and eye-hand coordination. Because they do not have good control of the strength of the pinch, they may sometimes pinch another child hard enough to hurt.

Holding a finger straight, infants poke at themselves and objects around them. They push and pull and may keep repeating their actions.

These infants are developing control of their arms, so now they can clap, bringing both hands to mid-body repeatedly. Their hands can grasp some objects, so they may bang objects together.

These children are beginning to use each hand for different tasks. They may pick up a toy with one hand, transfer it to the other hand to hold, and then pick up another toy. They may reach out and stack one block, transfer the other toy to that hand, and stack the second block.

Infants are now beginning to be able to stroke objects, controlling their arm and hand movements so that they can touch lightly over the surface of an object. They can explore objects now by touching lightly rather than by pinching.

Infants now can hold their own bottles if they are still using one. Allow the child this independence. Help the infant grasp the cup and then allow the child to drink by him- or herself, assisting only if necessary.

Infants now use both fingers and a spoon to eat and may use them at the same time. They are developing finger and arm control which helps in using a spoon and in picking up food with their fingers. Infants want to get the food into their mouths, and they use every way they can to accomplish this task.

Infants use their new teeth to bite anything put into their mouths. Check toys, materials, and utensils a child uses to determine that they can withstand biting.

Sleep patterns continue to change gradually. At this age infants take a morning and afternoon nap but have more awake time in which to be alert and to play. Each infant has a personal sleep schedule. It is affected by the child's own body needs for sleep as well as by the sleep routines at home. If the infant is awakened at 5:00 A.M. to get ready to come to child care, that child may need a morning nap earlier than an infant who was allowed to sleep until 7:00 A.M.

SUGGESTIONS FOR IMPLEMENTING CURRICULUM

	CHILD BEHAVIOR	MATERIALS	EXAMPLES OF CAREGIVER STRATEGIES
CDA **II . 4**	**Muscular Control** *TRUNK, LEG* Raises self to sitting position.	Flat surface.	Keep area clear of objects which would hurt the infant if child falls on them.
	Sits alone.		Provide short time to sit. Infant may tire soon.
	Stands holding on to furniture or hand.	Sturdy chair, bench, table.	Remove furniture which could tip over on infant.
	Stands without assistance.	Flat surface.	Allow infant to try to stand alone.
	Sits from standing.		Keep area clear of objects which could hurt infant. Infant often falls down when trying to sit down from standing.
	Squats and stands.		Watch sharp-cornered furniture. Pad corners as needed. Infant often stands up underneath furniture (tables) and bumps head.
	LOCOMOTION Crawls.	Obstacle-free space.	Allow infant to crawl. Play with infant to stimulate crawling. Place toys slightly beyond reach to stimulate crawling.
	Steps forward.	Obstacle-free space.	Hold infant's hand, provide furniture to lean on for support when stepping forward.
	Crawls up steps.	Low 2–4 step equipment.	Allow infant to crawl up steps. Watch so you can assist infant's getting back down safely. Barricade any steps you do not want the infant to use.
	Steps sideways.	Equipment, furniture to hold onto.	Allow infant to stand and step around furniture. Keep chairs, toys away from path.
	Walks with help.	Obstacle-free area.	Hold infant's hand(s). Slowly walk around allowing infant to step and balance as he or she needs to. Infant's swaying body will give you clues for stopping and starting.
	Climbs on furniture.	Low, sturdy furniture.	Infant can climb but has not learned how much space his or her body takes up so may climb into areas where does not fit. Watch, caution, and assist when necessary.

CHILD BEHAVIOR	MATERIALS	EXAMPLES OF CAREGIVER STRATEGIES
HAND		
Uses thumb and forefinger.	Toys, dolls.	Provide objects small enough to pinch and lift.
Uses thumb and two fingers.	Toys, dolls.	Provide objects small enough to pinch and lift.
Brings both hands to middle of body.	Banging objects, pot pie pans, blocks.	Play clapping, banging games with infant. Play Pat-a-cake game.
Uses finger to poke.	Pillow, ball, small box.	Provide soft objects to poke into. Watch carefully because infant may poke other children's face, eyes, etc.
Carries objects in hands.	Attractive objects small enough to grasp but too big to swallow.	Provide objects which can be carried. Play game of moving objects from one place to another nearby place.
Holds and uses pen, crayon.	Flat surface, fat felt marker, fat crayon, paper.	Provide materials and space. Demonstrate where marks go (on paper, not on floor or table). Remain with infant when child is using marker or crayon. Allow child to make the kind and number of marks he or she wants to. Praise child for the interest and effort. Put materials away when child decides he or she is finished.
Reaches, touches, strokes object.	Textured objects.	Provide objects of different textures. Infants can stroke, not just grasp and pinch. Demonstrate gentle stroking. Describe the texture, e.g., "the feather is soft." Allow infant to gently stroke many objects.
Uses one hand to hold object, one hand to reach and explore.	Objects small enough to grasp.	Provide several objects at once which stimulate infant's interest.
Stacks blocks with dominant hand.	Blocks, small objects.	Allow infant to choose which hand to use in stacking objects.
Takes off clothes.	Own clothes with big buttonholes, zippers.	Infant's fingers are beginning to handle buttons, zippers. Allow infant to play with these. Infant does not understand when to undress and when to keep clothes on. Discourage undressing when you want infant to stay dressed.
Sleeping		
May have trouble sleeping.	Calming music, musical toy.	Provide adequate time to spend with infant preparing for sleep. Rock, sing, talk, stroke.

CHILD BEHAVIOR	MATERIALS	EXAMPLES OF CAREGIVER STRATEGIES
Takes morning nap and after-noon nap. Seeks parent or caregiver presence.	Quiet, dim, clean sleeping space.	Respond immediately if infant awakens during regular sleep time. Rub child's back, talk quietly as you attempt to help infant go to sleep again. Determine infant's preferences for going to sleep. Feed, hold and rock, rub infant's back, hum and sing to help get the infant to sleep. Primary caregiver should prepare infant for sleep, put infant to bed, respond if sleep is interrupted, and get infant up from nap.
Eating Holds bottle.	Bottle.	Allow infant to hold bottle while you hold infant.
Holds cup.	Cup with special cover.	Allow infant to hold own cup. Assist when necessary, e.g., the spout is at infant's nose rather than mouth.
Holds and uses spoon.	Child-size spoon.	Provide food which can fit on spoon. Allow infant to use spoon to feed self. Assist when necessary with difficult food. Praise infant's efforts and successes. Child will hold spoon in one hand and eat with fingers of other hand.
Uses fingers to eat most food.	Finger food.	Wash hands and face **before** eating. Allow infant to use fingers to pick up food. Wash hands, face, chair, and whole area after eating time.
Starts establishing food preferences.		Identify and record infant's food likes and dislikes. Plan a balanced diet for child emphasizing foods child likes. Do not force foods child does not like.
May eat less.		Do not force eating. Infant's body may need less. Children make ad-justments in the amount they eat. Be sure children have food avail-able they like so they can make choices about **amount** rather than **kinds** of foods.

CHILD BEHAVIOR	MATERIALS	EXAMPLES OF CAREGIVER STRATEGIES
Teeth Begins to get teeth.	Teething ring, cold hard objects to bite, bib.	Provide objects safe to bite. Cold soothes the gums. Change bib as needed since drooling increases.

Emotional Development

Positive interactions with caregivers help infants develop good feelings about themselves. Infants express their happiness in many ways. They also express their anxiety and fears.

At this age infants are developing preferences. Providing toys they like not only adds to their pleasure in playing with the toys but also enhances their feelings of asserting some control over their world.

Developing physical skills make infants more independent in feeding and dressing themselves. Allowing them to accomplish as many tasks as possible on their own helps them strengthen their sense of independence.

Figure 10–2 Crawling enables the infant to explore a wide new world.

External controls like a verbal "no" or a firm look may sometimes cause infants to limit or change their behavior. Follow up your restrictive words or looks with an explanation. For example, when an infant throws food on the floor, the caregiver can say, "No. You need the carrots up here in your dish. Let's see you put a carrot in your mouth." Sometimes infants will stop their own negative action. You may see them pick up food or a toy, start to throw, and then stop their arm movement and put the object down carefully. This early self-restriction may be caused by distraction rather than self-control. Nevertheless, praise such actions to reinforce acceptable behavior.

The temperaments of infants produce varying responses to experiences. The high active infant who is crawling will spend much time and energy trying to crawl wherever you allow the child to go. His or her whole body is moving and developing physically. These children move into new areas and may keep changing their place in the environment frequently. The changing environment in turn stimulates their senses and their involvement with the world. The low active infant who is crawling will initiate crawling but move around less than a high active infant. These children may have the ability to move their whole bodies but may choose instead to use their eyes and hands and arms to search and interact in their space (see Figure 10–2, page 219).

Some infants approach new situations openly. When new solid foods and finger foods are introduced, they try them. They accept and eat many of the foods, and those they reject, they reject with minimal fussing. Other infants are hesitant or resist new situations. Each new food causes these infants to pull back and at first reject the new food. With encouragement these infants may taste the new food and then determine whether they like it or not. Sometimes they so actively resist a new food that it is difficult to get them to eat enough of it to develop an acceptance of it.

Variation in intensity of response often shows up when infants are pulling themselves up and falling down. Falling down, whether toppling forward or sitting down hard on their bottoms, always surprises infants. It is also sometimes painful. One infant will scream and cry loudly. Another may cry quietly or whimper or perhaps look surprised and upset but will not verbalize his or her discomfort.

Persistence at trying to stand upright and step forward leads toward walking. Very persistent infants will try again and again to stand or step. Falling down becomes a deterrent only after many tries. Other infants persist only a few times, then stop their efforts and change to some new task or interest.

SUGGESTIONS FOR IMPLEMENTING CURRICULUM

CHILD BEHAVIOR	MATERIALS	EXAMPLES OF CAREGIVER STRATEGIES
Types of Emotions-Feelings Shows happiness, joy, pleasure.		Share infant's feelings. Reflect back smile, positive tone of voice; hug, pat.

CHILD BEHAVIOR	MATERIALS	EXAMPLES OF CAREGIVER STRATEGIES
Shows anxiety.		Use calm, quiet talking, singing. Cuddle, stroke. Remove from situation if necessary.
Shows fear.		Determine and remove cause of fear if possible. Use calm, quiet talking, singing. Cuddle, stroke.
Shows anger, frustration; has tantrums.		Determine and remove cause if possible. Use calm talking, may sometimes hold and soothe infant. Help infant start a new activity. May sometimes ignore a tantrum.
Rejects items, situations.		Allow infant to make choices. Figure out alternative choices for situations he really needs, e.g., time or place choices.
Develops preferences with toys, people.		Identify and record infant's preferences. Make sure these toys are available frequently.
Shows independence—helps with feeding and dressing self.	Cup, spoon, clothes child can manipulate.	Allow infant to help feed and dress self. This takes much time and patience. Lengthen eating time to adjust to self-feeding skills.
Shows affection.		Accept and return affection with smile, hug, cuddle.
Begins developing self-esteem.		Provide positive affirmation of infant through your tone of voice, looks, touch.
Control of Emotions-Feelings Begins to learn to obey "No."		Use "No" sparingly so infants can determine important situations when they must control their behavior. Use firm, not angry voice. Use firm, not smiling look on your face.
Sometimes inhibits own behavior.		Praise infant for self-control, e.g., raised arm to throw book which then put down on table.
Obeys commands: No-No; Stop.		Use commands sparingly. Praise infants when they obey.
Temperament Activity level. Regularity.		List two of the infant's behaviors in each category which indicate the infant's basic style.

CHILD BEHAVIOR	MATERIALS	EXAMPLES OF CAREGIVER STRATEGIES
Approach or withdrawal as a characteristic response to a new situation. Adaptability to change in routine. Level of sensory threshold. Positive or negative mood. Intensity of response. Distractibility. Persistence and attention span.		List adjustments you need to make to help the infant cope with daily situations.

Figure 10–3 The crawling infant encounters other children.

Social Development

Interactions with others are increasing. The mobility infants now have enables them to encounter different people and to move away from them. These infants initiate interactions with others and respond to others' interactions with them (see Figure 10–3).

The infant's egocentric perspective is evident. These infants do not yet separate others' desires and needs from their own. Therefore, they do not consider or respond to someone else's requests. They are very possessive of materials and people. Such materials and people still seem part of the infant, not completely separate, and thus they seem to belong to the infant.

The caregiver is familiar to the infant and fosters a sense of security. The infant therefore tries to keep the caregiver in sight, reinforcing his or her feelings of security.

SUGGESTIONS FOR IMPLEMENTING CURRICULUM

CHILD BEHAVIOR	MATERIALS	EXAMPLES OF CAREGIVER STRATEGIES
Others Initiates interactions with others.		Respond to infant's behavior. Talk, play with infant. Allow infant access to other children and adults.
Responds.		Initiate talking and playing with infant.
May fear strangers.		Keep strangers from forcing themselves on infant, who may not want to be held by stranger.
Keeps parent or caregiver in sight.		Allow infant to follow you around. Arrange room so infant can see you from different areas of the room.
Initiates play.		Respond and play infant's game, e.g., Pat-a-cake.
Begins to identify with children of own sex.		Verbally label, e.g., "Audrey is a big girl"; "Rhodes is a big boy."
Becomes assertive.		Encourage infant's assertiveness. Observe to determine whether infant is getting aggressive and will need cautions.
Wants own pleasure; may not consider others.		Verbalize limits and help infant choose other activities, materials.
Imitates play.		Play games with infant, e.g., "Can you do this?" Wave hand, clap hands, etc.

CHILD BEHAVIOR	MATERIALS	EXAMPLES OF CAREGIVER STRATEGIES
Is possessive of people.		Verbally assure infant you will be here and will come back to talk, play with infant again.
Is possessive of materials.	Many toys.	Provide enough toys and materials so infant does not need to share.
May become shy, clinging.		Hold, hug, pat; allow infant to remain close; verbally assure infant you are here.
May demand attention.		Provide positive verbal attention even though you may be busy with another child.

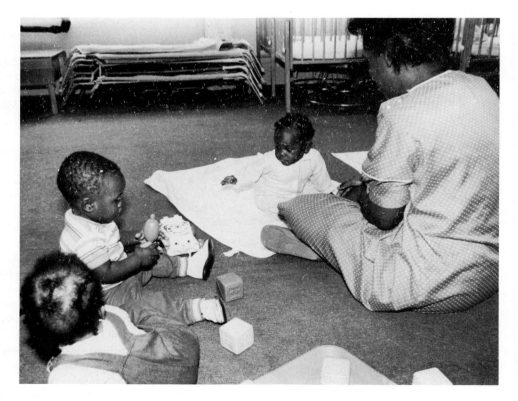

Figure 10–4 Other people and toys are beginning to be perceived as "not self" by the developing infant.

Cognitive Development

CDA
II.5

Assimilation and accommodation begin to operate independently. Infants of this age are beginning to separate their thinking about what they want to accomplish from how they can accomplish it.

The establishment of object permanence is the major development during this age range. Awareness of object permanence forms the basis for rapid development of representations in play and language.

These infants are constructing a concept of self separate from all other entities. People and toys will become real entities which continue to exist even when the infants cannot see them (see Figure 10–4). With this concept infants now actively search visually and manually for people or objects which are no longer visible. These infants are mentally constructing a representation of the person or object. This mental representation of the real entity forms the foundation for increasingly complex forms of representation. Along with thinking about other people as separate from themselves, these infants also begin to determine that others can cause actions. They will incorporate others' actions into their own play.

At this age the infant's imitations change: "...early imitation serves a learning function, that is, infants imitate to advance their comprehension and mastery of behaviors that interest them" (Anisfeld 1984, 44).

SUGGESTIONS FOR IMPLEMENTING CURRICULUM

CHILD BEHAVIOR	MATERIALS	EXAMPLES OF CAREGIVER STRATEGIES
Piaget's Stages of Sensorimotor Development *STAGE 4* (Coordination) Differentiates goals. Can focus on reaching and focus on toy.	Toys, visually attractive objects.	Place objects near infant.
Piaget's Concept of Object Permanence Establishes object permanence; object exists when it is no longer visible; child seeks toy that rolls behind box.		Play hiding games, e.g., hide the doll under the blanket; place the block behind you.
Causality Learns that others cause actions.		Verbalize caregiver's own actions, e.g., "I put the ball behind me."
Imitation and play Imitates other's actions; uses actions as play.		Introduce new copy games. Allow time and space for infant to play.

Language Development

Infants at this age use combinations of sounds, babbling, and words to converse with themselves and others (Wilson 1989). "Just as the sensorimotor exploration of objects lays the groundwork for object representation, so the sensorimotor exploration of speech lays the groundwork for speech representation" (Anisfeld 1984, 224).

Anisfeld identified levels of meaning, characterizing the first level as presymbolic uses of words. "The early words have a sign character. . . .They are *context bound*" (1984, 67). Infants learn to associate a word with a particular object or action. They respond to the word in that context but cannot identify it in other contexts. For example, each day the caregiver says "Sit in your chair" as she gets the infants ready for lunch. When told to "sit in your chair," Beverly looks to her chair. She does not look at other chairs around the room. "Chair" relates to a specific chair, not to a class of objects called "chairs." ". . .[C]hildren's early words are nonsymbolic because they function primarily as responses to specific stimulus contexts" (Anisfeld 1984, 69). An infant says the word in association with the context in which it was learned: ". . . the context-boundness of the first level results from a conceptual limitation. The child does not automatically conceive of words as independent of the specific contexts of their use" (Anisfeld 1984, 70).

Reading aloud to infants facilitates their language development. Linda Lamme recommends in *Growing Up Reading**

> Pointing to things in pictures and labeling them orally is especially important in the first year when your infant, though not yet talking, is acquiring so much language. Relate what is in the book to your infant's experience. "You have a ball just like that one!" Repetition is important also. After seeing a page several times, your infant will begin to recognize the pictures. You'll quickly come to realize your infant has distinct book preferences.
>
> The last guideline is: The earlier you begin to read aloud, the better. If your child can become used to having stories read aloud before he or she starts walking, reading-aloud sessions can be sustained during those mobile, early walking times. Children who are learning to walk have a hard time sitting still to listen to a story if they have not previously become hooked on book reading (1985, 51).

Scribbling is related to the language/reading/writing processes which the infant is developing. From her earlier work on infants, *Growing Up Writing*, Lamme has observed**

> Well before his first birthday, your child is ready to make marks on paper or chalkboard. Those first marks will be random scribbles. Your child won't even be watching as he is making the mark and will not see the connection between the mark on paper and the writing tool in his hand. This first stage of development is called "uncontrolled scribbling."

The outstanding feature of these early writing attempts is that they are more than random marks; they represent your child's intentions to create something. Scribbling has been termed "gesturing with a pencil." The role of scribbling in writing development has been compared with babbling in oral language development. In each case, there is probably some random sound or scribble made but, in both cases, your child is intending to communicate (1984, 38).

SUGGESTIONS FOR IMPLEMENTING CURRICULUM

CHILD BEHAVIOR	MATERIALS	EXAMPLES OF CAREGIVER STRATEGIES
Babbles.		Respond with talk.
Shouts.		Respond to infant's feelings.
Labels object sounds.	Bell, rattle.	Name important objects. Use one word. Then use in a sentence, e.g., "Bell" (while pointing to it). "Ramon has a bell."
Uses names: mama, dada.		Reinforce by talking about Mama and Dada.
Responds to familiar sounds.		Provide familiar music, routine changes. Acknowledge infant's response, e.g., "Tasha heard the spoons being put on the table."
Responds to familiar words.		Frequently use names or labels which infant is learning, e.g., ball, shoe, coat.
Responds to own name.		Use infant's name when you start talking with that child.
Makes sounds which reflect emotions.		Respond to the infant's message about how he or she feels. Name the emotions, e.g., "Garrett is angry."
Repeats syllables, words, e.g., bye-bye.		Label frequent behaviors and respond to infant's use, e.g., say "Bye-bye" and wave; repeat occasionally.
Makes sounds like conversation.		Respond verbally to infant's "conversation," e.g., "Holly is talking to her truck."
Repeats, practices word over and over.		Allow infant to play with words. Respond and praise occasionally.
Connect word with objects, e.g., says "kitty"—points to kitty.	Familiar toys, objects.	Point or touch objects you verbally label. Word is representing that particular object.
Chooses books	Picture books of familiar objects.	Point to picture of object and say name of object. Repeat often.
Scribbles randomly.	Paper, markers	Provide writing space and materials.

REFERENCES

Anisfeld, Moshe. 1984. *Language Development from Birth to Three.* Hillsdale, New Jersey: Lawrence Erlbaum.

Lamme, Linda Leonard. 1984. *Growing Up Writing.* Washington, D.C.: Acropolis Books Ltd.

Lamme, Linda Leonard. 1985. *Growing Up Reading.* Washington, D.C.: Acropolis Books Ltd.

Shirley, M. M. 1931. The first two years: A study of twenty-five babies. *Postural and Locomotor Development,* Volume 1. Minneapolis: University of Minnesota Press.

Wilson, L. C. 1989. Sounding off! *Pre-K Today.* 3(6): 51-53.

STUDENT ACTIVITIES

1. Observe one infant who is walking with support. Identify the following:
   a. what infant held onto for support
   b. where infant walked
   c. what you think caused infant to sit or fall down (lost balance, got tired, lost interest, wanted to get somewhere else fast).
2. Use narrative description to record your observations of one caregiver for five minutes. Then categorize the caregiver's behaviors which relate to social development.

INITIATING BEHAVIOR		RESPONDING BEHAVIORS	
Caregiver Behavior	Infant's Response	Infant's Initiating Behavior	Caregiver's Response

3. Observe one infant between 8 and 12 months of age. Record the infant's behavior in two five-minute sequences using narrative description. Transfer the descriptions to the Developmental Profile.
4. List five strategies which you competently use with infants between 8 and 12 months of age.
5. List strategies you need to develop and list ways you intend to develop them.

REVIEW

1. Why is sharing difficult for the infant between 8 and 12 months of age?
2. List five strategies you can use to facilitate the physical development of an infant in this age range; use this format:

	CAREGIVER STRATEGY	SPECIFIC PHYSICAL DEVELOPMENT
1.		
2.		
3.		
4.		
5.		

3. An 11-month-old is responding to labels of objects. Describe a game you can play with this child to stimulate the child's understanding and use of language.
4. Identify four ways an infant in this age range asserts independence.

11

The Child from Twelve to Eighteen Months of Age

OBJECTIVES

After completing this chapter, the caregiver shall

Identify and record sequences of change in the physical, emotional, social, cognitive, and language development of toddlers between 12 and 18 months of age.

Select materials appropriate to that age-level toddler's development.

Devise strategies appropriate to that age-level toddler's development.

CHILD DEVELOPMENT ASSOCIATE FUNCTIONAL AREAS

All CDA functional areas are integrated into the caregiver decisions and behaviors.

Review Chapter 6. Use Appendix A, The Developmental Profile, with each child. Children follow a **sequence** of development. There can be ranges in **rate** of development.

Andrea, 15 months old, stands looking around. She walks over to 2-year-old Jenny who is sitting on the sofa. She stands between Jenny's legs and bounces up and down to Hokey Pokey music from the record player. Andrea and Jenny dance around. Jenny lies down on the floor and Andrea crawls on top of her. Jenny moves and Andrea follows. They both lie quietly for a minute. Andrea walks to the toys. She picks up a toy plastic milk bottle and lifts it to her mouth to drink. She sits down and puts three lock blocks in the bottle. Allen, the caregiver, says, "Shake it, Andrea." She shakes the bottle, and it makes a noise. She shakes it again. She puts a pail over her head and walks around peeking under the edge of the pail and "talking." Andrea climbs into a child's rocking chair, turns around to sit down, and starts rocking. She "talks" and rocks and then climbs out of the chair and walks around, following Allen.

MATERIALS AND ACTIVITIES

CDA
I.3

Walking is a major development for toddlers at this age. They are fascinated with toys to pull or push as they toddle around (see Figure 11–1). They

Figure 11–1 Toddlers need toys and space which encourage walking.

climb over objects. They may ride wheeled toys. They grasp and throw and drop objects again and again. They are moving into imaginative play and need materials which can facilitate their play.

Types of Materials

Pull toys	Soft objects to throw
Push toys	Mirrors
Trucks, cars	Dolls
Low, riding wheel toys	Puppets
Low, 3-step stairs to climb	Puzzles
Blocks	Picture books and cards
Pail with objects to put in and take out	Paper, nontoxic markers, crayons
Water and sand toys and area	Audio records and tapes

Examples of Homemade Materials

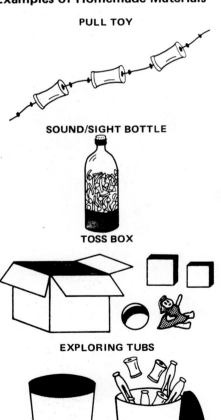

PULL TOY

Use plain or painted empty spools. Thread and knot spools on a length of clothesline rope.

SOUND/SIGHT BOTTLE

Use a clear plastic liter bottle (soft drink). Wash it thoroughly and allow to dry inside. Put inside material or objects which will make noise (sand, wooden or plastic blocks, metal bottle caps). Add confetti for color interest. Screw on bottle cap and glue securely. Tape over rough edges of cap.

TOSS BOX

Collect several small, soft toys and place in a cardboard box. Show child how to take out objects, stand away from the box, and throw the objects into the box. Paint the inside of the box to attract the child's attention as a "target."

EXPLORING TUBS

Place one solid object in a margarine tub. Put lid on. When children shake it, they hear a noise. Encourage the children to take off lid to discover what is inside. Put lid back on. Have several tubs available with different objects inside, e.g., plastic clothes pins, large wooden thread spools.

PICTURE CARD

Use a square of 2- or 3-ply cardboard. Place a photograph of a child on the cardboard and cover the whole square (front, back, and sides) with contact paper or laminating film. Also use colorful pictures cut from magazines. Select pictures which are simple and show one object, e.g., car, cat, flower, bird. Select pictures of objects the child is familiar with.

CLOTHING FRAME BOARD

Cover wood 12" x 12" x 2" with fabric. Glue one piece of fabric to each side of wooden frame with fabric opening at center of frame. Sew buttons on one side at center, buttonholes on other side. Or put on large snaps. Or sew in large-toothed zipper.

CAREGIVER STRATEGIES TO ENHANCE TODDLER DEVELOPMENT

Physical Development

An expanding world opens up to toddlers as they become mobile. They walk, lurch, run, fall, bump into things, and keep persisting in moving around in their world. They are unstable when they walk. They may topple over from stepping on an object or by leaning too far or walking too fast. They are learning to make adjustments so that they can remain upright. Their muscles are developing and coordinating gradually so in the next months their walking will become more stable (Wilson 1988).

Having developed control over reaching and grasping, it would seem that toddlers have become proficient in manipulation. There is one more skill, however, which they need. They now can reach to an object and grasp it. But they have trouble releasing it. You will see a toddler clutching a toy which he or she does not seem to want. When you try to take it away, the toddler's fingers seem "locked" around it. The flexor muscles in the fingers have to relax to let go of the object. It takes many months before these muscles have matured sufficiently to relax on command. Toddlers at this age develop finer control in reaching and grasping. However, since they have trouble releasing things from their hands, they often fling toys. Their arm movement is strong, but when the hand does not release the object adequately, the forward motion often propels the object out of the hand and toward anything in its path. These flying objects become dangerous among groups of children (see Figure 11–2).

Many toddlers are making a transition from very late morning and afternoon naps to one early afternoon nap. Arrange for these toddlers to eat their lunch a little earlier so they can finish before they fall asleep.

Figure 11–2 Toddlers fling toys to get them out of their hands.

CDA
II.4

SUGGESTIONS FOR IMPLEMENTING CURRICULUM

CHILD BEHAVIOR	MATERIALS	EXAMPLES OF CAREGIVER STRATEGIES
Muscular Control *TRUNK* Shows high energy, is active, moves from one activity to another.		Provide a variety of materials and activities so the child can change activities and play objects often. These toddlers frequently do not "make" anything or complete an activity. Schedule clean-up and help put away toys at end of playtime.

CHILD BEHAVIOR	MATERIALS	EXAMPLES OF CAREGIVER STRATEGIES
Raises self to standing.	Sturdy furniture to grasp; flat surface.	Provide space where toddlers can stand up safely. Caution them about standing up under furniture.
LOCOMOTION May prefer crawling to walking.		Allow toddler to crawl when child wants to. It is faster than walking when the child is just beginning to walk.
Walks alone.		Allow toddler to walk alone when child wants to. Provide a hand to hold on to when child seeks help.
Climbs up stairs with help.	Stairs.	Provide handrail or your hand to assist child with balance.
Climbs down stairs with help.	Stairs.	Provide handrail **and** your hand. Balance is still poor when walking down stairs.
Climbs over objects.	Low, sturdy furniture, equipment, boxes.	Provide low climbing equipment, furniture, e.g., stuffed footstool, sturdy cardboard boxes, covered foam incline.
HAND Uses thumb against fingers. Shows hand preference.	Small toys, crayons, pens.	Provide materials toddler can grasp. Allow toddler to use whichever hand he or she chooses.
Points with finger.	Pictures, books, objects.	Play pointing game, e.g., open picture book—"Point to the tree."
Carries, exchanges objects in hands.	Small toys.	Ask toddler to carry toys to another part of the room. Hand toddler another toy to carry.
Throws objects.	Soft, small objects.	Provide a place and target where toddler can throw objects.
Rolls and catches objects.	Large, small balls.	Sit on floor with legs open and outstretched and roll ball back and forth with toddler.
EYE-HAND COORDINATION Reaches and grasps accurately.	Toys, objects which hand can grasp.	Provide toys and objects in places where toddler can safely reach, grasp, lift, and move them.
Scribbles.	Paper, nontoxic markers, crayons.	Provide flat surface for toddler to use paper and marker or pen. Admire and praise the marks the toddler makes.

CHILD BEHAVIOR	MATERIALS	EXAMPLES OF CAREGIVER STRATEGIES
Helps in dressing, undressing.	Buttons, snaps, zipper cards, books, clothing frame board, large dolls with clothes.	Allow toddler to do as much as possible. Assist when toddler needs help.
Seeing Watches people, objects, actions.	Space with few visual obstructions.	Provide space where people are visible to toddler. Allow toddler to choose what to watch.
Bends, looks from different directions.		Place toys, materials in different places. Allow toddler to move materials. Toddler may look up from the floor, look down between legs, look sideways under a table.
Visually scans area around.		Allow toddler to look around. Toddler may gaze around for periods of time. Provide interesting visual stimuli.
Visually searches.		Toddler may look for specific object, person. Assist if child nonverbally or verbally requests your help.
Sleeping Begins to move from morning and afternoon nap to afternoon nap. May fall asleep during lunch.		Adjust eating and nap schedule so toddler does not miss lunch.
Eating Eats three meals.		Determine mealtime. Make adjustments for individual children as necessary.
Feeds self: uses cup, spoon, and fingers.	Food, plate, cup, spoon.	Allow toddler to feed self as much as possible. Assist when necessary.
Expresses food likes and dislikes.		Record food preferences. Provide foods child likes. Introduce new foods gradually. Combine foods child does not like with ones child does like to provide needed nutrition.
May eat less food.		Do not force eating. Make food as attractive as possible.

Emotional Development

Toddlers seek both dependence and independence. Many things in their world still cause them to be anxious. For many tasks they need help. The caregiver can provide toddlers with emotional strength and security, accepting toddlers' very real dependence (Wilson 1987). Toddlers also are trying to become independent. Emotionally they need support which affirms their importance as individuals who can make some choices and accomplish some tasks all by themselves. Their growing sense of achievement enhances their developing positive feelings of self-worth (see Figure 11–3).

Toddlers' anger and frustration may come out as temper tantrums. Distinguish between kinds of tantrums. Frustration tantrums may respond to changing the conditions which caused the child's frustration. Toddlers sometimes have tantrums in order to get their own way. Toddlers' manipulation tantrums sometimes have to be ignored. These children are seeking attention. Giving attention during the tantrum may reward and encourage future outbursts. Instead, the caregiver should provide positive attention soon after the tantrum is over.

Figure 11–3 The caregiver provides toys toddlers can use successfully, reinforcing the feeling of achievement.

Toddler negativism may be expressed by "No!" or in tantrums. Their pursuit of independence may carry over into doing the opposite of what was requested. Rephrase command statements and refocus attention to something of interest to the toddler. For example, you might rephrase "Put the doll away" to "Mary Jane, where can you find a place to put the doll down? She needs to go to sleep."

Children learn concepts of right and wrong from adults. Toddlers are just beginning to use words, and they respond to some labels and commands. But words alone will not control their behavior until they construct concepts of rightness and wrongness. These concepts are constantly being revised and expanded as the toddlers compare their behavior with adults' reaction to that behavior. At this age toddlers cannot separate themselves from their actions enough to understand the idea, "I like you but I do not like what you are doing." Therefore, caregivers need to find ways to help toddlers discriminate between right and wrong while still accepting each toddler as a worthy person no matter what his or her behavior is.

Children's ability to adapt to change in routine during this time of negativism may create problems. The toddler who is very adaptable may change routines easily or with a little fussing. For example, putting that toddler's chair in a different place in the room may create interest for the child. A toddler who has difficulty adapting to change may react negatively, resisting the moving of the chair by fussing or crying and even having a tantrum. This child may combine resistance to change with negativism.

A toddler's distractibility often can be used to stimulate attention and reduce frustrations and anger. Some toddlers who are less distractible may be able to focus attention on an activity which interests them without losing focus when someone nearby starts to sing. With these children you may not be able to distract their attention from using a toy another child has. However, an easily distractible child flits from activity to activity as something new attracts attention. When you need to distract such children from pulling a toy away from another child, these children easily turn their interest to a different toy you show them.

SUGGESTIONS FOR IMPLEMENTING CURRICULUM

CHILD BEHAVIOR	MATERIALS	EXAMPLES OF CAREGIVER STRATEGIES
Types of Emotion-Feelings Expresses emotions in behavior and language.		Determine and respond to toddler's emotions.
Recognizes emotions in others.		Be consistent in showing emotions, e.g., happiness—smile and laugh; anger—firm voice, no smile.

CHILD BEHAVIOR	MATERIALS	EXAMPLES OF CAREGIVER STRATEGIES
May fear strangeness.		Introduce new people, new experiences to toddler. Caution others not to "rush" the child. Allow child to approach or withdraw at own rate.
Shows excitement, delight.		Respond with similar excitement, e.g., touching a pretty flower, an animal.
Expresses sense of humor.		Giggle and laugh with toddler.
Shows affection.		Accept and return physical and verbal show of affection.
Displays negativism.		Provide honest, workable choices, e.g., "Do you want to run or walk to the table?"
Has tantrums.		Determine and remove cause if possible. Sometimes ignore. Proceed calmly with involvement with other children, activities.
Uses play to express emotions, resolve conflicts.	Blocks, dolls, home living, clothes, toy animals.	Provide props for acting out fear, frustration, insecurity, joy.
Seeks dependency, security with parent and caregiver.		Provide touching, holding, stroking interactions; respond quickly and consistently to toddler's needs.
Seeks to expand independence.		Allow toddler to attempt activities by him- or herself. Do not take over if toddler can be successful without you.
Control of Emotions-Feelings Begins to learn right and wrong.		Verbalize which behavior is right and which behavior is wrong. Give reasons. Since toddlers are only just beginning to conceptualize "right-wrong," they only occasionally can apply concept to control their own behavior.
Reinforces desired behavior.		Praise toddler for controlling own behavior.
Temperament Activity level. Regularity. Approach or withdrawal as a characteristic response to a new situation.		List two of the toddler's behaviors in each category which indicate the toddler's basic style. List adjustments you need to make to help the toddler cope with daily situations.

CHILD BEHAVIOR	MATERIALS	EXAMPLES OF CAREGIVER STRATEGIES
Adaptability to change in routine. Level of sensory threshold. Positive or negative mood. Intensity of response. Distractibility. Persistence and attention span.		

Social Development

Toddlers are egocentric; they see the world from their own point of view. In the first year and a half of life their bodies and the objects they play with are perceived to be part of "self." Gradually, as they develop the concept of object permanence, they differentiate "self" from other objects and people, which become "not self." This major development in toddlers provides the basis for life-long expansion of their concept of self and their interactions with others.

Toddlers behave differently toward different people. They recognize differences in people and adjust their interactions with them. They may be eager and excited with a familiar caregiver and quiet and withdrawn with a substitute.

Toddlers play with toys and materials and sing and talk usually by themselves in solitary play. They may look at other children and play near them, but they do not interact with them in play. Toddlers now engage in solitary play (playing alone) and parallel play (playing near but not with other children); they decide what kind of interaction they want with others (see Figure 11–4).

SUGGESTIONS FOR IMPLEMENTING CURRICULUM

CHILD BEHAVIOR	MATERIALS	EXAMPLES OF CAREGIVER STRATEGIES
Self Has concept of self.		Positively reinforce toddler as an individual.
Is egocentric: understands only own viewpoint.		Do not expect toddler to "feel sorry for" someone toddler has hurt. Toddler assumes everyone thinks and feels the way he or she does.

CHILD BEHAVIOR	MATERIALS	EXAMPLES OF CAREGIVER STRATEGIES
Others Seeks presence of parent or caregiver.		Allow toddler to follow you around. Tell child when you are going out of sight.
Plays games.		Play games with toddler. Respond and play child's games.
Occasionally shares.		Provide enough materials and equipment so sharing can be encouraged but not required.
Acts differently toward different people.		Expect different responses to different people. Accept toddler's choices.
Uses variety of behaviors to gain attention.		Identify toddler's usual behaviors to gain attention. Respond to any of those behaviors as quickly as possible.
May be shy with some people.		Do not force toddler to interact with all people. Allow child to keep a distance and watch.
Engages in parallel play.		Provide materials and space so toddlers can play with own materials but near each other.

Figure 11–4 The caregiver lets toddlers concentrate on exploring toys by themselves.

Figure 11–5 Toddlers learn about their physical world by putting themselves in different spaces.

Cognitive Development

Object permanence becomes more firmly established. At this age toddlers may search for an object they have seen moved and hidden again.

Toddlers of this age are interested in observing the effects of their own and others' actions. Exploration is done using trial and error. These little explorers try, and probe, and practice activities and observe the results of their actions. Logical reasoning is not a part of trying an action a different way (see Figure 11-5, page 241).

Now that toddlers are aware that others cause actions to occur, imitation of others' behaviors becomes a part of their play. They use some play behaviors repeatedly in the same pattern and develop their own ritual play.

SUGGESTIONS FOR IMPLEMENTING CURRICULUM

CHILD BEHAVIOR	MATERIALS	EXAMPLES OF CAREGIVER STRATEGIES
Piaget's Stages of Sensorimotor Development *STAGE 5* (Experimentation) *Object Permanence* Watches toy hid and moved. Looks for it where it was moved.	Blanket, paper; toys, dolls, spoon, interesting objects.	Play game with child. Hide the object while child watches. Let child watch you move the object to a different place under the blanket. Ask, "Where is it? Can you find it?" Observe and allow child to find the object. Praise child for good watching and thinking.
Causality Investigates cause and effect.		Allow and encourage child to search, identify relationship between an action and the effect of it, e.g., "What made the ball go under the table?"
Sees self as causal agent.		Verbally identify the child as cause of the action, e.g., "Laquata kicked the ball."
Explores various ways things happen.	Water toys, water basin.	Allow child time to play with the water and toys to discover different actions of water and of the objects in the water.
Employs active trial-and-error to solve problems.	Narrow-neck milk carton; different sizes and shapes of objects.	Provide time and materials which stimulate child to think and try out ideas. Ask questions but do not tell answers or show child.

CHILD BEHAVIOR	MATERIALS	EXAMPLES OF CAREGIVER STRATEGIES
Experiments.		Provide open-ended toys and materials which encourage several uses. Encourage child to see how many ways child can use them. Ask questions and allow time for child to experiment; ask "what happens?"
IMITATION AND PLAY Copies behaviors of others.		Encourage child to pretend: to drink from a pretend bottle like baby Gwen, to march like Pearl, to pick up toys. Think about your own behaviors; child will copy what you do. Be sure your actions are the kind of actions you feel comfortable seeing the child copy.
Turns play with imitation into rituals.		Allow child to repeat own play and develop own preferences. For example, child may see you hug a child who comes in the morning and imitate your hugging. Child may repeat this imitation and develop the ritual of hugging the child who has just arrived.

Language Development

Language in toddlers this age expands from less reliance on sounds and babbling to more use of recognizable words. Many word approximations are used and reinforced and become a usable part of toddlers' expressive vocabulary.

Toddlers use a word for many different things. "Wawa" may mean anything to drink. "Mama" may mean any woman. Word meaning is usually flexible (see Figure 11–6). The toddler may call anything that is round a "ball."

Reading and books can provide enjoyable experiences for toddlers. Several different kinds of children's literature interest toddlers.

Point-and-say books have pictures of familiar objects and little text. The object of reading this type of literature is to increase your child's vocabulary, to compare pictures in a book with known items in the environment, to familiarize the child with books, and to show your baby that books have meaning.

Nursery rhymes, chants, poems, and songs are best chanted or sung throughout the day rather than just presented at read-aloud sessions. Then, at a later time, it can be thrilling to watch your infant associate the rhymes that he or she already knows with the picture representing that rhyme in a book. Nursery rhymes help your child

Figure 11–6 "Bye-bye" combines words and actions, which helps to increase the toddler's vocabulary.

become familiar with the sounds of language. They assist the transition from telegraphic speech, where one word represents a sentence, to mature language, where each word is pronounced (Lamme 1985, 57–58).

Writing can be encouraged by allowing children to watch you as you write names, labels, and notes. The interrelationships among language, reading, and writing are evident at an early age.

At what age can you begin assisting your child in becoming a writer? You can begin by reading to your child at birth. All the reading you do during the first years aids writing development by exposing your child to writing. Just before one year of age, your baby can be given (under supervision) his first writing tools—water-soluble markers and large sheets of paper. His writing experiences will have begun (Lamme 1984, 17–18).

SUGGESTIONS FOR IMPLEMENTING CURRICULUM

CHILD BEHAVIOR	MATERIALS	EXAMPLES OF CAREGIVER STRATEGIES
Uses intonation.		Use intonation in your talk with toddler.
Babbles sentences.		Respond to toddler's babbling.
Repeats, practices words.		Repeat toddler's word. Occasionally expand into a sentence, e.g., "gone-gone"; "The milk is all gone."
Imitates sounds of other people, objects.		Enjoy toddler's sounds. Play sounds game—point to objects and make sound of object, e.g., dog barking.
Responds to word and gesture conversation.		Become very familiar with toddler's words and gestures. You often have to guess what toddler is saying. Make a statement or ask a question to determine if you interpret correctly, e.g., "Taylor wants to go outside."
Responds to many questions and commands child cannot say.		Choose a few questions and commands which you can use often and consistently. The toddler will learn what they mean through many experiences, e.g., "Go get your coat."
Uses word approximations for some words.		Watch the toddler's behavior to help you determine what the toddler is saying. Watch to see where child is looking, pointing, reaching. Say a word or sentence to test if you are interpreting the word correctly.
Uses words in immediate context.		Notice what the toddler is doing, saying, needing right now. Toddler's talk is about immediate needs and desires, not past or future situations.
Identifies familiar pictures	Pictures, picture book	Orally label objects. Ask toddler to point to or name familiar picture.
Uses markers, chalk	Markers, paper, chalk	Provide table space and materials. Write labels, sentences for child.

CDA
II . 6

REFERENCES

Lamme, Linda Leonard. 1984. *Growing Up Writing*. Washington, D.C.: Acropolis Books Ltd.

Lamme, Linda Leonard. 1985. *Growing Up Reading*. Washington, D.C.: Acropolis Books Ltd.

Wilson, L. C. 1987. Mommy, don't go! *Pre-K Today*. 2(1): 38–40.

Wilson, L. C. 1988. Gross-motor activities for toddlers. *Pre-K Today*. 2(7): 34–35.

STUDENT ACTIVITIES

1. Interview one caregiver. Ask the caregiver to describe the following:
   (a.) behaviors of a toddler between 12 and 18 months who is angry, and
   (b.) behaviors of the caregiver who is responding to the toddler's angry behavior.

   Write the caregiver's descriptions and then put an X beside the descriptions of the *physical* behaviors of the toddler and the caregiver.

BEHAVIOR OF ANGRY TODDLER	RESPONDING BEHAVIORS OF CAREGIVER

2. Listen to one toddler. Make a list of the child's words and "sentences." Watch the child's body language and nonverbals. Then write down the complete sentences you think the child meant (you must think about the context in which the toddler was talking).

WORDS, PHRASES	MEANING
Gone-gone	It is all gone; or, She went away.

3. Write one lesson plan to use with one toddler to help reinforce a word the toddler uses and to expand its use with sentences.
   Use the plan with the toddler.
   Evaluate the toddler's involvement.
   Evaluate the written lesson plan.

4. Observe one toddler between 12 and 18 months of age. Record the toddler's behavior in two five-minute sequences, using narrative description. Transfer the descriptions to the Developmental Profile.
5. List five strategies which you competently use with toddlers between 12 and 18 months of age.
6. List strategies you need to develop and list ways you intend to develop them.

REVIEW

1. If the toddler cannot say the name of an object or person, but you think the child understands the object-name match, how can you find out whether the child has connected the correct name with the correct object or person?
2. Describe something Juanita would do which shows you that she has developed the concept of the permanent object.
3. Describe two situations where the toddler interacts with others. Describe two situations where the toddler plays alone.
   With others
   1.
   2.
   Alone
   1.
   2.
4. List five safety precautions you need to take with the toddler between 12 and 18 months of age.
5. With the development of eye-hand coordination, what can toddlers do now that they could not do as well several months earlier?

12

The Child from Eighteen to Twenty-Four Months of Age

OBJECTIVES
After completing this chapter, the caregiver shall

Identify and record sequences of change in the physical, emotional, social, cognitive, and language development of children from 18 to 24 months of age.

Select materials appropriate to that age-level child's development.

Devise strategies appropriate to that age-level child's development.

CHAPTER OUTLINE
I. Materials and Activities
   A. Types of materials
   B. Examples of homemade materials
II. Caregiver Strategies to Enhance the Child's Development
   A. Physical development
   B. Emotional development
   C. Social development
   D. Cognitive development
   E. Language development

CHILD DEVELOPMENT ASSOCIATE FUNCTIONAL AREAS
All CDA functional areas are integrated into the caregiver decisions and behaviors.

Review Chapter 6. Use Appendix A, The Developmental Profile, with each child. Children follow a **sequence** of development. There can be ranges in **rate** of development.

Leonard, 23 months old, walks to a child-sized rocking chair, backs up to it and sits down. He rocks and watches the other children. He gets off the chair and sits on his legs to pick up blocks. He picks up a block wagon, stands up, and walks around. He holds the block wagon in his left hand, tries to put on another block with his right hand, and succeeds. He puts the wagon on the floor and pushes it. He takes off one block and then takes off five blocks; he puts them back on. Jasper walks past and Leonard says, "No, Jasper. That mine." Tracey takes the block wagon. Leonard reaches for it and says, "That mine." Leonard picks up the wagon and begins putting blocks in it. He picks up the block wagon and a bank bag, gets up and walks around, talking to himself.

MATERIALS AND ACTIVITIES

Walking, climbing, and riding materials and activities are enjoyable for children at this age. They are practicing their gross motor skills and developing increased competence in using them. Their finger and wrist muscles are developing so they can manipulate more complex objects. Their imaginations are expanding as they construct internal representations of their world.

Types of Materials

Textures
Snap toys
Large stringing beads
Blocks
Toy people
Caps or lids to twist off containers
Toys to throw
Tools: hammer, broom, shovel
Cars, trucks
Zippers
Hairbrush
Toothbrush
Low, wide balance beam
Sliding board
Pull and push toys
Balls
Low stairs

Tunnel
Riding toys and cycles
Water play equipment
Sand play equipment
Soap paint
Fingerpaint
Tempera paint
Puzzles
Books
Telephones
Dolls
Stuffed animals
Puppets
Music: records, tapes
Modeling dough
Markers, crayons, chalk, pens
Containers to fill and empty

Examples of Homemade Materials

STRINGING OBJECT

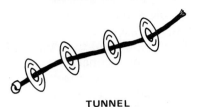

Slice a wooden spool crosswise in 3 or 4 sections. Tie a large knot on the end of a 1-foot length of clothesline rope.

TUNNEL

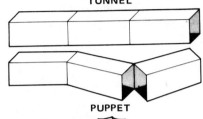

Use sturdy long rectangular cardboard box large enough for child to crawl through. Cut out ends and tape edges to keep from scraping child and also tearing box. Place several boxes end-to-end or in a square or zig-zag pattern.

PUPPET

Use a paper plate. The child tears colored paper and yarn and pastes the pieces on the paper plate. These puppets are safer without a wooden stick handle.

TARGET

Use a plastic pail (empty ice cream or peanut butter container). Place tennis balls, yarn balls in pail. Use a piece of yarn to mark where child will stand to throw objects into the pail.

Use an empty shoe box. Put in small items to throw: clothespins, spools. Store with box cover on.

CLAY DOUGH RECIPE

2 parts flour (2 cups)
1 part salt (1 cup)
Cooking oil (2 tablespoons)
Food coloring (drops)
Water (tablespoons)

Combine flour and salt.
Combine oil, food coloring, and water.
Pour liquids into flour-salt mixture. Stir to get pie dough consistency. If sticky, add more flour; if too dry, add more water. Store in a covered container in the refrigerator.

BOOK

Cut three pieces of sturdy cardboard. Select three magazine pictures which make a sequence. Glue one picture on each piece of cardboard. Cover the pictures and cardboard with contact film. Connect the pieces by punching holes in the side of the cardboard and tying together with yarn.

CAREGIVER STRATEGIES TO ENHANCE THE CHILD'S DEVELOPMENT

Physical Development

Children of this age are gaining much more stability and coordination. They can stand up, squat, reach over, and stand upright again without toppling. They climb up and down stairs by holding onto a rail or hand to maintain balance. They move rapidly, both walking and running. They jump with both feet (see Figure 12–1). They can kick a ball and pedal a cycle like a Big Wheel. They can throw objects at targets rather than randomly throwing and tossing, though they seldom hit the intended target.

These children's fine motor muscles are developing so they have increased control of their fingers and wrists. They probe and twist and turn objects (see Figure 12–2). They now can more easily release the objects they have

Figure 12–1 Toddlers can push and pull objects around the room.

Figure 12–2 The caregiver provides toys which fit together and encourage toddlers to twist and turn them.

grasped. The muscles relax, allowing them to drop or throw an object when they choose to. They also are more accurate in directing the dropped or thrown object.

Most children by now have established their handedness. Determine each child's dominant hand and allow the child to use it. The child may occasionally use the other hand when using a spoon, etc.; if the child occasionally chooses to do so, this will not be harmful. The caregiver should allow the child to develop and maintain the handedness which is comfortable. Do not attempt to make a left-handed child use utensils and toys with the right hand. That child's neurological patterns have developed with his or her left-handedness. Attempting to change a child's handedness causes both neurological and muscular stress.

SUGGESTIONS FOR IMPLEMENTING CURRICULUM

CHILD BEHAVIOR	MATERIALS	EXAMPLES OF CAREGIVER STRATEGIES
Muscular Control *LOCOMOTION* Walks forward. Walks backward. Walks sideways.	Flat floor, ground, clear of toys. Area clear of toys.	Keep area clear of toys or caution child about obstacles. Play with child: walk sideways, forward, backward.
Runs with stops and starts.	Clear area.	Provide *flat* running space. On incline child may run down too fast and fall on face.
Jumps with both feet.	Low steps, box, block, plastic crate.	Keep other children away from jumping spot when one child is jumping to the floor. Sometimes catch child as he or she jumps. Release and steady child so he or she can climb and jump again.
Kicks object.	Large ball: beach ball, nerf ball, soccer ball, volleyball, rubber ball.	Provide space where child can kick the ball and it will not go too far, e.g., into a big cardboard box or into a corner.
Walks up stairs holding railing; walks down stairs holding railing.	Steps and rail.	Provide equipment and time for child to safely walk up and down.
Pushes and pulls objects while walking.	Small wagons, strollers, pull toys, push toys which make noise, attract visual attention.	Provide clear space for walking where pushed and pulled toys have room to move without bumping and catching on equipment, furniture, rug.

CHILD BEHAVIOR	MATERIALS	EXAMPLES OF CAREGIVER STRATEGIES
Climbs.	Sturdy box, cubes, footstool, low climbing gym.	Provide equipment. Remain close by to assist getting down if needed.
Pedals cycle.	Low riding cycle; not high tricycle.	Provide space for fast and slow riding, for turning curves and in circles. Keep away children on foot.
ARM		
Throws object at target.	Bean bag, ball, box, cardboard or wood shape with large holes cut in it.	Place target at edge of play area so object is thrown away from children.
HAND		
Grasps and releases with developing finger muscles.	Small toys, objects, pail, box.	Provide objects for game of pick-up-and-drop.
Pulls zippers.	Zipper board, book, clothes with large zipper with tab.	Provide large zipper with tab large enough for small fingers to pinch and pull. Demonstrate where to hold fabric in other hand.
Helps dress and undress self.		Allow child to do as much as possible. Plan ahead to provide enough time for child who dresses and undresses slowly.
Scribbles.	Paper, pens, crayons, markers, pencils, flat hard surface.	Provide space and time to scribble. Show scribbling boundaries (edges of paper, not beyond edges).
Increases wrist flexibility; turns wrist to turn object.	Small objects to twist and turn; jars and screw-on lids.	Provide toys which stimulate manipulating, e.g., attractive, textured on several sides. Demonstrate twisting jar lid on and off.
Establishes right- or left-handedness.		Allow child to pick up objects and use them with hand child chooses. Do not change object into other hand.
Turns book pages.	Sturdy pages in books.	Read to child, carefully turning each page by grasping the upper right-hand corner and moving hand down to middle of page to gently turn the page.
Digs with tool.	Shovel, scoop, spoon; sand, dirt.	Provide tools which are not sharp and will not bend. Provide space designated for digging. Demonstrate where sand or dirt may and may not go.
Makes individual marks with crayon or pen.	Paper, pen, crayon, marker.	Listen if child talks about his or her marks. Praise child.

CHILD BEHAVIOR	MATERIALS	EXAMPLES OF CAREGIVER STRATEGIES
Sleeping May move from crib to bed or cot.	Firm cot, mattress.	Talk about the change **before** it happens. Emphasize child is getting bigger and now can use a **bigger** bed. Demonstrate where shoes go, where blanket is. Provide quiet talk, music, touch familiar to child.
Eating Controls cup and spoon better. May eat anything, then change to picky eating.		Emphasize how well child is using cup, spoon. Be patient with spills. Allow child to change eating behavior. Don't fuss at or push child. Child usually will get adequate nutrition if variety of foods are provided.
Teeth Has most baby teeth. Uses toothbrush.	Toothbrush, toothpaste, cup of water.	Assist when necessary with applying toothpaste and cleaning face afterwards.
Elimination May show interest in and readiness for toilet training.	Potty chair, training pants; slacks, leggings easy to remove.	Show child where potty chair is. Encourage child to use it. Praise child when he or she does. Do not push child. Many show interest in potty chair months before they are ready for actual transition to toilet-training. See Chapter 4 for the child who is ready for consistent toilet-training.

Emotional Development

Children of this age are continuing to develop positive and negative feelings about themselves. They interpret responses from caregivers and children as reflecting their self-worth.

Children's fantasies increase at this age. They are very real and may sometimes be frightening. The children often cannot be "talked out" of their fears. They need to accept security from the caregiver as they live with their fantasies.

Emotions are reflected in intense behaviors. These children swing between extremes, e.g., smiling, laughing—screaming, crying. Their basic pattern of intensity of response is affected by their swings into even more intensive behaviors. Those children who usually respond loudly may now scream and yell or laugh shrilly. The children who have a low intensity of response may use more energy and respond more loudly or actively than usual.

Distraction as a method of resolving conflicts over toys may no longer work. Both the easily distractible child and the not-so-easily distractible child can maintain attention on an object of interest. Their intense desire to play with the toy keeps their focus on the toy; they are not easily diverted to another object or activity.

CDA
Ⅲ . 8

SUGGESTIONS FOR IMPLEMENTING CURRICULUM

CHILD BEHAVIOR	EXAMPLES OF CAREGIVER STRATEGIES
Types of Emotions-Feelings Views internal feelings and external behavior as same.	Recognize that child does not feel angry and yet act happy.
Shows one or more emotions at same time.	Identify child's emotions. Respond to child's needs.
Continues to develop feelings about self.	Provide consistent behavior and feedback which helps child feel good about self; help child know he or she is a worthy person.
Changes feelings about self.	Reflect to child that child is still a loved person when child reflects negative or angry feelings about self.
Seeks approval.	Provide verbal and nonverbal approval of child as a person and of child's behavior when it is positive.
May develop new fears.	Listen to child's fears. Accept them as real. Comfort child. Reassure child of your concern and of your presence. May demonstrate object is harmless, e.g., siren toy. If you cannot convince child, remove the toy.
Increases fantasy.	Listen to child's fantasies. Accept them as real to child. Enjoy funny, happy fantasies. Comfort, reassure child of his or her safety when child has scary fantasies, e.g., "There's a monster in the kitchen."
May increase aggressiveness.	Remain nearby to caution, remind, and sometimes remove object or child from situation.
Seeks security in routines.	Provide consistent routines which child can use by self as child increases competence and seeks independence.
May become shy again.	Allow child to hold back or withdraw. Provide time for child to observe without having to enter into interactions with others.

CHILD BEHAVIOR	EXAMPLES OF CAREGIVER STRATEGIES
Sometimes rejects parent or caregiver.	Allow child to express rejection in words and behaviors. Continue to express your affection for child.
Control of Emotions-Feelings Uses reactions of others as a controller of own behavior.	Use words, facial expressions, gestures to indicate approval and disapproval of child's behavior.
May resist change.	Explain change **before** it happens. Provide reason for the change. Motivate by emphasizing specialness of the child who now is allowed to do something else.
Moves to extremes, from lovable to demanding and stubborn.	Allow child to express swings in behavior. Show acceptance of child as a person. Help child work on his or her demands and stubbornness by suggesting alternatives in behavior.
Temperament Activity level. Regularity. Approach or withdrawal as a characteristic response to a new situation. Adaptability to change in routine. Level of sensory threshold. Positive or negative mood. Intensity of response. Distractibility. Persistence and attention span.	List two of the child's behaviors in each category which indicate the child's basic style. List adjustments you need to make to help the child cope with daily situations.

Social Development

CDA
III . 9

Children of this age are continuing to develop a sense of self. They use words which identify them as separate people, e.g., "I, mine, me, you." These children are also expanding their relationships with others. They recognize others' feelings are being reflected in their behaviors and may respond by laughing, comforting, or crying. These children imitate their own behaviors and the behaviors of others. They try to please others and may help in situations where they are praised. They engage in parallel play (where they are near other children but play separately). They still have difficulty sharing toys and materials (see Figure 12–3).

Figure 12–3 Toddlers do not share toys easily, so the caregiver helps toddlers find other toys to use.

SUGGESTIONS FOR IMPLEMENTING CURRICULUM

CHILD BEHAVIOR	EXAMPLES OF CAREGIVER STRATEGIES
Self	
Is egocentric, sees things from own point of view.	Recognize that child thinks others think and feel the way he or she does. Help child identify own ideas and feelings.
May change identity of self from day to day.	Provide feedback to child about self so child can identify consistency within self.
Identifies materials as belonging to self.	Recognize and allow ownership of toys.

CHILD BEHAVIOR	EXAMPLES OF CAREGIVER STRATEGIES
Uses I, mine, me, you.	Verbally respond to child's use of pronouns, reinforcing distinction child makes between self and others.
Others Demands attention.	Both initiate and respond to child to provide attention to child's needs. Share looks, touch, words with child when you may be busy with another child.
Begins to be aware of others' feelings.	Help child identify and verbalize others' feelings which appear in their behavior, e.g., "Allen is crying; he is sad."
Believes people have changes in identity— change in role changes person.	Identify yourself in your different tasks, e.g., when you sweep and clean, when you cook, when you rock a child.
Expands social relationships.	Encourage child to interact with others. Be present and provide your support when child encounters a new child or adult.
Looks to others for help.	Consistently provide assistance when needed. Praise child for seeking help with something child would not be able to do for self, e.g., puts on shoe and then seeks help for tying laces instead of fussing and crying.
Imitates tasks of others.	Allow and enjoy child's watching you and others. Enjoy the imitations and don't be concerned that the imitation might be incomplete or inaccurate. The child will continue to watch and imitate.
Wants to help, assist with tasks, clean-up.	Encourage the child to help put toys away, clean up, etc. Work along with child. Child can be a very good helper if he or she sees how you do it.
May do opposite of what is requested.	Carefully word your requests. The child's negativism comes out in a frequent "no." Think of different ways to produce desired behavior without saying, "Do this."
Has difficulty sharing.	Provide enough toys and materials so child does not have to share. Suggest allowing another child to play with toy when child finishes. Provide alternative toys to child who must wait for desired toy.
Engages in parallel play.	Provide toys, materials, space for children to play near each other. Allow them to talk with each other. You talk to each of them. Allow them to choose if they want to trade toys or do something else.

Cognitive Development

CDA
II.5

Children of this age are gradually using **mental** trial and error. This is much faster than the sensorimotor trial and error where the children had to manipulate objects.

Object permanence is established. These children know that an object or person exists even when they cannot see it. They know that they exist separate from other people and objects (Wilson 1987).

Children of this age imitate past events. They remember the ideas by internal representation and reproduce them at a later time. For example, the caregiver washing the child's face is imitated later by the child as the child washes a doll's face.

Symbolic play is the child's representation of objects or feelings or ideas. Symbolic play serves several functions: Children can express conflicts and work them out in the pretend world. They can seek gratification of unsatisfied needs they feel they have, e.g., they play the baby to get extra nurturing they desire. They can pretend to be other people or objects, thereby reflecting their understanding of other people or objects as separate from themselves and trying behaviors similar to or different from their own.

SUGGESTIONS FOR IMPLEMENTING CURRICULUM

CHILD BEHAVIOR	EXAMPLES OF CAREGIVER STRATEGIES
Piaget's Stages of Sensorimotor Development *STAGE 6* (Representation) *Mental trial and error* Tries out ideas mentally, based on past concrete experiences.	Allow child time to figure out solutions. If child seeks assistance, help child think about the problem, e.g., "What can you use to reach that block?"
Object permanence Sees object disappear, mentally remembers object, and figures out where it went.	Allow child to think and search for object. Give clues, ask questions only after child has acted and still needs assistance.
Deferred imitation and symbolization Imitates past events.	Observe child's representations. Identify the ideas which seem very important to the child.
Symbolic play Resolves conflicts.	Allow child to act out conflict in play with toys and materials. Observe how child works out conflict so he or she feels better.
Compensates for unsatisfied needs.	Observe child's play. Identify consistent themes in child's play, e.g., child's talk and actions about being a good or a naughty child.
Tries roles.	Provide clothes, materials which help child pretend to be someone else.

Figure 12-4 The caregiver uses familiar objects to play choosing and naming games with toddlers.

Language Development

At this age children's vocabulary is expanding rapidly as they label objects which they now recognize as separate entities (see Figure 12-4). Children construct the principle that

> words are labels for socially defined classes of objects and events. This achievement is reflected in more systematic and productive extension of words and in accelerated growth of vocabulary. ... This is the time when children may tire their caregivers by constantly asking for the names of things (e.g., *what's this?*). They eagerly utter the words they hear and explore their uses (Anisfeld 1984, 86) (see Figure 12-5).

Children use their language to express needs and to direct others. They question as they seek to learn about their world (Wilson 1988).

Children of this age use nouns, verbs, and pronouns as they combine their words into two- and three-word sentences. These children produce *word sequences*, several words in sequence which convey a thought or action but are not regular sentence patterns. For example, Cameron says, "Key go car" when he sees his mother take the key ring out of her purse. She responds, "Yes, I have the key. We are going in the car."

Figure 12–5 The sandbox provides many opportunities for the caregiver to observe, question, label, and praise toddlers' actions.

These children follow simple one- and two-step oral directions. There are two broad classes of language functions: "the *cognitive function*—to name, indicate, describe, and comment; and the *instrumental function*—to request, reject, manipulate, and express desires. . . . [W]ords are used for cognitive purposes before they are used for instrumental purposes" (Anisfeld 1984, 91).

Caregivers and children use words to classify objects and actions. Words help children organize what they see and hear and do. Anisfeld reported that adults doing the following things helped young children develop their syntax:

- The adult speaks to children in short sentences.
- The adult articulates more clearly to young children than to others.
- The adult talks about the situation in which the child is involved.
- The adult expands what the child says: ". . . fills in the missing words as she echoes the child's utterance . . . ."

- The adult extends what the child says: "... continues a thought started by a child ...."
- The adult imitates what the child says: "... repeats all or part of what the child had said."

Pictures, books, and storytelling stimulate language interactions among caregivers and children. Lamme related several experiences which involved toddlers in the reading process.

> Pointing out things in pictures and encouraging your toddler to participate in the "reading" helps your child become more active in the reading process. Maybe you have tried to skip a page or shorten a story in an effort to speed up the bedtime ritual. Has your toddler surprised you by noticing and demanding the whole story? Even at these young ages, toddlers are actively listening to stories and remembering them word for word!
>
> Because reading sessions with your toddler are likely to be so short, it is important to read aloud frequently—several times during the day (1985, 52).

Choose reading materials for young children carefully. Stimulate the toddlers' interests in "reading" and hearing stories often.

> Your toddler will enjoy the classic fairy tales read over and over again. Stories like "The Three Little Pigs" or "The Three Billy Goats Gruff" will encourage your child to chant the repetitive parts as he or she sings and plays around the house. You and your toddler can act out the tales. If you make a flannel board with characters of these familiar stories or have puppets for the story characters, your child can experience the stories in lots of ways other than just by hearing them. Active involvement in the story plot is a real key for toddlers.
>
> Your toddler will enjoy books that are small in size because they are easy to carry around the house....
>
> Your toddler will still enjoy much of the literature that appealed to him or her as an infant—nursery rhymes especially. Some toddlers can proceed through a favorite Mother Goose collection and chant each rhyme.
>
> Your toddler will also enjoy bigger books which are "two laps wide" for lap reading. Many children's picture books are wider than they are long so that you can spread the book out and see the pictures. *The Very Hungry Caterpillar* by Eric Carle is a book which has manipulative pages as well. It is a most popular toddler read-aloud book (Lamme 1985, 58–59).

Toddlers experiment with markers, chalk, and crayons as their interest in scribbling continues. Encourage their scribbling by providing time and attention to their use and enjoyment of writing.

> Your child may be far more interested in the process of making scribbles than in the product produced by those scribbles. You, however, may want to write your child's name in the corner of the picture, letting him watch as you write. As scribble pictures get framed, mounted or displayed, your youngster soon learns that his scribble pictures are valued. He will want to draw more, not only because scribbling is so innately pleasurable but also because his scribbling attracts your positive attention.
>
> Don't ask your child what his scribbles are. The scribbles at this stage do not represent anything. Rather, comment on what is apparent—lines from top to bottom or across the page, dots, and colors. You might say, "I like your orange and brown picture," or "What beautiful blue lines!" (Lamme 1984, 39).

SUGGESTIONS FOR IMPLEMENTING CURRICULUM

	CHILD BEHAVIOR	MATERIALS	EXAMPLES OF CAREGIVER STRATEGIES
CDA II.6	Uses language to reflect own meaning; expects others to have same meaning.		Recognize limited meaning of child's use of words. Be careful not to read extra meaning into what the child says.
	Expands vocabulary rapidly, labeling objects.		Verbally label and also point, touch objects and actions in child's world. Also expand the label into a sentence, e.g., "Ball. Michael has a ball."
	Points to objects and pictures named by others.		Play games, look at pictures, read books; say, "Point to the bird" or "Where is the car?"
	Learns social words—hello, please, thank you.		Consistently use social words in their correct context. Say "please" and "thank you" to the child. When child requests item, repeat request and add the word "please," e.g., "Carrot please."
	Uses language to express needs, desires.		Listen to child's expression of needs. Verbally respond so child knows that his or her words get your attention and you understand them. Use words and actions to meet child's needs or explain why you cannot meet them, e.g., "The milk is all gone."
	Uses language to direct others.		Listen to child's commands. Respond verbally and with actions following child's directions or explain why you are not, e.g., "Here is a napkin" when child asks for one.
	Questions, asks "What's that?"		Answer child's occasional and persistent questions. This is how the child learns labels and other information about the world. Provide simple answers, not complicated ones, e.g., "That is a flower" rather than a description of petals, leaves, stem, etc.
	Uses nouns, verbs, pronouns.		Speak normally with the child so child can hear complete sentence patterns.

CHILD BEHAVIOR	MATERIALS	EXAMPLES OF CAREGIVER STRATEGIES
Is learning prepositions.		Use in natural contexts, e.g., "The ball rolled under the table"; "Put the book on the shelf."
Calls self by name.		Use the child's name when talking directly to child.
Follows one-step direction.		Use simple directions and praise when the child follows them, e.g., "Please put the truck here."
Follows two-step direction.		Make sure child is aware you are giving directions. Use simple directions, e.g., "Please pick up this book and put it on the shelf."
Makes two- and three-word sentences.		Use both short and long sentences with the child. Praise child and respond to child's sentences, e.g., *Child:* "Coat on?" *Caregiver:* "Yes, you need your coat on."
Looks at books.	Cloth or paper or cardboard picture books.	Read books with child. Demonstrate proper care of books. Allow child to look at books alone.
Listens to stories and rhymes.		Tell stories which child can understand. Use rhymes, poems.
Scribbles	Markers, chalk, crayons, paper.	Provide writing space and materials. Show interest and approval of scribbling. Share scribbling with others.

REFERENCES

Anisfeld, Moshe. 1984. *Language Development from Birth to Three.* Hillsdale, New Jersey: Lawrence Erlbaum.

Lamme, Linda Leonard. 1984. *Growing Up Writing.* Washington, D.C.: Acropolis Books Ltd.

Lamme, Linda Leonard. 1985. *Growing Up Reading.* Washington, D.C.: Acropolis Books Ltd.

Wilson, L. C. 1987. Peek-a-boo... I see you! *Pre-K Today.* 1(6): 32–33.

Wilson, L. C. 1988. What's in the box? *Pre-K Today.* 2(4): 38–39.

STUDENT ACTIVITIES

1. Observe one caregiver for ten minutes. Use narrative description to write down everything caregiver did and said. Then categorize the behavior:

CAREGIVER BEHAVIOR (WHAT CAREGIVER DID)	CAREGIVER INITIATED	WITH WHOM?	CAREGIVER RESPONDED	TO WHOM?	AREA(S) OF CHILD DEVELOP-MENT INVOLVED

2. Identify one characteristic temperament of one child (by records, caregiver information, or your own observation). Observe to see how the caregiver makes adjustments in the routine or expectations of the child to the situation and how the caregiver helps the child make adjustments. For example, the caregiver may tell a low active child several minutes early that it is time for the child to put on outdoor clothing.
3. Make one toy and allow two children this age to use it. Observe and write down how they used it, what they said, and your judgment about whether they seemed interested, challenged, bored using it. Also evaluate the toy's construction.

TOY	HOW USED?	CHILD'S COMMENTS	INTERESTING/ CHALLENGING/ BORING?	STURDY, TORN, BROKEN?

4. Observe one child between 18 and 24 months of age. Record the child's behavior in two five-minute sequences, using narrative description. Transfer the descriptions to the Developmental Profile.
5. List five strategies which you competently use with children between 18 and 24 months of age.
6. List strategies you need to develop and list ways you intend to develop them.

REVIEW

1. List three physical changes which enable the child to become more independent.
2. Chris and Marlin both pick up a car and start pulling on it. What can you do and what can you say which shows appropriate understanding of their needs and desires?
3. List three ways symbolic play helps a child.
4. Identify two possible developments in the child's language and state two strategies for each that a caregiver can use to facilitate that development.

CHILD'S DEVELOPMENT OF LANGUAGE		CAREGIVER STRATEGIES	
1.		1. 2.	
2.		1. 2.	

13

The Child from Twenty-Four to Thirty Months of Age

OBJECTIVES

After completing this chapter, the caregiver shall

Identify and record sequences of change in the physical, emotional, social, cognitive, and language development of children from 24 to 30 months of age.

Select materials appropriate to that age-level child's development.

Devise strategies appropriate to that age-level child's development.

CHAPTER OUTLINE

CHILD DEVELOPMENT ASSOCIATE FUNCTIONAL AREAS

All CDA functional areas are integrated into the caregiver decisions and behaviors.

Review Chapter 6. Use Appendix A, The Developmental Profile, with each child. Children follow a **sequence** of development. There can be ranges in **rate** of development.

Twenty-six-month-old Cathy picks up a fire truck and walks up on the porch with it. She pushes it around on the floor, then picks it up and takes it out into the yard. Ms. Susan asks her what she has. Cathy responds, "A truck," and smiles. Ms. Susan asks what kind of truck. Cathy says, "Red," and smiles. Cathy picks up a ball and says, "Watch me throw it." She moves the fire truck and tells Ms. Susan "Can't find ladder." Ms. Susan gives her the ladder and starts to put it on the fire truck. Cathy requests, "Let me do it." Cathy puts a toy fireman in the truck and plays with it. She says to Ms. Susan, "See the truck," and then, "See if it goes?" As Cathy plays with the fire truck, the ladder falls off again and she says, "Oh, no" and looks at Ms. Susan. She takes the truck to Ms. Susan to fix the ladder, saying "It fall off" and pointing to the ladder. She watches Ms. Susan fix the ladder and plays with it again. Another child gets the fire truck and begins to play with it. Cathy tells the child, "I want the truck, Bill." Bill gives the fire truck back to Cathy, who says, "Thank you, Bill."

MATERIALS AND ACTIVITIES

Riding toys are favorites at this age (see Figure 13–1). The children also use climbing and jumping equipment frequently. Kicking and throwing are more accurate than before and are enjoyed by the children. Finger, hand, and wrist movements not only grasp and release but also coordinate with vision, enabling the children to string beads and to use crayons and other drawing and writing tools. These children take pleasure in manipulating objects and

Figure 13–1 The caregiver provides riding toys of different sizes for young children.

Figure 13–2 The young child is becoming more coordinated and can stoop and stand easily.

materials. They focus on the process rather than on producing a product. They respond to and also create music. They enjoy symbolic play. They can find meaning in pictures and books representing ideas with which they are familiar.

A regular schedule and routine provide stability for toddlers and caregivers as they engage in learning experiences and enrich each others' lives (Wilson 1987, 38).

Types of Materials

Balance beam	Large pegs and boards
Climbing equipment	Large beads and string
Bouncing equipment	Markers, crayons, pens, chalk
Rocking boat	Modeling dough
Wagon	Construction material: wood, styro-
Cycles	foam, glue
Wheeled toys	Rhythm instruments
Items to throw	Records
Balls	Tape recordings
Blocks	Puppets
Trucks, cars	Dress-up clothes
Dolls, people, animals	Pictures
Jars with twist lids	Books
Items to put together or pull apart	Puzzles
Knobs	Matching games

Examples of Homemade Materials

BALANCE BEAM

Tape masking tape on the floor to indicate the line where the child can walk.

In the yard partially bury a tree trunk so that several inches remain above ground. Place so that no branch stubs are on the top walking surface.

PEG BOARD

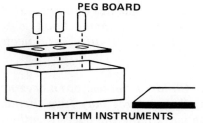

Cut a piece of heavy cardboard to fit in the bottom of a box (shoe, gift, hamburger). Cut holes in the cardboard. Cut 1/2-inch dowel rod into 1 1/2–2-inch lengths. Paint if desired. Store cardboard and pegs in the box and put on lid.

RHYTHM INSTRUMENTS
MARACAS

Collect gourds in the fall. Allow to dry. The seeds will rattle when the gourd is shaken.

DRUM

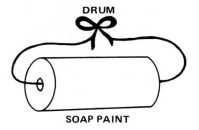

Poke a hole through both ends of an oatmeal box. Pull a strong string through the box and both ends and extend 12–24 inches (measure on one of your children). Tape the box lid onto the box. Tie a knot or leave the ends loose and tie a bow each time you put it around a child's neck.

SOAP PAINT

Use 1 part soap flakes, 1 part water, and food coloring. Beat the mixture with a hand egg beater. Skim off soap suds to paint on table top or shelf paper or freezer paper.

FINGER PAINT

Use liquid starch, dry tempera paint, and soap flakes. Pour out about a tablespoon of liquid starch on shelf or freezer paper. Sprinkle dry paint on starch. Sprinkle soap flakes on starch. Children mix ingredients as they paint.

TEMPERA PAINT

Mix 1/2 cup dry tempera paint and 1/2 cup dry detergent. Add water until mixture is thick but not runny. Keep in covered jar.

PUPPETS

Use paper sandwich bags. Child can use crayons or glue on paper to decorate puppet. Help child fit hand in bottom of sack.

CLOTH BOOK

Use pinking shears to cut heavy cloth to make several pieces the same size. Stack the pieces and sew down the middle by machine or by hand. Cut out colored pictures from magazines or cards. Glue one picture per page. Make a theme book, e.g., children riding, or use pictures of different objects or activities.

GROUP BOOK

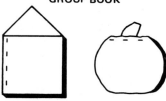

Make a group book. Children can tear out magazine pictures of objects; the pictures may fit a theme. Glue to pieces of paper. Staple the pages together. Write the title page. Write what children dictate to you for the other pages. (Paper may first be cut into shape which matches the theme, e.g., pumpkin; leaf.)

PUZZLE

Cut out one uncluttered colored picture from a magazine.

a. Glue it to a piece of cardboard.

b. Cover the picture and cardboard with contact film. Pencil the picture into three to five sections which are visually recognizable (head, legs, tail). Cut around the picture and cut it into the pieces.

c. Cut the remaining hole slightly larger.

d. Glue the remainder of the cardboard onto a second piece of cardboard the same size. Fit the puzzle pieces into place. If necessary, trim so the pieces come out easily.

MATCHING GAME

Cut two 2-inch squares from pages of a wallpaper sample book. Make about six sets, using different pages. Store the pieces in an envelope. To play, mix up the pieces and then select squares which match.

MATCHING GAME

Select four picture sets of objects which are alike, e.g., two cardinals, two mice, two daisies, two German Shepherds. Glue one of each set onto the bottom of a styrofoam tray. Glue the other four pictures onto cardboard and cut into small squares. Glue part of an envelope in the tray to hold the loose cardboard pieces.

Activities Ideas

These children are constructing physical knowledge, logico-mathematical knowledge, and social arbitrary knowledge. The following are examples of activities that help the children construct knowledge.

CDA
II.5

EXPLORATION		
Cooking		
Recipe chart	Stir	See
Oral language	Beat	Hear
Measure	Smell	Taste
Sift	Feel	
Growing Plants		
Carrot	Bean sprouts	Observations
Sweet potato	Food	Comparisons
Beans	Care	Charting
Lettuce	Rate of growth	

**CDA
II.7**

REPRESENTATIONS

Oral Language

Conversation	Poetry	Singing and rhythms
Information gathering	Nursery rhymes	Dramatic play
Story telling	Fingerplays	

Objects
Painting rocks, seeds, pine cones
Creating prints with potatoes, carrots, celery; footprints, handprints, fingerprints

Pictures
Magazines, photographs
Art media: crayons, painting, tear and paste

Books
Wordless picture books
Naming objects books
Books with a storyline to read or tell in your own words

CAREGIVER STRATEGIES TO ENHANCE THE CHILD'S DEVELOPMENT

Physical Development

Children of this age can stand, bend, walk, run, and jump. They are more flexible and stable in their movements than before (see Figure 13–2, page 268). Their eye-hand coordination is more accurate so they can reach and grasp objects. They are able to fit objects together and like to put them together and pull them apart. They use either their right or left hand most, having by now established handedness. These children are visually fascinated with some new items. They may stare and stare. They use a spoon when eating and are learning to use a fork. Many children this age have all twenty baby teeth. These children may learn to brush their teeth. Many children this age are ready for toilet-training.

SUGGESTIONS FOR IMPLEMENTING CURRICULUM

CHILD BEHAVIOR	MATERIALS	EXAMPLES OF CAREGIVER STRATEGIES
Muscular Control *MOVEMENT* Bends at waist.	Dropping and picking up objects: pail and plastic rings.	Play game with child. Observe appropriateness of materials, interest of child.
Climbs.	Low objects: steps up to slide, tires.	Select safe materials and safe height.

CHILD BEHAVIOR	MATERIALS	EXAMPLES OF CAREGIVER STRATEGIES
Jumps.	Two- to three-step equipment.	Keep floor or ground space clear where jumping. Block off higher levels so jump is safe distance for muscles and balance.
Stands on one foot.	Song for lifting one foot.	Make up rhyme or song about standing on one foot. Child will stand on one foot for only a few seconds. Praise child. Encourage child to try again.
ARM Throws.	Target—large paper sack or plastic basin. Nerf ball, yarn ball.	Provide space for child to throw objects at target. Decorate target so child is aiming at hoop or door.
HAND Touches.	Textured objects: sandpaper, fur, corduroy, egg carton bottom, juice can.	Make feely box. Allow child to pull out object to touch and see. Label object for child. Label texture for child.
Twists.	Jars and cans with lids; large plastic nuts and bolts.	Provide objects which twist on and off easily.
Eating Uses spoon.	Spoon that fits child's hand.	Provide food which can be spooned easily.
Is learning to use fork.	Fork that fits child's hand.	Provide food which will stay on fork.
Uses fingers.		Cut solid food in small pieces so can be picked up with fingers.
Teeth Has all twenty baby teeth. Brushes teeth.	Toothbrush, toothpaste.	Assist with toothpaste and water.
Elimination Is learning to use toilet.	Training pants, potty chair or adapter seat.	Ask whether child needs to go to toilet. Assist with clothes. Assist with handwashing. Clean up potty chair or toilet seat. **Wash your hands.**
Has completed toilet training.	Training pants, potty chair or toilet.	Ask whether child needs to go to toilet before and after nap, before outside play. Assist with clothes as needed. Assist with handwashing. Clean up, and **wash your hands.**

Figure 13-3 Friends show affection for each other.

Emotional Development

Feelings about the self continue to develop: positive and negative self-image, competence, acceptance. Children this age are becoming more independent at the same time they recognize their need for help. They attempt to please and show affection (see Figure 13-3). They may be aggressive, then shy. Routines provide children this age with consistency and security.

  The regularity or irregularity of body functions at this age affects toilet-training. If a child is very regular and has a bowel movement at about the same time every day, the caregiver can check with the child at that time to suggest it is time to go to the toilet. If the child is very irregular, it is difficult for the caregiver and child to anticipate and be more tuned to body feelings.

SUGGESTIONS FOR IMPLEMENTING CURRICULUM

CHILD BEHAVIOR	EXAMPLES OF CAREGIVER STRATEGIES
Types of Emotions-Feelings Feels comfortable with self.	Provide experiences where child can succeed often, feel pleasure with self.

CHILD BEHAVIOR	EXAMPLES OF CAREGIVER STRATEGIES
Feels positive self-worth.	Provide child positive feedback. Reinforce other people's reflections of child as a worthy person.
Feels negative self-worth.	Be sensitive to child's frustrations with tasks and with social encounters. Provide reassurance of child's worth.
Control of Emotions-Feelings Expresses emotions.	Accept child's feelings as honest rather than manipulative.
Temperament Activity level. Regularity. Approach or withdrawal as a characteristic response to a new situation. Adaptability to change in routine. Level of sensory threshold. Positive or negative mood. Intensity of response. Distractibility. Persistence and attention span.	List two of the child's behaviors in each category which indicate the child's basic style. List adjustments you need to make to help the child cope with daily situations.

Social Development

These children's sense of ownership now includes both what is mine and what is yours. Because they still have difficulty sharing, they often engage in parallel play. The children recognize some emotions in others and may express comfort and concern for others. They may help with tasks.

Playing and learning are one and the same for toddlers. In addition to learning about their surroundings, toddlers are developing socially. Play gives them a variety of opportunities and situations to develop a sense of themselves and of others in their world (Wilson 1988, 36).

SUGGESTIONS FOR IMPLEMENTING CURRICULUM

CHILD BEHAVIOR	EXAMPLES OF CAREGIVER STRATEGIES
Self Realizes own skills.	Provide materials and equipment which child can use to own satisfaction. Provide challenging materials which child can use.
Others Shows independence.	Allow child to accomplish as many tasks as possible by self. Assist when asked or when you anticipate you are needed.

CHILD BEHAVIOR	EXAMPLES OF CAREGIVER STRATEGIES
Acts to please adult.	Provide verbal and nonverbal positive feedback to child. Recognize child's need for your attention and approval. Plan activities child can help you with (clean-up).
Shows feelings to others.	Show feelings to child. Show appropriate actions with feelings, e.g., happy—laugh, physical excitement; sad—hug, pat, listen. Praise child when child uses those behaviors.
Recognizes emotions in others.	Label children's behaviors. Verbalize about feelings of others. Provide appropriate responses to behaviors. Praise child when child identifies others' emotions. Praise when child responds to others' emotions.
Understands "mine," "yours."	Reinforce possession by child and others. It is "mine" while using it.
Shares some.	Provide materials and equipment so some sharing is necessary. Praise child who shares. Verbalize reasons for sharing. Recognize, however, that not all children can share yet.
Helps others.	Provide opportunities for purposeful helping—clean up, passing out items, assisting with clothing. Praise and thank for helping behaviors.
Engages in parallel play.	Plan space and materials so child can play close to others without having to interact in play.

Cognitive Development

Many children between 24 and 30 months are entering Piaget's *preoperational stage* of cognitive development. The first substage of the preoperational stage is the **preconceptual**, which occurs from about 2 to 4 years of age. These children can mentally sort some objects and actions. The mental symbols are partly detached from experience. Early nonverbal classifications are called graphic collections, where the children focus on figurative properties. These children form some verbal preconcepts. But the meaning of words may fluctuate from one time to another. Verbal reasoning is from particular to particular.

Preconceptual children are constructing and organizing knowledge about a wide range of areas in their world. They are beginning to classify objects and to develop very limited ideas of quantity, number, space, and time.

The development of the symbolic function occurs in the preconceptual stage. It involves the following mental representations, presented here in increasing complexity. In the child's **search for hidden objects** the object remains permanent (does not cease to exist) in the child's thinking even when the child cannot see it. These experiences form the bases for more

Figure 13–4 A box and a hat become a firetruck and firehat in the child's symbolic play.

specific representational thinking. In **deferred imitation** the child imitates another person's behavior even when that person is no longer present. A child engaged in **symbolic play** may give the caregiver a stone and tell the caregiver to eat this apple; the stone represents the real object (see Figure 13–4). The child's **drawings** may be scribbles, experiments with the media, or they may begin to be representations; a child may point to a mark he or she has made on a piece of paper and say his or her own name. **Mental images** are "pictures in the mind with which children can carry out action sequences internally" (Wadsworth 1978, 64). **Language** (words) represent objects or behaviors. As children develop language, they use **verbal evocation,** "the ability to verbalize events not occurring at the time" in verbal representation (Wadsworth 1978, 64).

Children at this age are active explorers, seeking information through manipulating and observing their world. As problem-solvers, they now move beyond trial and error to mental manipulation of ideas and physical manipulation of objects to construct their reasoning.

SUGGESTIONS FOR IMPLEMENTING CURRICULUM

CHILD BEHAVIOR	EXAMPLES OF CAREGIVER STRATEGIES
Piaget's Preoperational Stage, Preconceptual Substage. *NONVERBAL CLASSIFICATION* Makes graphic collections.	Allow child to create own classifications.

CHILD BEHAVIOR	EXAMPLES OF CAREGIVER STRATEGIES
VERBAL PRECONCEPTS	
Uses words differently at different times.	Listen and ask for clarification of words used differently.
Uses words with private meanings.	Listen to child's words in context; reword or question to find meaning.
Begins to label classes of objects.	Repeat and identify class of object. Extend child's label to include other objects.
Focuses on one attribute.	Reinforce classifications. Child has not yet formed stable classes of objects.
VERBAL REASONING	
Reasons from particular to particular.	Understand and accept child's classification of behaviors which seem alike. Ask for clarification if needed.
QUANTITY	
Understands some, more, gone, big.	Use quantity words in context with objects. Respond and expand child's use.
NUMBER	
Understands more.	Use objects to identify "more."
SPACE	
Understands up, down, behind, under, over.	Use spatial-position words with actions, e.g., "I will lift you up. I am putting you down on the floor."
TIME	
Understands now, soon.	Label actions in terms of time, e.g., "Let's wash your hands now."

Language Development

Children of this age are rapidly increasing their vocabulary. Building on their use of language to name objects with single words, they proceed to a more complex structuring of language, the sentence. Anisfeld says that they *construct* sentences; they do not *reproduce* sentences from memory (1984, 113). Thus, the child has to think and select words which express the child's ideas in ways others can understand.

Anisfeld has identified several types in the child's development of syntax:

Demonstrative naming: The first word in a demonstrative-naming phrase points out an object; the second names it, e.g., "this ball" or "here spoon."

Attribution: Children give objects a specific attribute, often using an adjective-noun combination, e.g., blue shoes. The attribute "blue" distinguishes one particular pair of shoes from all other items in a class of things called "shoes."

Figure 13–5 The repetitive lyrics of a song help a child learn proper word patterns.

Possession: Children make special associations between a person and an object, often using a two-word sentence, e.g., "mommy chair."

Action: Action sentences separate the action from the actor and from the object and explore the relations among these three. Children's descriptions of their own or other's actions at this age include sentences like "ride big-wheel" and "I jump."

Recurrence: A recurrence sentence tells of a thing or event which happens again. Children often use "more" to express this, e.g., "more juice," "more ride."

Negation: The negative sentences of children this age usually say that something desired or expected is not there or has disappeared or that the child cannot, is not permitted to, or does not want to do something. A child may say, "no car" or "no hit."

Children use many sentences which contain specific word patterns. They hear others use word patterns and then use these same word patterns over and over in their process of constructing language (see Figure 13–5). Thus they learn to use word-order patterns common to their language, but they cannot tell you the basic rule or principle of word order they are using.

Another kind of patterning which children learn is prosodic patterning. They learn stress and intonation of word parts, words, and sentences along with the words themselves and syntax. For example, "MY ball" means something different from "my **ball**." Children learn to use the appropriate stress and intonation to express their specific ideas.

Many sentences young children use are incomplete. Very young children use subject-and-verb and verb-and-object sentences but seldom use subject-verb-and-object sentences. They also often omit function words like **on, in, a,** and **the.** This is because they have to plan and coordinate all the parts (words) of their sentences. The more words they use, the more difficult it is for them to construct a sentence.

Children also extend their construction of language to include two ways of forming new words. They begin to use the plural and the past tense forms of words. By now children understand that there is more than one hand, or eye, or foot. They listen to others talking and learn that the word changes when referring to more than one hand. They then construct their words to include plurals, e.g., hands, eyes, etc. However, at this age they apply the same plural rule to all words, making possible words like "foots." Applying the same kind of pluralization to all words is called overregularization or overgeneralization. When children can distinguish between what is happening now and what has happened previously, they can begin to use some words which are in the past tense, such as "I jumped." They also overregularize past tense forms, constructing words like "goed" and "seed."

Books contain language patterns which serve as examples to children who are busily constructing language; therefore, you should read to children often. Children also can read books with pictures. These experiences provide practice in putting thoughts into oral language. Books will soon be selected frequently by toddlers.

> Books with bright illustrations are especially appropriate for toddlers who are "reading" the pictures, rather than the words. . . .
> At the age of the "terrible twos" your toddler will learn that one way to acquire positive attention is to carry a book up to you and ask to be read to. Your two-year-old has discovered "favorite" books, which need to be read frequently (Lamme 1985, 60).

Written language is becoming more a part of the children's world. They see print at home, along the highway, and in other homes or centers. They look at the print in a book as the caregiver reads the story or tells the storyline. They see their own names on each of their own papers. They are eager to make their own marks. Writing opportunities can be provided to them in several ways.

> Find or make a chalkboard—the larger the better for very young children. You can make one by painting a large, very sturdy piece of cardboard with chalkboard paint. Since your youngster is standing up and using pressure to write and draw, make the board very sturdy. One that bounces will be hard to write on and may frustrate children.
> Put the chalkboard in a central location where it will get lots of use. A hallway or a child's room is a good place. Buy thick, soft chalk because regular-size chalk breaks easily. Although it's messier, soft chalk makes dark marks more easily than hard chalk.

Another way to give your child experience with drawing is to let him "paint" with water on a wall or chalkboard. Take the chalkboard outside for this activity. Use brushes that are light enough for your child to handle easily (Lamme 1984, 19–20).

Some children may be doing controlled scribbling which has several characteristics.

Gradually, after much playing around with markers, chalk, and crayons, your child's scribbles become more controlled. He begins to see the relationship between the marks he is making on paper and the writing utensil in his hand. His scribbles are more systematic.... The lines go up and down. . .or in circles. Dots may surround the picture.... He systematically scribbles with each marker in the box.... Later, as part of the scribble pattern, circles, triangles, arrows, and squares may emerge (Lamme 1984, 39–40).

SUGGESTIONS FOR IMPLEMENTING CURRICULUM

CHILD BEHAVIOR	MATERIALS	EXAMPLES OF CAREGIVER STRATEGIES
Uses demonstrative naming.	Toys, objects.	Point to and label objects, e.g., "a foot," "a hand," "a nose." Extend to sentence: "Mary has a foot; Myron has a foot."
Uses attribution.	Toys, objects.	Combine labels, e.g., "red car," "big book." Extend to sentence: "Ray has the red car; Twila has the green car."
Uses possession.	Toys, objects.	Identify and label "Roger's shoe, Jenny's shoe."
Uses action.	Toys, objects.	Identify and label own and child's actions: "Urvi sits on the floor." "Stewart is eating."
Uses recurrence.		Use word patterns which indicate repeating or additional, e.g., At snack ask each child if he or she wants **more** apple.
Uses negation.		Use "no" with action, e.g., "No hitting; no kicking." Follow up commands with reasons.
Learns word order.		Use proper word order, e.g., "The truck moves." Extend child's "Move truck" to "Yes, the truck moves."
Learns prosodic patterning.		Use expression when talking. Accent the proper syllables. Child will imitate you.
Uses subject-verb pattern.		Use whole sentences. Expand child's sentences.

CHILD BEHAVIOR	MATERIALS	EXAMPLES OF CAREGIVER STRATEGIES
Uses verb-object pattern.		Use whole sentences. Expand child's sentences.
Omits function words.		Use whole sentences. Expand child's sentences.
Selects and uses books	Picture books, story books	Read aloud. Listen to child "read."
Controls scribbling	Markers, crayons, chalk, chalkboard, paper	Provide materials and space. Write labels, notes to child. Share child's scribbling.

REFERENCES

Anisfeld, Moshe. 1984. *Language Development from Birth to Three.* Hillsdale, New Jersey: Lawrence Erlbaum.

Lamme, Linda Leonard. 1984. *Growing Up Writing.* Washington, D.C.: Acropolis Books Ltd.

Lamme, Linda Leonard. 1985. *Growing Up Reading.* Washington, D.C.: Acropolis Books Ltd.

Wadsworth, Barry J. 1978. *Piaget for the Classroom Teacher.* New York: Longman.

Wilson, L. C. 1987. Planning the toddler day. *Pre-K Today.* 2(2): 38–39.

Wilson, L. C. 1988. When toddlers play. *Pre-K Today.* 2(5): 36–37.

STUDENT ACTIVITIES

1. Observe a child this age for fifteen minutes during play time. Write a narrative description.
   a. Categorize the child's social behaviors.
   b. List behaviors which indicate preconceptual classifications.
   c. Categorize the child's speech using the above types of syntax.
   d. List the kinds of representations the child used.
2. Make a theme picture book. Use it with a child. Observe the child's emotional reactions. Observe the child's language. Involve the child in rereading the book.

REVIEW

1. List two developing physical accomplishments of a child this age.
2. Describe a situation where the child is asserting independence.
3. In each of the following areas list two concepts the child is constructing:
    a. quantity
    b. number
    c. space
    d. time
4. Write an example of the following language patterns:
    a. demonstrative naming
    b. attribution
    c. possession
    d. action
    e. recurrence
    f. negation

14

The Child from Thirty to Thirty-Six Months of Age

OBJECTIVES

After completing this chapter, the caregiver shall

Identify and record sequences of change in the physical, emotional, social, cognitive, and language development of children from 30 to 36 months of age.

Select materials appropriate to that age-level child's development.

Devise strategies appropriate to that age-level child's development.

CHAPTER OUTLINE

I. Materials and Activities
   A. Types of materials
   B. Examples of homemade materials
   C. Activities ideas
II. Caregiver Strategies to Enhance the Child's Development
   A. Physical development

   B. Emotional development
   C. Social development
   D. Cognitive development
   E. Language development

CHILD DEVELOPMENT ASSOCIATE FUNCTIONAL AREAS

All CDA functional areas are integrated into the caregiver decisions and behaviors.

Review Chapter 6. Use Appendix A, The Developmental Profile, with each child. Children follow a **sequence** of development. There can be ranges in **rate** of development.

Jeffrey, 35 months old, is playing in the playyard. He sits on a bigwheel and rolls backward, gets off and runs around with other children, picks at the ground and finds a roly poly which he takes to show the caregiver, walks around showing the roly poly to others, sits on a small trike, takes the roly poly and puts him by a tree trunk, sits on the ground, climbs a tree, climbs down and runs after a soccer ball, plops on a bigwheel, and then kicks a soccer ball back and forth with another child. At another time he again plays with a roly poly. When asked where the roly poly is, he stops, puts his hands up in the air and says, "He's dead." He finds another roly poly and shows it to the caregiver, saying, "He might be sleeping. Wake up roly poly." The bug moves and rolls up again. Jeffrey says, "He went to sleep again."

MATERIALS AND ACTIVITIES

Children this age are active, eager learners. They practice newly acquired skills and develop new ones. They like large muscle activity and are developing their fine muscles for more controlled manipulation of objects. They enjoy imaginative play. Their play incorporates their imagination, their language, and their understanding of themselves and others. They explore their world. They represent their ideas not only in play and language, but they also recognize pictures. They construct sentences to share their ideas (see Figure 14–1). They listen to stories and enjoy and participate in rhymes, fingerplays, music, and singing.

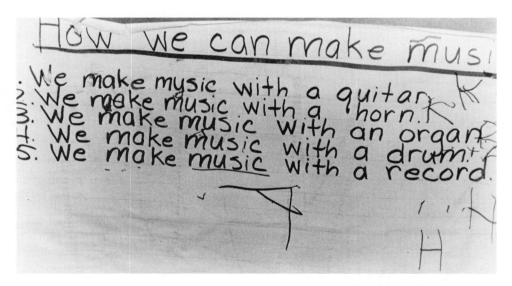

Figure 14–1 Language experience charts expose the young child to the process of writing what is spoken.

Types of Materials

Riding toys
Wagon
Trucks for hauling
Rocking boat
Tunnel, barrel to crawl through
    and on
Cardboard blocks
Wooden unit block set
Wooden people
Wooden animals

Markers, crayons, chalk, pens
Wooden beads and string
Rhythm instruments
Records
Tapes
Dramatic play props
Puppets
Books
Materials to explore—feel, measure,
    use

Examples of Homemade Materials

PROP BOXES

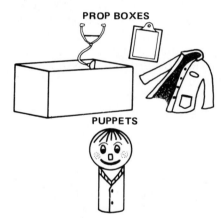

Gather props for one specific story or role. For example, put in a shoebox a stethoscope, white shirt, and small pad of paper for doctor props. In a larger box put a child-sized fire fighter's hat, boots, and poncho.

PUPPETS

Use cardboard tubes from paper towels. Cut paper to make face. Child uses markers or crayon to make face and clothes features. Glue face on tube.

BOOK: JOURNAL

Sew or staple sheets of unlined paper together. Each morning ask child to identify one toy or activity he or she wants to play with. Write a sentence identifying what the child chose. Allow the child to scribble, draw on the page. Read sentence to child. Label book "Juan's book," "Orelia's book." Send home each Friday.

WOODEN PEOPLE OR ANIMALS

Draw or cut out of a magazine pictures of people: infants, children, adults; fire fighter, police officer, doctor; or of animals or other objects: cars, houses, etc.

Glue picture on a piece of 1-inch thick white pine board. With a jigsaw, cut around the outside of the picture on three sides, cutting the bottom straight across. Sand the edges smooth. Apply two coats of nontoxic sealer. The object will stand up by itself.

Activities Ideas

Keeping records of informal observations as well as on the Developmental Profiles will assist you in planning appropriate experiences for each child. Plan for a holistic curriculum. Identify your children's interests. Use these to focus your thematic units. Plan mostly individual activities. Some short small-group activities may be included, e.g., reading or telling a story, singing a song, saying a rhyme or fingerplay. Each small-group activity is appropriate also for use with individuals.

Children construct physical knowledge by moving objects and observing changes in objects. They observe the effects of their "pulling, pushing, rolling, kicking, jumping, blowing, sucking, throwing, swinging, twirling, balancing, and dropping" objects (Kamii and DeVries 1978, 6). They observe changes in objects: for example, when they put a drop of blue food coloring in a clear glass of water. Offer materials and activities which help children discover the physical characteristics of objects.

Children construct logico-mathematical knowledge by inventing relationships among objects. Comparisons of quantity, number, space, and time are explorations into relating two or more objects or events in a new and abstract way. Children can seek relationships among any kinds of materials. Games and activities which use the invented relationships help stimulate and reinforce their constructions. For example, a bulletin board of all the children's handprints provides opportunities for each child to place his or her hands over other children's handprints and make comparisons.

Children learn social-arbitrary knowledge from other people. They learn language from people. They learn the names of objects, meanings of words, intonations in pronouncing words, and word order and syntax from others. They learn the rules for living from others. They learn valuing from others. The caregiver bears the major responsibility in the child care program for providing this information and helping the child construct social-arbitrary knowledge. The child's physical, emotional, social, and cognitive development are all involved in constructing social-arbitrary knowledge.

CAREGIVER STRATEGIES TO ENHANCE THE CHILD'S DEVELOPMENT

Physical Development

Children of this age are increasing their stability in both fast and slow movements. They walk evenly both quickly and slowly. They run quickly and usually maintain their balance. They jump up and down. They jump off objects. And they jump forward. They can twist and turn to dress and undress. And they can use their small muscles to hold clothes and attempt

Figure 14-2 The caregiver allows the child to use crayons in either or both hands even though handedness may be established.

Figure 14-3 The caregiver shares the child's enthusiasm in discovery.

buttoning, snapping, and zippering. They practice their physical skills. Right- or left-handedness is now established, though children use both hands in many activities (see Figure 14-2).

At this age children can establish sleep routines which they can do themselves. Before nap they can go to the bathroom and wash their hands. They can sit on their cots, take their own shoes off, and put the shoes under the cot. They can lie down with their heads near their name tapes. When they awaken, they can go to the bathroom and return to put on their shoes. If others are still sleeping, they can choose a quiet activity, e.g., looking at books or listening to a story or music with earphones.

Most children have completed toilet-training by 36 months of age. They need to wear clothes which they can remove quickly and easily. They need easy access to the bathroom. And they need occasional questions and reminders to go to the bathroom.

CDA Ⅱ.4

SUGGESTIONS FOR IMPLEMENTING CURRICULUM

CHILD BEHAVIOR	EXAMPLES OF CAREGIVER STRATEGIES
Muscular Control *MOVEMENT AND COORDINATION* Walks evenly. Runs.	 Provide uncluttered floor space. Provide space and games for appropriate running.

CHILD BEHAVIOR	EXAMPLES OF CAREGIVER STRATEGIES
Jumps in place and forward. Dresses and undresses self with assistance.	Play games, sing songs which encourage jumping. Allow time for child to manipulate clothes. Demonstrate how to hold button and buttonholes, zipper and cloth, etc.
HAND Has established handedness.	Allow child to select hand to use.
Sleeping Assists with preparation routines.	Plan time in schedule for children to do as much of routines as possible. It takes longer for a child to wash and dry hands than if you help, but child needs to be independent and to develop skills. Help with tight snaps, etc.
Elimination Is in process of or has completed toilet-training.	Provide assistance when needed. Assist with clothes, handwashing when needed. Clean up area. **Wash your hands.**

Emotional Development

Children of this age express their emotions and feelings strongly. They let you know how they feel and then may move beyond their anger or happiness and soon express a different feeling.

These children's negativism is expressed in several ways. Sometimes negative behavior is a way of asserting themselves and their independence.

These children are enthusiastic learners, enjoying themselves and their discoveries. Their developing mastery of skills enhances their feelings of competence, self-worth, and acceptance of self (see Figure 14–3).

These children may become physically aggressive. Their widening world presents many new experiences. They may use aggression in their attempts to feel they have some control of their world.

Persistence in continuing a task enables these children to discover many things. As they explore, their persistence will probably enable them to accomplish enough so that they have the feeling that "I did it" or "See what I found out." Children who persist for only a short time may be unable to finish tasks or make discoveries which provide them with that feeling of accomplishment and worth. Children with long attention spans have opportunities to learn from their own extended actions as well as from others. A short attention span limits a child's exposure and involvement in many activities.

SUGGESTIONS FOR IMPLEMENTING CURRICULUM

CHILD BEHAVIOR	EXAMPLES OF CAREGIVER STRATEGIES
Types of Emotions-Feelings Reacts strongly.	Accept child's initial response. Help child keep within bounds of appropriate behavior, e.g., let child express anger by vigorously riding a bigwheel for a while.
Acts negatively.	Rephrase suggestions to child. Stimulate interest in a different activity.
Learns enthusiastically.	Reinforce child's excitement with learning. Provide opportunities for challenging experiences.
Is mastering skills.	Provide toys, equipment, materials which child needs to use often to master skills.
Control of Emotions-Feelings Is physically aggressive.	Provide activities for child to work out feelings and need to control.
Temperament Activity level. Regularity. Approach or withdrawal as a characteristic response to a new situation. Adaptability to change in routine. Level of sensory threshold. Positive or negative mood. Intensity of response. Distractibility. Persistence and attention span.	List two of the child's behaviors in each category which indicate the child's basic style. List adjustments you need to make to help the child cope with daily situations.

Social Development

Egocentrism continues to be present in the preconceptual substage. Even though young children can distinguish themselves from others, they are only slowly developing the ideas that follow from this. They are just beginning to understand that others have feelings. They assume that when they speak, everyone understands the exact meanings of their words; they do not realize that others may give different meanings to the same words or experiences.

Young children interpret changes in appearance to mean changes in the basic object or person. "Preconceptual children generally do not see things or people as having a core and consistent identity over time" (Cowen 1978, 133). This fluctuation includes their concepts of self. "They seem to have little idea that their 'self' of a few days ago is relevant to what is happening now, today" (Cowen 1978, 133).

Figure 14-4 The caregiver is available to share materials and attention.

Children continue to identify their selfness within their world. Their toys are a part of themselves, and they remain very possessive of the toys and materials they are using. However, their strengthening sense of self also provides a foundation for expanding interactions with others. These children are increasingly aware of others as individuals. They use adults as resources, seeking assistance from them when the children decide they need help (see Figure 14-4). They become directive with others, exerting control over people, animals, and toys as they learn ways to control their world. Children this age sometimes recognize others' needs and may help with tasks or initiate or respond with assistance.

These children's self-control is increasing. Their desire for instant gratification is being modified so they sometimes accept delayed gratification. They may take turns occasionally. At times they may decide to share. And they may play cooperatively for short periods of time.

SUGGESTIONS FOR IMPLEMENTING CURRICULUM

CHILD BEHAVIOR	EXAMPLES OF CAREGIVER STRATEGIES
Self Acts possessive.	Provide enough toys and materials so child can control use of some for a period of time.
Others Seeks assistance.	Allow child to use you as a resource. Help where needed. Do not take over.
Directs others.	Provide opportunities for child to exert acceptable control over others.
Helps others.	Praise child's spontaneous helping. Ask for assistance so child can help with routines, etc.
Control of Self Plays cooperatively.	Provide toys, materials, and time.
Shares.	Encourage by providing opportunities to share, e.g., eating orange or apple slices.
Takes turns.	Use daily routines to help control wait time, e.g., taking turns to wash hands.

Cognitive Development

Children at this age are curious, exploring problem-solvers. They are seeking to discover what makes things tick, what objects are made of, and how actions happen. They use observing, questioning, manipulating, classifying, and measuring to learn about their world.

Figure 14–5 Block carts can provide cues for matching shapes.

In the preconceptual stage children may attempt to put objects in an order, like biggest to smallest buttons, but unless the materials present cues, such as fitting together, the children are not able to determine the logic of ordering. Arranging objects in a series is guesswork for young children because they do not understand the relationships in a series of objects.

These children continue to construct physical knowledge about the properties of objects (see Figure 14–5). They construct logico-mathematical knowledge about relationships. And they construct social-arbitrary knowledge about language and social rules and values.

CDA
II . 5

SUGGESTIONS FOR IMPLEMENTING CURRICULUM

CHILD BEHAVIOR	EXAMPLES OF CAREGIVER STRATEGIES
Piaget's Preoperational Stage, Preconceptual Substage	
NONVERBAL CLASSIFICATION	
Makes graphic collections.	Encourage child to use art media to represent. Listen to child's explanation of own classification system.
VERBAL PRECONCEPTS	
Uses words differently at different times.	Observe context of talk. Ask for clarification of meaning if necessary.
Labels objects in one class.	Remember that child's meaning may not be as inclusive as yours. Determine exactly what child meant.
VERBAL REASONING	
Thinks one action is like another action.	Observe the behavior which precedes a child's talking. Determine how child is drawing relationships among his or her actions.
Reasons from effect to cause.	Think backward from action to previous action to understand child's reasoning.
QUANTITY	
Understands some, more, gone, big.	Use words labeling quantity. They are a part of the daily experiences.
NUMBER	
Understands more.	Use words labeling number as a comparative. Use daily situations, e.g., "There are more rocks in this pail than in that pail."
SPACE	
Understands up, down, behind, under, over.	Label child's actions when child is moving into different positions in space, e.g., "Merrilee is behind the box. Ashton is under the box."
TIME	
Understands now, soon, before, after.	Use time words in daily experiences, e.g., "We wash our hands before we eat." "We go to the bathroom after naptime."

Language Development

Children this age continue to increase their vocabulary. Their daily experiences provide opportunities for them to construct meanings of new objects and to extend previously learned concepts. The labeling process is now part of children's construction of the identity of objects.

These children continue to overregularize words. However, more and more of their plural words are formed correctly. These children are very gradually constructing concepts of time. The past is still an abstraction they are attempting to understand. They still overregularize past tense words, saying things like, "Jim bited me" and "I bringed these out."

Sentence length increases as the children increase their use and familiarity with frequently used vocabulary, word-order patterns, and stress and intonation patterns. They speak more complete sentences and are able to express several ideas in a sequence of sentences.

Dramatic play provides opportunities to combine language with imagination. These children can describe their actions and say what they think others might say. They are practicing their language and fitting it into a social context.

Books play an increasingly important role. Reading aloud provides book language patterns. Reading the pictures encourages self-expression. And talking about the story or the pictures facilitates comprehension of the language (see Figure 14–6).

Scribbling continues as the child is involved in the writing process. Each child is developing scribbling at his or her own rate.

Figure 14–6 Big books stimulate involvement in making and reading familiar stories.

Children are scribblers from the time they hold a writing tool until after they learn to write their names. There is a progression to their scribbles which moves from random scribbling, to controlled scribbling, to the naming of scribbling, to writing mock letters and words, to learning, finally, how to write. It is important not to underestimate the value of scribbling as a foundation for writing (Lamme 1984, 37).

You model many uses of writing for children. You write their names. You write a note to their parents. You write sentences on their art work papers. You write dictated sentences on their pages of scribbling. You write charts about daily experiences; for example, planting beans and writing on the chart what they look like each day. In this way, the children experience meaningful uses of writing.

CDA
II. 6

SUGGESTIONS FOR IMPLEMENTING CURRICULUM

CHILD BEHAVIOR	MATERIALS	EXAMPLES OF CAREGIVER STRATEGIES
Increases vocabulary Associates word and object.		Introduce new objects to see and feel and use. Label objects and actions with single words and use in sentences.
Improves syntax Word order		Repeat child's sentence, using proper word order.
Two- and three-word sentences		Respond to child's meaning. Extend his sentence.
Longer sentences		Respond to child's meaning. Commend his ideas.
Improves word forms Uses plurals		Use correct plural form. When child says "foots," restate "See your feet."
Uses past tense		Use correct past tense. When child says "He bited me," restate, "He bit you? Show me where he bit you."
Improves reading skills Listens to stories, "reads" pictures, storybooks	Records, pictures, picture books	Read aloud. Listen to child "read." Use expression. Tell or read story line.
Uses controlled scribbling	Markers, chalk, crayons, pencil, paper	Write to child. Write notes to child and others. Label objects. Write dictated sentences.

REFERENCES

Cowen, Philip A. 1978. *Piaget with Feeling.* New York: Holt, Rinehart & Winston.

Kamii, Constance, and DeVries, Rheta. 1978. *Physical Knowledge in Pre-school Education: Implications of Piaget's Theory.* Englewood Cliffs, New Jersey: Prentice-Hall.

Lamme, Linda Leonard. 1984. *Growing Up Writing.* Washington, D.C.: Acropolis Books Ltd.

STUDENT ACTIVITIES

1. Observe one child for ten minutes in a playyard. Write a list of the activities the child does. Identify equipment and materials used.
2. Observe one child for ten minutes in a playyard. Tally the times the child shares a toy or equipment. Tally the times the child plays **with** another child.
3. Observe a caregiver for five minutes. Write down the dialogue the caregiver has with a child or with several children. Categorize the caregiver's statements which imitate, expand, or extend the child's statements.
4. Observe children at play. List their language and actions which indicate their developing concepts of quantity, number, space, and time.
5. Plan and use one activity with a child to facilitate the child's constructing physical knowledge.
6. Plan and use one activity with a child to facilitate the child's constructing logico-mathematical knowledge.
7. Plan and use one activity with a child to facilitate the child's constructing social-arbitrary knowledge.

REVIEW

1. List three tasks children this age can complete by themselves.
2. List four tasks children can assist you with.
3. Describe one way to deal with an angry child.
4. Write one example of a child's statement which uses a word which the child has given a meaning different from that which adults give the word.
5. Compare how children learn physical knowledge, logico-mathematical knowledge, and social-arbitrary knowledge.

APPENDIX A

Developmental Profiles

APPROXIMATELY BIRTH TO FOUR MONTHS OF AGE

CHILD BEHAVIOR	DATE FIRST OBSERVED	PRACTICING	PROFICIENT
Physical Development			
MUSCULAR CONTROL			
Reflex			
Grasp reflex.			
Startle reflex.			
Tonic neck reflex.			
Head and neck			
Turns head.			
Holds head upright with support.			
Lifts head slightly when on stomach.			
Holds head to sides and middle.			
Holds up head when on back and on stomach.			
Holds head without support.			
Trunk			
Holds up chest.			
Sits with support.			
May attempt to raise self.			
May fuss if left lying down with little chance to sit up.			
Holds up chest and shoulders.			
Leg			
Rolls from stomach to back.			
Arm			
Moves randomly.			
Reaches.			

CHILD BEHAVIOR	DATE FIRST OBSERVED	PRACTICING	PROFICIENT

Hand

  Opens and closes.

  Keeps hands open.

  Plays with hands.

  Uses hands to grasp object.
    Whole hand and fingers against thumb.

    Thumb and forefinger.

    Holds and moves object.

Eye–hand coordination

  Moves arm toward object: may miss it.

  Reaches hand to object: may grab or miss it.

SEEING

  Focuses 8 inches from eyes.

  Follows with eyes.

  Stares.

  Sees objects beyond 8 inches.

  Looks from object to object.

  Looks around; stops to focus on object which has caught attention; then looks at something else; continual visual searching.

HEARING

  Responds to voice.

  Hears range of sounds.

  Calms while hearing low-pitched sounds.

  Becomes agitated while hearing high-pitched sounds.

  Locates sound.

SLEEPING

  Sleeps much of the day and night.

  Takes a long morning nap and a long afternoon nap.

  May have irregular sleep habits.

EATING

  Takes bottle on demand.

CHILD BEHAVIOR	DATE FIRST OBSERVED	PRACTICING	PROFICIENT

ELIMINATION
    Begins to establish predictable eating and elimination pattern.
    Establishes regular time for bowel movements.

Emotional Development
TYPES OF EMOTIONS-FEELINGS
    Shows excitement.
    Shows stress.
    Shows enjoyment.
    Shows anger.
    Shows fear.
    Protests.

CONTROL OF EMOTIONS-FEELINGS
    Seems to occur automatically.
    Decreases crying.
    Increases sounds (talking).
    Reflects sounds (talking).
    Comforted by holding.

TEMPERAMENT (List two behaviors which indicate basic style)
    Activity level.
    Regularity.
    Approach or withdrawal as a characteristic response to a new situation.
    Adaptability to change in routine.
    Level of sensory threshold.
    Positive or negative mood.
    Intensity of response.
    Distractibility.
    Persistence and attention span.

Social Development
ATTACHMENT
    Shows special closeness to parent.
    Develops familiarity with one primary caregiver.

CHILD BEHAVIOR	DATE FIRST OBSERVED	PRACTICING	PROFICIENT

SELF

Becomes aware of hands and feet.

Smiles spontaneously.

Smiles at self in mirror.

OTHERS

Establishes eye contact with another person.

Recognizes voice of parent.

Smiles at people (social smile).

Watches people.

Talks (cooing) to people.

Shows longer attentiveness when involved with people.

Recognizes parent visually.

Recognizes individual people.

Behaves differently with parent than with others.

Interacts with people.

Laughs.

Differentiates self from parent.

Initiates talking to others.

Plays with toys.

Cognitive Development
SENSORIMOTOR STAGE 1

Reflexive actions.

Passive to active search.

SENSORIMOTOR STAGE 2

Small, gradual changes come from repetition.

Coordination of behaviors, e.g., sound-looking.

Puts hand, object in mouth and sucks on it.

Moves hand, object where can see it.

Produces a pleasurable motor activity and repeats activity.

CHILD BEHAVIOR	DATE FIRST OBSERVED	PRACTICING	PROFICIENT

OBJECT PERMANENCE

Follows moving object with eyes until object disappears. Looks where object disappeared.

Loses interest and turns away. Does not search for it.

Language Development

PHYSICAL COMPONENTS INVOLVED IN LANGUAGE COMMUNICATION

Back of throat.

Nose.

Mouth cavity.

Front of mouth.

Tongue.

Lips.

Saliva.

ACTIONS INVOLVED IN LANGUAGE COMMUNICATION

Changes air flow: through nose; through mouth.

Uses tongue to manipulate air flow, saliva.

Plays with tongue—twists, turns, sticks it out, sucks on it.

Uses saliva in various places and changes sounds: gurgle in back of throat; bubbling in center of mouth; hissing, spitting with partially closed lips and tongue.

INITIATING–RESPONDING

Initiates making sounds.

Responds vocally to another person.

Makes sound, repeats sound, continues practicing sound and lengthening to longer amounts of time.

Imitates a few sounds he or she already knows.

Experiments with sounds.

CHILD BEHAVIOR	DATE FIRST OBSERVED	PRACTICING	PROFICIENT

CRYING

Cries apparently automatically in distress, frustration.

Cries differently to express hunger, discomfort, anger.

Cries to gain attention.

Cries less as vocalizing increases.

COOING

Coos in vowellike sounds.

Adds pitch.

APPROXIMATELY FOUR TO EIGHT MONTHS OF AGE

CHILD BEHAVIOR	DATE FIRST OBSERVED	PRACTICING	PROFICIENT

Physical Development
MUSCULAR CONTROL

Head and neck

Holds head up independently.

Holds head in midline position.

Holds head up when on back, stomach, and sitting.

Trunk

Holds up chest, shoulders; arches back, hips.

Sits with support.
    May attempt to raise self.
    May fuss if left lying down with little chance to sit up.

Leans back and forth.

Sits in a chair.

Sits unsupported for short time.

Pushes self to sitting position.

Leg

Lifts legs when on back and stomach.

Rolls from stomach to back.

Straightens legs when standing.

Stamps feet when standing.

CHILD BEHAVIOR	DATE FIRST OBSERVED	PRACTICING	PROFICIENT
Rolls from back to stomach.			
Raises to hands and knees.			
Stands with support.			
Pulls self to standing.			
Locomotion			
Kicks against surface to move.			
Rocks on hands and knees.			
Creeps on stomach.			
Uses legs to pull, push self when sitting.			
Arm			
Visually directs reaching, hitting.			
Throws objects.			
Hand			
Grasps objects with whole hand and fingers against thumb.			
Uses thumb and forefinger.			
Picks up object with one hand; passes it to the other hand.			
Uses objects in both hands.			
Grasps and releases objects.			
Drops objects.			
SEEING			
Focuses on objects near and far.			
Distinguishes color, distance; depth perception.			
Distinguishes visually attractive objects.			
Has visual preferences.			
HEARING			
Listens to own voice.			
Listens to others' voices.			
Looks around to locate sound.			
SLEEPING			
Takes a long morning nap and a long afternoon nap.			
EATING			
Begins solid foods (new tongue and swallowing technique).			

CHILD BEHAVIOR	DATE FIRST OBSERVED	PRACTICING	PROFICIENT
Drinks from cup (new tongue and swallowing technique).			
Eats at "mealtimes"—solid foods, milk, juice.			
Feeds self finger foods.			
TEETH			
First teeth emerge: 2 middle lower, 2 middle upper.			
ELIMINATION			
Decreases number of times of urination and bowel movements.			
Emotional Development			
TYPES OF EMOTIONS-FEELINGS			
Shows pleasure in watching others.			
Shows pleasure in repetitive play.			
Shows depression.			
Shows fear: of strangers; of falling down.			
Shows frustration with stimulation overload.			
Shows happiness, delight, joy, humor.			
Shows rage.			
CONTROL OF EMOTIONS-FEELINGS			
Sometimes stops crying when talked to, sung to.			
TEMPERAMENT (List two behaviors which indicate basic style)			
Activity level.			
Regularity.			
Approach or withdrawal as a characteristic response to a new situation.			
Adaptability to change in routine.			
Level of sensory threshold.			
Positive or negative mood.			
Intensity of response.			
Distractibility.			
Persistence and attention span.			

CHILD BEHAVIOR	DATE FIRST OBSERVED	PRACTICING	PROFICIENT

Social Development

ATTACHMENT

Shows strong attachment to parent.

Differentiates response to parent.

Shows familiarity with one specific caregiver.

Shows intense pleasure and frustration to person with whom attached.

SELF

Recognizes self in mirror.

Seeks independence in actions.

Plays self-designed games.

OTHERS

Observes others.

Imitates others.

Recognizes children.

Plays with people.

Seeks parent's and caregiver's attention by movement, sounds, smiles, cries.

Follows parent and caregiver to be in same room.

Resists pressures from others regarding feeding and eating.

Acts shy with some strangers.

Cognitive Development

SENSORIMOTOR STAGE 3

Produces a motor activity, catches interest, and intentionally repeats the activity over and over.

Repeats interesting action.

Develops hand-eye coordination further. Looks for object, reaches for it, and accurately touches it.

Imitates behavior can see or hear.

OBJECT PERMANENCE: STAGE 3

Visually follows object.

Searches visually for short time when object disappears.

CHILD BEHAVIOR	DATE FIRST OBSERVED	PRACTICING	PROFICIENT
Does not search manually.			
Sees part of object; looks for whole object.			

Language Development

Coos vowellike sounds for many minutes.			
Babbles syllablelike sounds.			
Responds to talking by cooing, babbling, smiling.			
Imitates sounds.			
Initiates sounds.			
Makes vowel sounds.			
Looks for person speaking.			
Looks when name is called.			
Makes consonant sounds.			
Babbles conversation with others.			
Reflects happiness, unhappiness in sounds made.			
Babbles two- and three-syllable sounds.			
Uses intensity,			
volume,			
pitch,			
rhythm.			

APPROXIMATELY FROM EIGHT TO TWELVE MONTHS OF AGE

CHILD BEHAVIOR	DATE FIRST OBSERVED	PRACTICING	PROFICIENT

Physical Development
MUSCULAR CONTROL

Trunk and leg

Raises self to sitting position.			
Sits alone.			
Stands holding on to furniture or hand.			
Stands without assistance.			
Sits from standing.			
Squats and stands.			

CHILD BEHAVIOR	DATE FIRST OBSERVED	PRACTICING	PROFICIENT
Locomotion			
Crawls.			
Steps forward.			
Crawls up steps.			
Steps sideways.			
Walks with help.			
Climbs on furniture.			
Hand			
Uses thumb and forefinger.			
Uses thumb and two fingers.			
Brings both hands to middle of body.			
Uses finger to poke.			
Carries objects in hands.			
Holds and uses pen and crayon.			
Reaches, touches, strokes object.			
Uses one hand to hold object, one hand to reach and explore.			
Stacks blocks with dominant hand.			
Takes off clothes.			
SLEEPING			
May have trouble sleeping.			
Takes morning nap and afternoon nap.			
Seeks parent or caregiver presence.			
EATING			
Holds bottle.			
Holds cup.			
Holds and uses spoon.			
Uses fingers to eat most food.			
Starts establishing food preferences.			
May eat less.			
TEETH			
Begins to get teeth.			

CHILD BEHAVIOR	DATE FIRST OBSERVED	PRACTICING	PROFICIENT

Emotional Development

TYPES OF EMOTIONS-FEELINGS

Shows happiness, joy, pleasure.

Shows anxiety.

Shows fear.

Shows anger, frustration.
May have tantrums.

Rejects items, situations.

Develops preferences with toys, people.

Shows independence—helps with feeding and dressing self.

Shows affection.

Begins developing self-esteem.

CONTROL

Learning to obey "No."

Sometimes inhibits own behavior.

Obeys commands: No-No, Stop.

TEMPERAMENT (List two behaviors which indicate basic style)

Activity level.

Regularity.

Approach or withdrawal as a characteristic response to a new situation.

Adaptability to change in routine.

Level of sensory threshold.

Positive or negative mood.

Intensity of response.

Distractibility.

Persistence and attention span.

Social Development

OTHERS

Initiates interactions with others.

Responds.

May fear strangers.

Keeps parent or caregiver in sight.

Initiates play.

CHILD BEHAVIOR	DATE FIRST OBSERVED	PRACTICING	PROFICIENT

Begins to identify with children of own sex.

Becomes assertive.

Wants own pleasure; may not consider others.

Imitates play.

Is possessive of people.

Is possessive of materials.

May become shy, clinging.

May demand attention.

Cognitive Development
SENSORIMOTOR STAGE 4

Differentiates goals
Can focus on reaching and focus on toy.

Object permanence
Object permanence established; object exists when it is no longer visible; child seeks toy that rolls behind object.

Causality
Understands that others cause actions.

Imitation and play
Imitates other's actions; uses actions as play.

Language Development
Babbles.

Shouts.

Labels object sounds.

Uses names: mama, dada.

Responds to familiar sounds.

Responds to familiar words.

Responds to own name.

Makes sounds which reflect emotions.

Repeats syllables, words, e.g., bye-bye.

Makes sounds like conversation.

Repeats, practices word over and over.

Connects word with objects: says word and points to object.

APPROXIMATELY TWELVE TO EIGHTEEN MONTHS OF AGE

CHILD BEHAVIOR	DATE FIRST OBSERVED	PRACTICING	PROFICIENT

Physical Development

MUSCULAR CONTROL

Trunk

Shows high energy, is active, moves from one activity to another.

Raises self to standing.

Locomotion

May prefer crawling to walking.

Walks alone.

Climbs up stairs with help.

Climbs down stairs with help.

Climbs over objects.

Hand

Uses thumb against fingers.

Shows hand preference.

Points with finger.

Carries, exchanges objects in hands.

Flings objects.

Throws objects.

Rolls and catches objects.

Eye-hand coordination

Reaches and grasps accurately.

Scribbles.

Helps in dressing, undressing.

SEEING

Watches people, objects, actions.

Bends, looks from different directions.

Visually scans surrounding area.

Visually searches.

SLEEPING

Begins to move from morning and afternoon nap to afternoon nap.

EATING

Eats three meals.

Feeds self; uses cup, spoon, and fingers.

CHILD BEHAVIOR	DATE FIRST OBSERVED	PRACTICING	PROFICIENT
Expresses food likes and dislikes.			
May eat less food.			

Emotional Development
TYPES OF EMOTIONS-FEELINGS

Expresses emotions in behavior and language.

Recognizes emotions in others.

May fear strangeness.

Shows excitement, delight.

Expresses sense of humor.

Shows affection.

Displays negativism.

May have tantrums.

Uses play to express emotions, resolve conflicts.

Seeks dependency, security with parent and caregiver.

Seeks to expand independence.

CONTROL OF EMOTIONS-FEELINGS

Begins to understand right and wrong.

Reinforces desired behavior.

TEMPERAMENT (List two behaviors which indicate basic style)

Activity level.

Regularity.

Approach or withdrawal as a characteristic response to a new situation.

Adaptability to change in routine.

Level of sensory threshold.

Positive or negative mood.

Intensity of response.

Distractibility.

Persistence and attention span.

CHILD BEHAVIOR	DATE FIRST OBSERVED	PRACTICING	PROFICIENT

Social Development
SELF
    Has concept of self.

    Is egocentric: understands only own viewpoint.

OTHERS
    Seeks presence of parent or caregiver.

    Plays games.

    Occasionally shares.

    Acts differently toward different people.

    Uses variety of behaviors to gain attention.

    May be shy with some people.

    Engages in parallel play.

Cognitive Development
SENSORIMOTOR DEVELOPMENT: STAGE 5
    Object permanence
        Watches toy hid and moved.

        Looks for it where moved.

    Causality
        Investigates cause and effect.

        Sees self as causal agent.

        Explores various ways things happen.

        Employs active trial-and-error to solve problems.

        Experiments.

    Imitation and play
        Copies behaviors of others.

        Turns play with imitation into rituals.

Language Development
    Uses intonation.

    Babbles sentences.

    Repeats, practices words.

    Imitates sounds of other people, objects.

CHILD BEHAVIOR	DATE FIRST OBSERVED	PRACTICING	PROFICIENT
Responds to word and gesture conversation.			
Responds to many questions and commands child cannot say.			
Uses word approximation for some words.			
Uses words in immediate context.			
Identifies familiar pictures.			
Uses markers.			

APPROXIMATELY EIGHTEEN TO TWENTY-FOUR MONTHS OF AGE

CHILD BEHAVIOR	DATE FIRST OBSERVED	PRACTICING	PROFICIENT
Physical Development			
MUSCULAR CONTROL			
Locomotion			
Walks forward.			
Walks backward.			
Walks sideways.			
Runs with stops and starts.			
Jumps with both feet.			
Kicks object.			
Walks up stairs holding railing; walks down stairs holding railing.			
Pushes and pulls objects while walking.			
Climbs.			
Pedals cycle.			
Arm			
Throws object at target.			
Hand			
Grasps and releases with developing finger muscles.			
Pulls zippers.			
Helps dress and undress self.			
Scribbles.			
Increases wrist flexibility, turns wrist to turn object.			

CHILD BEHAVIOR	DATE FIRST OBSERVED	PRACTICING	PROFICIENT
Establishing right- or left-handedness.			
Turns book pages.			
Digs with tool.			
Makes individual marks with crayon or pen.			

SLEEPING

May move from crib to bed or cot.

EATING

Controls cup and spoon better.

May eat anything, then change to picky eating.

TEETH

Has most baby teeth.

Uses toothbrush.

ELIMINATION

May show interest in and readiness for toilet training.

Emotional Development

TYPES OF EMOTIONS-FEELINGS

Views internal feelings and external behavior as same.

Shows one or more emotions at same time.

Continues to develop feelings about self.

Changes feelings about self.

Seeks approval.

May develop new fears.

Increases fantasy.

May increase aggressiveness.

Seeks security in routines.

May become shy again.

Sometimes rejects parent or caregiver.

CONTROL OF EMOTIONS-FEELINGS

Uses reactions of others as a controller of own behavior.

May resist change.

CHILD BEHAVIOR	DATE FIRST OBSERVED	PRACTICING	PROFICIENT
Moves to extremes, from lovable to demanding and stubborn.			

TEMPERAMENT *(List two behaviors which indicate basic style)*

Activity level.

Regularity.

Approach or withdrawal as a characteristic response to a new situation.

Adaptability to change in routine.

Level of sensory threshold.

Positive or negative mood.

Intensity of response.

Distractibility.

Persistence and attention span.

Social Development

SELF

Is egocentric, sees things from own point of view.

May change identity of self from day to day.

Identifies materials as belonging to self.

Uses I, mine, me, you.

OTHERS

Demands attention.

Begins to be aware of others' feelings.

Believes people have changes in identity.

Expands social relationships.

Looks to others for help.

Imitates tasks of others.

Wants to help, assists with tasks.

May do opposite of what is requested.

Difficulty sharing.

Engages in parallel play.

CHILD BEHAVIOR	DATE FIRST OBSERVED	PRACTICING	PROFICIENT

Cognitive Development
SENSORIMOTOR DEVELOPMENT: STAGE 6

Mental trial and error
   Tries out ideas mentally, based on past concrete experiences.

Object permanence
   Sees object disappear, mentally remembers object and figures out where it went.

Deferred imitation and symbolization
   Imitates past events.

   Engages in symbolic play.

   Resolves conflict.

   Compensates for unsatisfied needs.

   Tries roles.

Language Development
Uses language to reflect own meaning; expects others to have same meaning.

Expands vocabulary rapidly, labeling objects.

Points to objects and pictures named by others.

Learns social words—hello, please, thank you.

Uses language to express needs, desires.

Uses language to direct others.

Questions.

Uses nouns,

verbs,

pronouns.

Is learning prepositions.

Calls self by name.

Follows directions of one-step or two-steps.

CHILD BEHAVIOR	DATE FIRST OBSERVED	PRACTICING	PROFICIENT
Uses two-word sentences; three-word sentences.			
Looks at books.			
Listens to stories and rhymes.			
Scribbles.			

APPROXIMATELY TWENTY-FOUR TO THIRTY MONTHS OF AGE

CHILD BEHAVIOR	DATE FIRST OBSERVED	PRACTICING	PROFICIENT

Physical Development
MUSCULAR CONTROL

Movement
Bends at waist.
Climbs.
Jumps.
Stands on one foot.

Arm
Throws.

Hand
Touches.
Twists.

EATING
Uses spoon.
Is learning to use fork.
Uses fingers.

TEETH
Has all twenty baby teeth.
Brushes teeth.

ELIMINATION
Is learning to use toilet.
Has completed toilet-training.

Emotional Development
TYPES OF EMOTIONS-FEELINGS

Self-esteem
Feels comfortable with self.
Feels positive self-worth.
Feels negative self-worth.

CHILD BEHAVIOR	DATE FIRST OBSERVED	PRACTICING	PROFICIENT

CONTROL OF EMOTIONS-
FEELINGS
   Expresses emotions.

TEMPERAMENT (List two behaviors
which indicate basic style)
   Activity level.

   Regularity.

   Approach or withdrawal as a
   characteristic response to a new
   situation.

   Adaptability to change in
   routine.

   Level of sensory threshold.

   Positive or negative mood.

   Intensity of response.

   Distractibility.

   Persistence and attention span.

Social Development
SELF
   Realizes own skills.

OTHERS
   Shows independence.

   Acts to please adult.

   Shows feelings to others.

   Recognizes emotions in others.

   Recognizes the difference between
   "mine" and "yours."

   Shares.

   Helps others.

   Engages in parallel play.

Cognitive Development
PREOPERATIONAL STAGE:
PRECONCEPTUAL

   Nonverbal classification
      Makes graphic collections.

   Verbal preconcepts
      Uses words differently at differ-
      ent times.
      Uses words with private meanings.

CHILD BEHAVIOR	DATE FIRST OBSERVED	PRACTICING	PROFICIENT
Labels objects in one class.			
Focuses on one attribute.			
Verbal reasoning			
Reasons from particular to particular.			
Quantity			
Understands some,			
more,			
gone,			
big.			
Number			
Understands more.			
Space			
Understands up,			
down,			
behind,			
under,			
over.			
Time			
Understands now,			
soon.			
Language Development			
Uses demonstrative naming.			
Uses attribution.			
Uses possession.			
Uses action.			
Uses recurrence.			
Uses negation.			
Learns word order.			
Learns prosodic patterning.			
Uses subject–verb.			
Uses verb–object.			
Omits function words.			
Selects and uses books.			
Uses controlled scribbling.			

APPROXIMATELY THIRTY TO THIRTY-SIX MONTHS OF AGE

CHILD BEHAVIOR	DATE FIRST OBSERVED	PRACTICING	PROFICIENT

Physical Development
MOVEMENT AND COORDINATION
    Walks evenly.

    Runs.

    Jumps in place and forward.

    Dresses and undresses self with assistance.

    Has established handedness.

SLEEPING
    Assists with preparation of routines.

ELIMINATION
    Is in process of or has completed toilet-training.

Emotional Development
TYPES OF EMOTIONS-FEELINGS
    Reacts strongly.

    Acts negatively.

    Learns enthusiastically.

    Is mastering skills.

CONTROL OF EMOTIONS-FEELINGS
    Is physically aggressive.

TEMPERAMENT (List two behaviors which indicate basic style)
    Activity level.

    Regularity.

    Approach or withdrawal as a characteristic response to a new situation.

    Adaptability to change in routine.

    Level of sensory threshold.

    Positive or negative mood.

    Intensity of response.

    Distractibility.

    Persistence and attention span.

CHILD BEHAVIOR	DATE FIRST OBSERVED	PRACTICING	PROFICIENT
Social Development			
SELF			
Acts possessive.			
OTHERS			
Seeks assistance.			
Directs others.			
Helps others.			
CONTROL OF SELF			
Plays cooperatively.			
Shares.			
Takes turns.			
Cognitive Development			
PREOPERATIONAL STAGE: PRECONCEPTUAL			
Nonverbal classification			
Makes graphic collections.			
Verbal preconcepts			
Uses words differently at different times.			
Labels objects in one class.			
Verbal reasoning			
Thinks one action like another action.			
Reasons from effect to cause.			
Quantity			
Understands some,			
more,			
gone,			
big.			
Number			
Understands more.			
Space			
Understands up,			
down,			
behind,			
under,			
over.			

CHILD BEHAVIOR	DATE FIRST OBSERVED	PRACTICING	PROFICIENT
Time			
Understands now,			
soon,			
before,			
after.			
Language Development			
INCREASES VOCABULARY			
IMPROVES SYNTAX			
Word order.			
Two- and three-word sentences.			
Longer sentences.			
IMPROVES WORD FORMS			
Plurals.			
Past tense.			
IMPROVES READING SKILLS			
Listens to stories, "reads" pictures, storybooks.			
USES CONTROLLED SCRIBBLING			

APPENDIX B

CDA Competency Standards for Infant/Toddler Caregivers in Center-Based Programs

The CDA Competency Standards are the national standards used to evaluate a caregiver's performance with children and families during the CDA assessment process. The Competency Standards are divided into six **competency goals**, which are statements of a general purpose or goal for caregiver behavior. The competency goals are common to all child care settings. The six goals are defined in more detail in 13 **functional areas**, which describe the major tasks or functions that a caregiver must complete in order to carry out the competency goals.

Each functional area is explained by a **developmental context**, which presents a brief overview of child development from birth to 3 years and provides a rationale for the functional area definition and examples of competent caregiver behavior that follow. Three different developmental levels are identified: young infant (birth-9 months), mobile infant (6-18 months), and toddler (16-36 months). The age ranges overlap because children develop at different rates, but the descriptions of these levels emphasize the unique characteristics and needs of children at each stage of development.

Each functional area is further explained by a list of sample caregiver behaviors. These examples describe behavior that demonstrates that a caregiver is acting in a competent way or exhibiting a skill in a particular functional area. During the assessment process, most Candidates will exhibit other competent behavior, and a competent Candidate might not demonstrate all the examples listed under a functional area. The examples are organized according to developmental stages of children from birth to 3 years in order to emphasize the importance of the special skills needed to work with young infants, mobile infants, and toddlers. Special bilingual specialization examples are presented for several functional areas.

The samples of caregiver competency included in the standards should serve as a basis for recognizing other, more specific behaviors that are important to the individual Candidate. A competent Candidate might not demonstrate all the examples listed in the following pages. CDA Candidates, other members of the Local Assessment Team, and individuals conducting or participating in CDA training will be able to think of many different ways to demonstrate skill in the six competency goals and 13 functional areas.

Competent caregivers integrate their work and constantly adapt their skills—always thinking of the development of the whole child. In all functional areas, it is important for competent caregivers to individualize their work with each child while meeting the needs of the group. In every area, too, caregivers must promote multiculturalism, support families with different languages, and meet the needs of handicapped children and children with special needs. And, while demonstrating skills and knowledge, competent caregivers must also demonstrate personal qualities, such as flexibility and a positive style of communicating with young children and working with families.

Competency Goal I

To Establish and Maintain a Safe, Healthy Learning Environment

1. FUNCTIONAL AREA: SAFE

Candidate provides a safe environment to prevent and reduce injuries.

DEVELOPMENTAL CONTEXT:

One of the most essential services for children is to ensure their safety and well-being. Indoor and outdoor areas should be free of dangerous conditions and materials. Adults should teach children about safety and comfort children when hurt. Adults should be attentive and have the skills and knowledge to prevent injuries and to handle emergencies, accidents, and injuries appropriately when they occur. In a safe environment, children will learn gradually to protect themselves and look out for others.

Young infants (birth-9 months) must be attended to carefully. A safe and secure environment is essential to their development. Because of infants' vulnerability and relative helplessness, adults must attend to each individual infant in order to ensure his/her continued safety.

Mobile infants (6-18 months) are changing each day. As their rapidly increasing motor skills lead them into new areas, adults must anticipate new hazards that may arise.

Toddlers (16-36 months) are increasingly curious about their world. They stretch boundaries and test everything in their surroundings. Adults must be attentive to their activities and ensure their safety while giving them simple explanations for safety precautions.

For example, the competent Candidate working with infants and toddlers:

☐ Keeps both the inside of the center and the outdoor play area free of debris, structural hazards, unguarded space heaters, tools, and dangerous substances, such as medicine, cleaning products, matches, chipping paint, toxic plants, small objects that could be swallowed, balloons, and plastic bags.

☐ Ensures that safety equipment, such as fire extinguishers and smoke detectors, are in place and operable and knows how to use them.

☐ Maintains an easily accessible and current list of phone numbers for contacting parents and emergency services, including poison control, fire company, and medical help.

☐ Uses diagrams, pictures, and words understood by children and adults to post instructions and practice procedures for fires and other emergencies, including safety procedures for handicapped children.

☐ Plans and practices monthly fire drills for moving all children in care to safety as quickly as possible.

☐ Ensures that outdoor play equipment is safe for small children and in good repair.

☐ Responds immediately and sympathetically to a child's injury or fear of injury and encourages the same response by the children.

☐ Takes safety precautions in a reassuring manner without overprotecting or making children fearful.

☐ Anticipates and makes plans to prevent potentially dangerous situations, such as children being left alone or separated while on a field trip.

☐ Maintains first aid supplies (including gauze, tape, syrup of ipecac, tweezers, scissors, and soap) and knows basic first aid procedures appropriate for young children, such as how to handle choking, treating cuts, etc.

☐ Uses safe auto and bus travel procedures, including use of appropriate car seats for children.

☐ Discusses safety information with parents and tells them about resources, such as poison control centers, that provide services to families in their own language.

☐ Makes areas safe for children at different developmental stages; for example, putting safety gates on stairways; covering electrical outlets with safety plugs; inspecting children's equipment (such as cribs and car seats) at least weekly; and securing, rearranging, or removing furniture that could fall or be pulled over.

☐ Supervises all children's activities indoors and outdoors.

☐ Keeps informed about safety standards for toys and equipment and shares this information with parents.

☐ Adapts the indoor and outdoor environment for the safety of children with handicaps.

☐ Requires parents to authorize in writing all persons allowed to pick children up from the program.

The competent Candidate working with **young infants** also, for example:

☐ Locks side rails on cribs in "up" position when children are napping.

☐ Places infants in a comfortable and safe position for sleeping.

☐ Stays with infants on changing table or when bathing.

The competent Candidate working with **mobile infants** also, for example:

☐ Holds child's hand when near dangerous areas, such as roads, deep water, or steps.

☐ Knows children's individual differences in their tendency to bite, climb, and escape. Watches or stays close to children to anticipate and respond to these actions.

The competent Candidate working with **toddlers** also, for example:

☐ Helps toddlers stop dangerous actions toward themselves and others.

☐ Explains cause and effect in dangerous situations in simple language, demonstrating as much as possible.

☐ Teaches safe use of playground equipment.

In addition, the competent Candidate working towards the **bilingual specialization**:

☐ Explains and practices safety procedures such as fire drills using the language best understood by the children.

2. FUNCTIONAL AREA: HEALTHY

Candidate promotes good health and nutrition and provides an environment that contributes to the prevention of illness.

DEVELOPMENTAL CONTEXT:

Good health involves sound medical and dental practices and good nutrition. Adults should model and encourage good health and nutrition habits with children. Food should be nutritious, prepared carefully, and served in a relaxed atmosphere. Prompt care should be given to children who are or become ill or hurt. Children need a clean environment that is properly lighted, ventilated, and heated or cooled. Indoor and outdoor areas should be free of materials or conditions that endanger children's health. Care of the child's physical needs communicates positive feelings about his/her value and influences the child's developing identity and feelings of self-worth. Parents and caregivers should exchange information about children's physical health frequently.

Young and mobile infants (birth-18 months) need affectionate and competent physical care geared to their individual needs and rhythms. Adults can help infants regulate their eating, sleeping, and other activities gradually, while continuing to balance the infant's and the group's needs.

Toddlers (16-36 months) imitate and learn from the activities of those around them. Good health habits can be established through modeling and encouraging tooth brushing, hand washing, nutritious eating, etc.

For example, the competent Candidate working with infants and toddlers:

☐ Learns about good nutrition for children from birth through 5 years old and helps plan age-appropriate, nutritious meals and snacks. While respecting family customs and habits, the caregiver shares nutrition information with parents and encourages them to provide healthy foods when they contribute food to the center.

☐ Conducts activities in a positive, relaxed, and pleasant atmosphere to reduce tension and stress.

☐ Washes hands after toileting a child, helping child blow nose, and before food preparation and eating.

☐ Attends to each child's physical needs, such as toileting, eating, exercising, and napping.

☐ Provides affection for all children.

☐ Provides adequate ventilation and lighting, comfortable room temperatures, and good sanitation.

☐ Makes sure play areas and materials are cleaned daily.

☐ Establishes procedures for care of sick children; for example, isolating a child with a contagious illness from well children, contacting parents and medical providers, and administering medicine.

☐ Helps children develop basic health habits.

☐ Keeps handy current emergency telephone numbers for each child's parent(s), nearest relative, and medical providers.

☐ Communicates frequently with parents about children's health, nutrition, communicable diseases, and medications and cooperates with parents and health specialists.

☐ Follows center procedures for maintaining health records and administering medication and first aid and cooperates with health and nutrition staff.

☐ Establishes a relaxed mealtime routine that makes eating pleasant for each child.

☐ Limits sugar, salt, processed foods, unnecessary chemical additives, and artificial coloring and flavoring in meals and snacks and encourages parents to do the same.

☐ Informs parents about health resources, such as physicians or community clinics, that provide services to families in their primary language.

☐ Recognizes unusual behavior and physical symptoms in children and encourages parents to obtain appropriate treatment.

☐ Works cooperatively with health professionals and parents to meet the needs of children with handicapping conditions.

☐ Recognizes symptoms of possible abuse and neglect and is alert to play or behavior that indicates physical or sexual abuse. If physical or sexual abuse is suspected, the competent Candidate seeks out resources for information and support, follows state law in response, responds sensitively to child's and family's needs, and cooperates in carrying out treatment plans.

The competent Candidate working with **infants** also, for example:

☐ Cleans with sanitizing solution, at least daily, all toys and objects used and "mouthed" by infants.

☐ Makes provisions for sanitary diaper changing and disposal.

☐ Washes hands thoroughly before and after each diaper change and before each feeding.

☐ Supports mothers who wish to continue breast feeding infants.

☐ Follows a sanitary procedure for preparing, storing, and labeling baby bottles.

☐ Responds to infant's individual rhythms, while working towards regularity in feeding, sleeping, and toileting.

☐ Manages group so as to be able to concentrate on the individual feeding of infants and to hold infants for bottle feeding.

☐ Recognizes rashes and skin irritations and works with parents to prevent and treat them.

☐ Works cooperatively with parents and shares information frequently concerning nutrition, weaning, and introducing solid foods, while showing respect for different practices and values.

☐ Offers children opportunities to gradually feed themselves, providing finger foods and adequate time for pleasurable feeding.

☐ Does not put children to bed with a bottle unless it contains water.

The competent Candidate working with **toddlers** also, for example:

☐ Uses role playing, modeling, visual material, and real objects to teach healthy physical, mental, dental, and nutritional practices.

☐ Plans health care and educational activities that integrate health and nutrition information from the children's cultures with medically accepted health and nutrition practices.

☐ Has age-appropriate expectations of toddlers' abilities and helps them to develop self-help skills in eating, toileting, washing hands, tooth brushing, etc.

☐ Works with parents in planning for toilet learning, respects different family practices and expectations, and is sensitive to each child's readiness.

☐ Understands toddlers' explorations, concerns, and curiosities about their own and others' bodies and responds with information at their level; for example, explaining the physical differences between boys and girls matter-of-factly in simple terms.

The competent Candidate working towards the **bilingual specialization**, for example:

☐ Provides written health information for parents (e.g., notices about immunizations) in both languages.

3. FUNCTIONAL AREA: LEARNING ENVIRONMENT

Candidate uses space, relationships, materials, and routines as resources for constructing an interesting, secure, and enjoyable environment that encourages play, exploration, and learning.

DEVELOPMENTAL CONTEXT:

Children of all ages learn from their own experience and by imitation. Adults can guide and encourage children's learning by ensuring that the environment is emotionally supportive; invites active exploration, play, and movement by children; and supports a broad array of experiences. A reliable routine together with a stimulating choice of materials, activities, and relationships enhances children's learning and development.

Young infants (birth-9 months) begin to learn from their immediate surroundings and daily experiences. The sense of well-being and emotional security conveyed by a loving and skilled caregiver creates a readiness for other experiences. Before infants can creep and crawl, adults should provide a variety of sensory experiences and encourage movement and playfulness.

Mobile infants (6-18 months) are active, independent, and curious. They are increasingly persistent and purposeful in doing things. They need many opportunities to practice new skills and explore the environment within safe boundaries. Adults can share children's delight in themselves, their skills, and discoveries, gradually adding variety to the learning environment.

Toddlers (16-36 months) are developing new language skills, physical control, and awareness of themselves and others each day. They enjoy participation in planned and group activities, but they are not yet ready to sit still or work in a group for very long. Adults can support their learning in all areas by maintaining an environment that is dependable but flexible enough to provide opportunities for them to extend their skills, understanding, and judgment in individualized ways.

For example, the competent Candidate working with infants and toddlers:

☐ Uses materials, books, and equipment that are stimulating to each child and suitable to individual learning styles, including those of handicapped children.

☐ Uses materials that demonstrate acceptance of each child's sex, family, race, language, and culture.

☐ Provides easily accessible learning materials (e.g., puzzles, crayons and markers, books) that children can explore by themselves as well as putting some materials away for special times or for use at later stages of development.

☐ Organizes space into identifiable areas that encourage appropriate and independent use of materials.

☐ Balances active and quiet, free and structured, individual and group, indoor and outdoor activities.

☐ Provides many opportunities for children to develop their senses and ability to concentrate.

☐ Observes individual children and the group frequently and modifies the environment to meet their changing abilities, needs, and interests.

☐ Varies routines spontaneously to take advantage of unusual opportunities; e.g., goes outside in the snow, invites a visiting grandmother to share stories or songs with children, lets the children watch workers and machinery on the street, or plays with one child for an extra period of time when additional adults are available to care for group.

☐ Supports relationships between adults and children, as well as between children in care, as an important aspect of the learning environment.

☐ Schedules day so there is time for individual attention to each child.

☐ Encourages children to become involved in activities that extend their attention spans.

☐ Provides simple and consistent routines for mealtimes, naps, preparing to go out, changing activities, clean up, etc., supporting children's learning through these routines.

☐ Makes and helps parents make toys and equipment from easily available materials for use in the home and center.

The competent Candidate working with **young infants** also, for example:

☐ Changes an infant's position and location often during the day and responds to the child's developing skills, such as sitting up, rolling over, reaching for objects, and making noises.

☐ Provides a learning environment for nonmobile infants that encourages mouthing, reaching, batting, grasping, babbling, and social interaction.

☐ Understands and respects the individual eating and sleeping needs of healthy infants.

☐ Carries the child about in arms, on a hip, or in a sling frequently.

☐ Takes the infant out of doors to experience various temperatures, light variations, breezes, etc.

☐ Provides the infant with the sights and sounds of other living things—humans, animals, and plants—including caregiver's own face.

☐ Recognizes the importance of a consistent relationship between a caregiver and infant and makes caregiver-child interaction the base of the infant's learning environment.

The competent Candidate working with **mobile infants** also, for example:

☐ Arranges room so that mobile infants have an area for free movement protected from older children.

☐ "Baby-proofs" the environment so that there are many opportunities for child-initiated learning and limit-setting is minimized.

☐ Understands that intense feelings and rapid changes in mood and energy influence the child's response to the environment and adjusts routines, activities, and materials supportively.

The competent Candidate working with **toddlers** also, for example:

☐ Expands the learning environment to include the community when possible; for example, trips to the local shops, walks around the block, community events.

☐ Introduces a variety of materials and opportunities for learning based on an understanding of toddlers' developmental level, abilities, and interests; for example, provides water play in an area that can get wet, covers children's clothes with plastic smocks or removes clothing in warm weather, and limits such play to a few children so each has plenty of room and free use of utensils.

☐ Provides a step stool when necessary so that children can use toilet and wash hands independently as soon as possible.

In addition, the competent Candidate working towards the **bilingual specialization**, for example:

☐ Uses objects, music activities, and celebrations that are meaningful to young children to encourage development of both languages and cultures.

☐ Helps parents identify resources in their homes, families, and community that will support the development of both languages.

☐ Establishes and maintains a routine for use of the second language in daily activities.

Competency Goal II

To Advance Physical and Intellectual Competence

4. FUNCTIONAL AREA: PHYSICAL

Candidate provides a variety of equipment, activities, and opportunities to promote the physical development of children.

DEVELOPMENTAL CONTEXT:

Physical development is an essential part of the total development of children. Developing physically includes using large and small muscles, coordinating movements, and using the senses. Large-motor development includes strengthening and coordinating the muscles and nervous system, controlling large motions using the arms, legs, torso, or whole body. Small-motor development involves the ability to control and coordinate small, specialized motions using the eyes, mouth, hands, and feet. Adults should provide materials, equipment, and opportunities for indoor and outdoor activities that encourage this development and recognize and respect the wide differences in individual rates of physical development.

Young infants (birth-9 months) begin all learning through physical movement, taste, touch, smell, sight, and sound. By moving their arms, hands, legs, and other body parts, by touching and being touched, infants develop an awareness of their bodies and their ability to move and interact with the environment. By using their mouths to explore, hands to reach and grasp, whole bodies to roll over and sit up, they master the necessary skills needed for developmental stages that follow.

Mobile infants (6-18 months) delight in practicing and achieving new physical skills: crawling, standing, sitting down, cruising, and walking. They interact with their environment in a practical way, using all their senses to examine and manipulate objects, and begin to understand cause and effect, space, and distance in this way.

Toddlers (16-36 months) continue to master physical skills at their own individual rates. Their learning and interaction with the environment continue to be active. Although they are gaining greater control and satisfaction through use of their small muscles (e.g., painting, drawing, or working with puzzles), they need opportunities to exercise their large muscles often each day.

For example, the competent Candidate working with infants and toddlers:

☐ Arranges and encourages physical activities, knowing how children's physical development affects their cognitive, social, and emotional development.

☐ Observes and evaluates children's developmental levels in order to provide activities for physical skills and development of the senses at the appropriate level for each child.

☐ Plans and participates daily in appropriate large-muscle activities (e.g., playing ball, running, jumping, climbing with children, both indoors and outdoors).

☐ Provides a variety of activities from children's culture(s), such as dances, music, fingerplays, and active games.

☐ Provides opportunities for children to develop their senses by noticing colors, smelling odors, distinguishing sounds, feeling and touching a variety of objects, and tasting different foods.

☐ Communicates to children and their parents the importance of outdoor play and physical activity for healthy growth and development.

☐ Plans for and supports children's changing needs for active play, quiet activity, and rest.

☐ Supports and encourages, but never forces, children who are fearful of physical activity because of illness, accidents, abuse, limited opportunity, or overprotective caregivers and parents.

☐ Observes and evaluates children's physical development, recognizes signs of possible physical handicaps and developmental delays, refers parents to appropriate services, and follows up on referrals or individual development plans.

☐ Adapts the program to meet the special needs of children with handicaps, taking into account the importance of physical development to self-concept and social development.

☐ Avoids overprotecting children with handicaps, supports their independence, includes them in physical activities with other children (making modifications only when necessary), and encourages parents to do the same.

The competent Candidate working with **young infants** also, for example:

☐ Gives infants freedom and opportunities to move and explore in a variety of safe spaces, e.g., bare floor, carpet, mattress, grass.

☐ Maximizes warm and loving physical contact with infants, providing variety in physical contact from soothing to stimulating, depending on the infant's readiness and need.

☐ Provides appropriate activities and materials to help infants develop small muscles by grasping, dropping, pulling, pushing, throwing, fingering, mouthing.

The competent Candidate working with **mobile infants** also, for example:

☐ Encourages active manipulation of a variety of objects and the use of tools; for example, strings to pull toys, a pail to carry objects, a shovel to scoop sand.

☐ Shares children's pleasure in and provides them safe opportunities to practice repeatedly creeping, crawling, cruising, walking, climbing, descending stairs, and other physical movements.

☐ Provides opportunities for the development of eye-hand coordination in ways that are challenging and satisfying for the child; for example, fitting objects into a hole in a box, self-feeding.

The competent Candidate working with **toddlers** also, for example:

☐ Increases variety of opportunities for large- and small-muscle activity and sensory development as children are ready, e.g., introducing ride-on toys, play dough, puzzles, listening games, fingerplays, boxes for climbing.

☐ Cooperates with parents in toilet learning when toddlers appear to be ready.

5. FUNCTIONAL AREA: COGNITIVE

Candidate provides activities and opportunities that encourage curiosity, exploration, and problem solving appropriate to the developmental levels and learning styles of children.

DEVELOPMENTAL CONTEXT:

Exploring and trying to understand the world is natural and necessary for children's cognitive or intellectual development. As children learn and grow, their thinking capacities expand and become more flexible. Adults should support and guide this process by responding to children's interests with new learning opportunities and to their questions, with information and enthusiasm. Cognitive growth also requires healthy development in other areas: consistent physical growth, secure emotional behavior, and positive social interaction.

Young infants (birth-9 months) begin cognitive or intellectual learning through their interactions with caring adults in a secure environment. Some of their early learning includes becoming familiar with distance and space relationships, sounds, similarity and differences among things, and visual perspectives from various positions (front, back, under, and over).

Mobile infants (6-18 months) actively learn through trying things out; using objects as tools; comparing; imitating; looking for lost objects; and naming familiar objects, places, and people. By giving them opportunities to explore space, objects, and people and by sharing children's pleasure in discovery, adults can build children's confidence in their ability to learn and understand.

Toddlers (16-36 months) enter into a new and expansive phase of mental activity. They are beginning to think in words and symbols, remember, and imagine. Their curiosity leads them to try out materials in many ways, and adults can encourage this natural interest by providing a variety of new materials for experimentation. Adults can create a supportive social environment for learning by showing enthusiasm for children's individual discoveries and by helping them use words to describe and understand their experiences.

For example, the competent Candidate working with infants and toddlers:

☐ Observes children's play frequently to assess their cognitive development and readiness for new learning opportunities.

☐ Uses techniques and activities that stimulate children's curiosity, inventiveness, and problem-solving and communication skills.

☐ Gives children time and space for extended concentrated play and adjusts routines and schedules for this purpose.

☐ Provides opportunities for children to try out and begin to understand the relationships between cause and effect and means and ends.

☐ Understands the importance of play and often joins children's play as a partner and facilitator.

☐ Uses the center environment, everyday activities, and homemade materials to encourage children's intellectual development.

☐ Helps children discover ways to solve problems that arise in daily activities.

☐ Supports children's repetitions of the familiar and introduces new experiences, activities, and materials when children are interested and ready.

☐ Recognizes differences in individual learning styles and finds ways to work effectively with each child.

☐ Encourages active learning, rather than emphasizing adult talking and children's passive listening.

☐ Obtains (or makes) and uses special learning materials and equipment for children whose handicaps affect their ability to learn.

☐ Provides equipment and materials that children can explore and master by themselves.

☐ Is alert to the task a child is attempting and provides appropriate support.

☐ Recognizes learning problems and makes referrals according to center policy.

The competent Candidate working with **young infants** also, for example:

☐ Talks to infants, describing what they feel, hear, touch, and see.

☐ Encourages manipulation and inspection of a variety of objects.

☐ Provides opportunities for infants to interact with adults and children and watch interactions of adults and children.

☐ Encourages infants in imitating others.

☐ Plays with infants frequently.

The competent Candidate working with **mobile infants** also, for example:

☐ Talks, sings, plays with, and reads to mobile infants.

☐ Gives children more space to explore as they become more mobile.

☐ Gives children many opportunities to figure out cause and effect, how things work.

☐ Provides many experiences with moving, hiding, and changing objects.

The competent Candidate working with **toddlers** also, for example:

☐ Encourages children to ask questions and seek help and responds to them in ways that extend their thinking; for example, "That's a good question; let's see if we can find out."

☐ Asks questions that have more than one answer, encouraging children to wonder, guess, and talk about their ideas; for example, "What do you think might happen...?" or "How do you feel when...?"

☐ Encourages children to name objects and to talk about their experiences and observations.

☐ Provides opportunities to organize and group, compare and contrast thoughts, words, objects, and sensations.

☐ Involves toddlers in projects such as cooking, gardening, and repairing, when possible.

☐ Reduces distractions and interruptions so that toddlers have opportunities to extend their attention span and work on one activity, such as block building or water play, for a long period of time.

In addition, the competent Candidate working towards the **bilingual specialization**, for example:

☐ Provides learning experiences that lead to the understanding of basic concepts in the language most familiar to each child.

☐ Encourages learning of both languages through everyday experiences and activities.

6. FUNCTIONAL AREA: COMMUNICATION

Candidate actively communicates with children and provides opportunities and support for children to understand, acquire, and use verbal and nonverbal means of communicating thoughts and feelings.

DEVELOPMENTAL CONTEXT:

Communication between people can take many forms, including spoken words or sounds, gestures, eye and body movements, and touch. Children need to understand verbal and nonverbal means of communicating thoughts, feelings, and ideas. Adults can help children develop their communication skills by encouraging communication and providing ample opportunity for children to listen, interact, and express themselves freely with other children and adults.

Young infants (birth-9 months) need adults who are attentive to their nonverbal and pre-verbal communication. Adults can provide better care when they respond sensitively to the individual signals of each infant. Infants' early babblings and cooings are important practice for later word expression. Infants' speech development is facilitated by an encouraging partner who responds to their beginning communications and who talks with them about themselves and their world.

Mobile infants (6-18 months) begin to jabber expressively, name familiar objects and people, and understand many words and phrases. Adults can build on this communication by showing active interest in children's expressions, interpreting their first attempts at words, repeating and expanding on what they say, talking to them clearly, and telling simple stories.

Toddlers (16-36 months) increase their vocabularies and use of sentences daily. There is a wide range of normal language development during this time; some children are early, and some are late talkers. Adults should communicate actively with all toddlers—modeling good speech, listening to them carefully, and helping them with new words and phrases. Language should be used in a variety of pleasurable ways each day, including songs, stories, directions, comfort, conversations, information, and play.

For example, the competent Candidate working with infants and toddlers:

☐ Has realistic expectations for each child's understanding and use of speech based on knowledge of language development and the individual child.

☐ Talks often with individual children and stimulates conversation among children and with adults in the room.

☐ Provides activities that encourage children to develop listening and comprehension skills.

☐ Helps children connect word meaning(s) to experiences and real objects.

☐ Recognizes, understands, and respects local speech patterns and idioms.

☐ Respects the language of non-English-speaking families, encourages them to communicate freely with their children in the language parents prefer, and helps them find opportunities to learn English.

☐ Is aware of the caregiver's role as a language model for children and uses affectionate and playful tones, clear speech, and responsive conversation.

☐ Listens attentively to children, tries to understand what they want to communicate, and helps them to express themselves.

☐ Shares children's communication/language achievements with parents.

☐ Uses a variety of songs, stories, books, and games—including those from the children's cultures—for language development.

☐ Talks with children about special experiences and relationships in their families and home lives.

☐ Recognizes possible impairments or delays that affect hearing and speech, helps families find resources, cooperates with treatment plans, and finds ways to communicate positively with these children.

The competent Candidate working with **young infants** also, for example:

☐ Responds to the infant's cooing sounds and imitates them, encouraging a "conversation" in which the infant can often take the lead.

☐ Talks to infants about what they can see and what is happening while giving physical care, such as diapering and feeding.

☐ Talks with parents about the meaning of an infant's beginning communications, such as different kinds of crying.

☐ Responds to infant's body signs and nonverbal cues that signal discomfort, excitement, pleasure, etc., and describes the infant's feeling out loud.

☐ Sings to infants or uses voice in interesting ways that encourage infants to listen.

The competent Candidate working with **mobile infants** also, for example:

☐ Responds enthusiastically to an infant's first words.

☐ Uses gestures to demonstrate the meaning of words to infants.

☐ Names and talks about infants' feelings, behaviors, activities, clothing, body parts, etc. to help expand their vocabularies.

☐ Elaborates on children's short phrases to help them express intended meaning.

The competent Candidate working with **toddlers** also, for example:

☐ Uses everyday conversations with children to enrich and expand their vocabulary.

☐ Provides opportunities for children to represent their ideas nonverbally through activities such as painting, music making, and creative movement.

☐ Helps children learn, understand, and use words to express thoughts, ideas, questions, feelings, and physical needs.

☐ Writes toddlers' "stories" and labels their drawings, showing the relationship between spoken and printed words.

☐ Looks at picture books and magazines with children to stimulate talking.

In addition, the competent Candidate working towards a **bilingual specialization**, for example:

☐ Demonstrates ability to understand, speak, read, and write in both languages.

☐ Understands the principles and characteristics of bilingual language development in children and explains these to parents.

☐ Assesses each child's language abilities and uses activities that are appropriate to the child's level of development in each language.

☐ Helps children associate word meanings in both languages with familiar objects and experiences.

☐ Encourages children who are fluent in either language to help less fluent children.

☐ Helps parents understand the importance of children's learning the first language and culture and their role in providing experiences to meet this goal.

☐ Helps parents understand the child's attempts at communication in the second language.

☐ Allows children opportunities to express themselves in the language of their choice.

☐ Encourages English-speaking children and families to learn the second language.

☐ Uses lullabies, songs, games, stories, books, and fingerplays from both languages, asking parents for examples from their childhood.

☐ Makes sure there are consistent language models for both languages used in the program, through selection and use of materials and personnel.

☐ Takes an active role in labeling children's actions and surroundings in their first language and encourages children to use these words.

7. FUNCTIONAL AREA: CREATIVE

Candidate provides opportunities that stimulate children to play with sound, rhythm, language, materials, space, and ideas in individual ways and to express their creative abilities.

DEVELOPMENTAL CONTEXT:

All children are imaginative and have creative potential. They need opportunities to develop and express these capacities. Creative play serves many purposes for children in their cognitive, social, physical, and emotional development. Adults should support the development of children's creative impulses by respecting creative play and by providing a wide variety of activities and materials that encourage spontaneous expression and expand children's imagination.

Young and mobile infants (birth-18 months) are creative in their unique and individual ways of interacting with the world. Adults can support their creativity by respecting and enjoying the variety of ways very young children express themselves and act on their environment.

Toddlers (16-36 months) are interested in using materials to create their own product—sometimes to destroy and create it again or to move on. For example, they become absorbed in dipping a brush in paint and watching their stroke of color on paper. They use their voices and bodies creatively: swaying, chanting, and singing. They enjoy making up their own words and rhythms as well as learning traditional songs and rhymes. Adults can provide raw materials and opportunities for toddlers' creativity and can show respect for what they do. Make-believe and pretend appear gradually, and adults can join in imaginative play, while helping toddlers distinguish between what is real and what is not.

For example, the competent Candidate working with infants and toddlers:

☐ Recognizes that the process of creating is as important—and sometimes more important—than the product.

☐ Understands that each child's creative expression is unique and does not encourage uniformity.

☐ Allows time for spontaneous and extended play within the daily routine.

☐ Includes a variety of music, art, literature, dance, role playing, celebrations, and other creative activities from the children's culture(s) in program activities.

☐ Participates in make-believe games with children.

☐ Models and encourages children's creativity in language; for example, through rhymes, imaginative stories, and nonsense words.

☐ Provides unstructured materials (such as blocks, paint, clay, or musical instruments) that are appropriate for children at different ages.

☐ Encourages thorough, repeated exploration of creative materials whenever possible; for example, by letting a block structure stand so that building can continue the next day or by letting one child play with soap suds for an extended period of time.

☐ Models creativity by using homemade materials and found objects.

☐ Helps parents understand the importance of creative expression in children's development and the need to provide children with opportunities for creative activities such as storytelling, playing make-believe, using art materials.

☐ Encourages children to try new and different activities.

☐ Provides for "messy" activities with children, such as water and sand play, finger painting, and drawing with markers.

The competent Candidate working with **young and mobile infants** also, for example:

☐ Recognizes that exploration and discovery by infants through their movements, voice, and expression are creative acts.

☐ Is alert and responsive to infants' initiatives to play, move, and use materials, gradually introducing new things to be combined and used in ways that infants can invent; for example, pieces of fabric of different colors and textures, rhythm instruments or objects that make different noises, assorted empty food containers.

☐ Provides a variety of music and rhythm experiences for infants.

☐ Shares infants' joy in a variety of ways—clapping, smiling, hugging—in order to encourage their spontaneity and creativity.

The competent Candidate working with **toddlers** also, for example:

☐ Introduces a variety of art materials gradually, allows toddlers time to explore them in their own ways, and shows interest in what they do.

☐ Provides and rotates a variety of male and female dress-up clothes and other "props," including those from the children's culture(s).

☐ Plays make-believe with each toddler, following the child's lead and taking care not to overstimulate or frighten the child.

☐ Keeps informed about cultural resources in the community and uses them with children when possible.

In addition, the competent Candidate working towards the **bilingual specialization**, for example:

☐ Helps children develop creative abilities through activities and discussion in both languages.

☐ Helps children identify and imitate creative forms found in the art, music, and dance of their cultures.

Competency Goal III

To Support Social and Emotional Development and Provide Positive Guidance

8. FUNCTIONAL AREA: SELF

Candidate provides physical and emotional security for each child and helps each child to know, accept, and take pride in himself or herself and to develop a sense of independence.

DEVELOPMENTAL CONTEXT:

All children need a physically and emotionally secure environment that supports their developing self-knowledge, self-control, and self-esteem and, at the same time, encourages respect for the feelings and rights of others. Knowing one's self includes knowing about one's body, feelings, and abilities. It also means identifying one's self as a girl or boy and a member of a family and a larger cultural community. Accepting and taking pride in one's self comes from experiencing success and being accepted by others as a unique individual. Self-esteem develops as children master new abilities, experience success as well as failure, and realize their effectiveness in handling increasingly challenging demands in their own ways.

Young infants (birth-9 months), during the first few weeks and months, begin to build a sense of self-confidence and security in an environment where they can trust that an adult will lovingly care for their needs. The adult is someone who feeds the child when hungry, keeps the child warm and comfortable, soothes the child when distressed, and provides interesting things to look at, taste, smell, feel, hear, and touch.

For mobile infants (6-18 months), a loving caregiver is a "home base" who is readily available and provides warm physical comfort and a safe environment to explore and master. This emotional stability is essential for the development of self-confidence as well as language, physical, cognitive, and social growth.

Toddlers (16-36 months) become aware of many things about themselves, including their separateness from others. A sense of self and growing feelings of independence develop at the same time that toddlers realize the importance of parents and other caregivers. The healthy toddler's inner world is filled with conflicting feelings and ideas: independence and dependence, confidence and doubt, fear and power, hostility and love, anger and tenderness, aggression and passivity. The wide range of toddlers' feelings and actions challenge the resourcefulness and knowledge of adults who provide them emotional security.

For example, the competent Candidate working with infants and toddlers:

☐ Treats each child as an individual with his or her own strengths and needs and unique characteristics.

☐ Is sensitive to differing cultural values and expectations concerning independence and expression of feelings.

☐ Addresses each child by name, talks with each child every day, and encourages each child to call other children and adults by name.

☐ Has affectionate and appropriate physical contact with each child daily in ways that convey love, affection, and security.

☐ Helps children through periods of stress, separation, transition, and other crises.

☐ Offers children, when possible, choices in activities, materials, and foods and respects their choices.

☐ Encourages and helps children practice skills when eating, getting dressed, using toys and equipment, cleaning up, and helping others.

☐ Gives one-to-one attention to each child as much as possible.

☐ Enjoys children and directly expresses the enjoyment to them.

☐ Delights in each child's success, expresses kindness and support when a child is having trouble, and helps him/her learn from mistakes.

☐ Helps children recognize and accept their feelings, such as joy, affection, anger, jealousy, sadness, and fear, and express feelings in culturally appropriate ways.

☐ Models the recognition and expression of feelings by naming her/his own feelings while expressing them.

☐ Provides many opportunities for all children, including those with handicaps, to feel effective, experience success, and gain the positive recognition of others.

☐ Understands the effect of abuse and neglect on children's self-concept and works sensitively with such children.

The competent Candidate working with **young infants** also, for example:

☐ Listens carefully to an infant's cry and makes decisions quickly and appropriately: allows an infant to cry briefly when settling into sleep, comforts an infant who is distressed, or feeds an infant who is hungry.

☐ Does not substitute food for affection.

☐ Provides basic physical care (feeding, bathing, dressing, diapering) gently and pleasantly, respecting the tempo and sensitivities of the baby.

☐ Holds the infant close, allowing him/her to feel the caregiver's body warmth and heartbeat and to feel comfortable in the adult's arms.

☐ Creates a personal relationship with each infant and knows the kind of cuddling, stroking, talking, and playing that brings comfort and good feelings to each individual infant.

The competent Candidate working with **mobile infants** also, for example:

☐ Removes the exploring infant from an obstacle that is too frustrating, comforts the child, and provides an alternative activity.

☐ Recognizes periods when the child has difficulty separating from parents or is fearful of new adults and is supportive of the child.

☐ Talks to child frequently about his/her family—where they are, when they will come back, and what they do together.

☐ Communicates, with eyes and voice, attention and interest to an exploring child at a distance from the caregiver.

☐ Welcomes a child who comes for nurturing with a loving voice, hugging, or stroking.

The competent Candidate working with **toddlers** also, for example:

☐ Responds to toddler's intense feelings of love, joy, loneliness, anger, and disappointment with sympathetic attention.

☐ Provides opportunities for toddlers to learn to help themselves, such as taking off jackets or pouring juice, and shares children's pleasure in new skills.

☐ Helps the toddler understand his/her own feelings and express feelings in acceptable ways.

☐ Supports child's developing awareness of him/herself as a member of a family and of an ethnic or social group by talking about families (using photographs, mirrors, or other appropriate objects) and by celebrating cultural events with children.

☐ Uses books, pictures, stories, and discussion to help children identify positively with the events and experiences of their lives; for example, single-parent families, extended families, divorce, moving, or birth of siblings.

In addition, the competent Candidate working towards a **bilingual specialization**, for example:

☐ Helps children feel good about themselves as speakers of each language.

☐ Supports the child's attempt to use the second language.

☐ Helps each child deal with the stress of separation, using the child's first language and a tone and style compatible with the family's.

9. FUNCTIONAL AREA: SOCIAL

Candidate helps each child feel accepted in the group, helps children learn to communicate and get along with others, and encourages feelings of empathy and mutual respect among children and adults.

DEVELOPMENTAL CONTEXT:

Children need to develop social skills that help them work and play cooperatively and productively with other children and adults. To do this, children need to feel secure themselves, value other people, and enjoy positive social interaction.

Young infants (birth-9 months) enter the world with a capacity and a need for social contact. Yet each one is unique in styles of interacting and readiness for different kinds of interactions. Infants need both protective and stimulating social interactions with a few consistent, caring adults who get to know them as individuals. The adults' understanding response to their signals increases infants' participation in social interactions and their ability to "read" the signals of others.

Mobile infants (6-18 months) are curious about others but need assistance and supervision in interacting with other children. They continue to need one or a few consistent adults as their most important social partner(s).

Toddlers' (16-36 months) social awareness is much more complex than that of younger children. Toddlers can begin to understand that others have feelings too—sometimes similar to and sometimes different from their own. They imitate many of the social behaviors of other children and adults. As toddlers become increasingly interested in other children, adults should guide and support their interactions, recognizing that they continue to rely upon familiar adults for emotional stability.

For example, the competent Candidate working with infants and toddlers:

☐ Learns about children's stages of social development and helps children and parents deal with such typical issues as separation anxiety, negative behavior, shyness, sexual identity, and making friends.

☐ Has realistic expectations for young children's social behavior based on their level of development.

☐ Serves as a social model by building a positive relationship with each child and parent and by maintaining positive relationships with other adults in the center.

☐ Responds quickly and calmly to prevent children from hurting each other.

☐ Helps children learn to respect the rights and possessions of others, in light of local expectations regarding sharing.

☐ Encourages children to ask for, accept, and give help to one another.

☐ Encourages children to make friends.

☐ Helps the children become aware of their feelings and those of others by talking about feelings with each child.

☐ Encourages children to express their feelings and assert their rights in socially acceptable ways.

☐ Encourages play and relationships among all children across racial, language, ethnic, age, and gender groupings, including children with handicaps.

The competent Candidate working with **young infants** also, for example:

☐ Recognizes that infants need a consistent social partner (caregiver) who is dependable, warm, and loving.

☐ Responds to social gestures and noises of infants and elaborates appropriately, playing responsive social games.

☐ Takes advantage of opportunities for social play during feeding, bathing, dressing, and other aspects of physical care.

☐ Makes eye contact often.

The competent Candidate working with **mobile infants** also, for example:

☐ Structures periods of time for social interaction with other children, remains available to protect, comfort, or facilitate, but does not interfere unless necessary.

☐ Provides infants with opportunities to observe social interactions among older children and among adults.

☐ Provides more than one attractive toy to minimize conflicts and waiting.

☐ Engages in social play with children that supports their developing social skills; e.g., taking turns with a ball, conversing at mealtime, sharing a snack, putting toys away.

☐ Encourages children to comfort and help each other.

The competent Candidate working with **toddlers** also, for example:

☐ Encourages children to interact with each other in playful and caring ways.

☐ Understands that sharing, taking turns, and playing with others is difficult for toddlers and encourages their attempts to use words to resolve conflicts.

☐ Encourages cooperation rather than competition.

☐ Helps toddlers understand that sometimes they must wait for attention because of other children's needs.

In addition, the competent Candidate working towards a **bilingual specialization**, for example:

☐ Understands that the social roles and expectations for bilingual children in their family setting may be different from those of the child care program and helps the children to behave appropriately in each.

10. FUNCTIONAL AREA: GUIDANCE

Candidate provides a supportive environment in which children can begin to learn and practice appropriate and acceptable behaviors as individuals and as a group.

DEVELOPMENTAL CONTEXT:

Knowing what behavior is appropriate or acceptable in a situation is an important skill. Children develop this understanding when consistent limits and realistic expectations of their behavior are clearly and positively defined. Understanding and following simple rules can help children develop self-control. Children feel more secure when they know what is expected of them and when adult expectations realistically take into account each child's development and needs.

Young infants (birth-9 months) begin to adapt their rhythms of eating and sleeping to the expectations of their social environment through the gentle guidance of sensitive caregivers who meet their needs. The basic trust in adults and the environment that is established at this time directly affects the child's responsiveness to positive guidance later and promotes the development of self-discipline.

Mobile infants (6-18 months) want to do everything, but they have little understanding about what is permissible and cannot remember rules. Adults can organize the environment in ways that clearly define limits and minimize conflicts. While respecting the child's experiments with saying "no," they can reinforce positive social interaction (e.g., hugging) and discourage negative behaviors (e.g., biting).

Toddlers (16-36 months) move through recurring phases of extreme dependence and independence as they gain new skills and awareness. They require an understanding caregiver who remains calm and supportive during their struggle to become independent. Adults must be resourceful in recognizing and encouraging self-reliant behavior while setting clear limits.

For example, the competent Candidate working with infants and toddlers:

☐ Knows a variety of positive guidance methods—such as listening, reinforcement, and redirection—and uses each appropriately.

☐ Relates guidance practices to knowledge of each child's personality and level of development.

☐ Avoids negative methods, such as spanking, threatening, shouting, isolating, or shaming children.

☐ Establishes guidelines for children's behavior that encourage self-control and are simple, reasonable, and consistent.

☐ Alerts children to changes in activities or routines well in advance and handles transitions from one activity to another with clear directions and patience.

☐ Is able to modify play when it becomes overstimulating for any of the children.

☐ Builds a trusting relationship with children as a foundation for positive guidance and self-discipline.

☐ Anticipates confrontations between children and defuses provocative behavior.

☐ Addresses the problem behavior or situation rather than labeling the child involved.

☐ Accepts children's sad or angry feelings, provides acceptable outlets for children to express them, and teaches words for feelings.

☐ Helps parents develop realistic expectations for children's behavior in ways that help avoid disciplinary problems, e.g., discussing how long children can sit still.

☐ Encourages parents to talk about childrearing, guidance, and self-discipline and refers them to classes, books, and other resources, as appropriate.

☐ Knows parents' disciplinary methods and expectations and selects those appropriate for use in the center.

☐ Recognizes that sometimes serious behavior problems are related to developmental or emotional problems and works cooperatively with parents towards solutions.

☐ Is aware of each child's limitations and abilities, uses guidance techniques accordingly, and explains rules at child's level of understanding.

The competent Candidate working with **young infants** also, for example:

☐ Creates an environment of love and trust through warmth and responsive caring.

☐ Guides infants gradually into regular sleeping and eating patterns while remaining responsive to individual needs.

☐ Responds to infants' needs for comfort and protection.

The competent Candidate working with **mobile infants** also, for example:

☐ Says "no" when necessary for guidance and safety, moves the child or dangerous object, and gives a simple explanation.

☐ Has realistic expectations about children's attention spans, interests, social abilities, and physical needs.

☐ Redirects children gently while explaining limits.

☐ Gives children real choices and accepts the choices made; for example, "Do you want to read a book with me or play on the climber?" or "Shall we have the apples or bananas for snack today?"

The competent Candidate working with **toddlers** also, for example:

☐ Lets toddlers solve some of their own problems.

☐ Limits inappropriate behavior in ways that show respect and support for the toddler's sense of dignity.

☐ Avoids power struggles with toddlers who say "no" or refuse to cooperate, using redirection, distraction, acceptance, or active listening.

☐ Explains the reasons for limits in simple words, demonstrating whenever possible.

☐ Uses firm and friendly techniques, such as reminding and persuading, when rules are forgotten or disobeyed.

☐ Uses positive language with children; for example, "walk" rather than "don't run."

In addition, the competent Candidate working towards a **bilingual specialization**, for example:

☐ Uses the language in which each child understands expectations, limits, and guidance.

Competency Goal IV

To Establish Positive and Productive Relationships with Families

11. FUNCTIONAL AREA: FAMILIES

Candidate maintains an open, friendly, and cooperative relationship with each child's family, encourages their involvement in the program, and supports the child's relationship with his or her family.

DEVELOPMENTAL CONTEXT:

Today's families take many different forms. Each family has primary responsibility for its own children, and parents may share this responsibility for their children with others. The parents and the caregiver become partners who communicate respectfully and openly for the mutual benefit of the children, the family, and the caregiver. Caregivers also recognize that parenthood, too, is a developmental process and that they can support parents in their role.

Young infants (birth-9 months) are establishing patterns of sleeping, waking, eating, playing, and social activity. They can be supported in developing some stability in these routines by the sensitive and consistent responses of adults. Parents and caregivers can respond more appropriately to the infant's signals when they share details with each other about the baby's day—sleeping, eating, diapering, activities, and moods.

Mobile infants (6-18 months) may have difficulty separating from the parents even when the caregiver is a familiar and trusted person. Caregivers and parents need to discuss ways of handling this, recognizing that it may be upsetting both for the adults and the child. Caregivers should recognize the potential for competition between themselves and parents and work to avoid it. Caregivers and parents also need to agree on reasonable and safe limits as children begin to explore and wander.

Toddlers (16-36 months) develop their own special routines and rituals in order to feel more organized and secure. It is essential that parents and caregivers share common understanding of the child's patterns and provide constant, dependable support for the toddler's growth towards self-definition.

For example, the competent Candidate working with infants and toddlers:

☐ Recognizes that children's primary caregivers may be single mothers or fathers, both parents, stepparents, grandparents, uncles, aunts, sisters, brothers, foster parents, or guardians.

☐ Helps parents understand the development of their child and understand the child's point of view.

☐ Provides opportunities for parents and other family members to share their skills and talents in the program.

☐ Recognizes that caregivers can support parents in their role.

☐ Offers parents information about health and social services and other resources in the community.

☐ Respects each family's cultural background, religious beliefs, and childrearing practices.

☐ Observes strict confidentiality regarding children and families and makes parents aware of this policy.

☐ Suggests activities and materials that parents can share with their children at home.

☐ Encourages parents to talk about important family events and their children's special interests and behavior at home and shares information frequently with parents about the child's experiences in the center.

☐ Is able to discuss problem behavior with parents in a constructive, supportive manner.

☐ Supports parents in making arrangements for school or an alternative child care program when necessary.

☐ Develops attachment towards children without competing with parents.

☐ Encourages parents to visit the center, participate in activities, and make suggestions for the daily program.

☐ Respects and tries to understand the parents' views when they differ from the program's goals or policies and attempts to resolve the differences.

☐ Tells parents about children's achievements and shares their pleasure in new abilities.

☐ Helps parents with separations from child, recognizing parents' possible concerns about leaving their child.

☐ Supports children and families under stress, working cooperatively with other professionals, as appropriate.

☐ Helps parents recognize their feelings and attitudes about handicaps.

☐ Helps parents identify resources to diagnose and treat children with handicaps.

☐ Helps parents obtain clear and understandable information about their children's handicaps and information about the family's legal right to services.

☐ Encourages and assists parents to communicate confidently about their children with government and other community agencies.

The competent Candidate working with **young infants** also, for example:

☐ Supports parents in becoming involved observers of their infant.

☐ Exchanges information regularly with parents about the child's life at home and in the center, including routines and changes in care, favorite activities, etc.

☐ Responds with interest and information to concerns of parents about sleep, waking, feeding, or particulars related to infant's needs and development.

☐ Shares parents' desire to understand meaning of baby's cries and to respond sensitively.

☐ Makes suggestions to parents about how to stimulate infants' vision, touch, and hearing at home.

The competent Candidate working with **mobile infants** also, for example:

☐ Recognizes the recurring stress of separation for child and parents and attempts to ease it for them.

☐ Helps parents understand child's possible fear of strangers.

☐ Helps parents to provide safe home environment for mobile infant.

☐ Talks with parents of mobile infants about the beginning of independence and the child's use of the word "no."

☐ Decides with parents what limits to set.

☐ Suggests use of household items to provide a stimulating environment and to encourage the curiosity of mobile infants.

The competent Candidate working with **toddlers** also, for example:

☐ Discusses child's rituals and routines with parents.

☐ Discusses with parents the reasons for toddlers' emotional outbursts and negative behaviors and possible ways of handling them.

☐ Explains the toddler's pride and interest in imitating adults and learning to use tools to make things.

☐ Sends home projects made by the children.

☐ Helps parents find ways to enjoy time with their toddlers and to help toddlers relax after time in group setting.

☐ Coordinates toilet learning plans with parents and frequently communicates on child's progress.

☐ Supports toddler's sense of belonging to his/her family.

In addition, the competent Candidate working towards a **bilingual specialization**, for example:

☐ Communicates orally and in writing regularly with parents and children in their preferred language.

☐ Helps parents understand the program goals for bilingual development.

☐ Knows parents' views on such issues as the use of first and second languages within the program, childrearing, and biculturalism and incorporates their views into program planning.

☐ Communicates with parents regularly about child's bilingual development and helps them find ways to support this within the family.

☐ Supports families' desires to communicate their language and cultural heritage to their children through cultural practices.

Competency Goal V

To Ensure a Well-Run, Purposeful Program Responsive to Participant Needs

12. FUNCTIONAL AREA: PROGRAM MANAGEMENT

Candidate is a manager who uses all available resources to ensure an effective operation. The Candidate is a competent organizer, planner, record keeper, communicator, and a cooperative coworker.

DEVELOPMENTAL CONTEXT:

Running an effective program requires a systematic approach. A systematic approach means that the Candidate can determine the needs of her/his operation, families, and children; can make plans based on those needs; and can keep accurate records of needs, plans, and practices.

Such a systematic approach should be applied to keeping records of attendance, fees, health status, and home visits. It should include specific plans for meeting the needs of children and their families and coordinating communication among involved adults through written information, meetings with parents and resource persons, and frequent informal discussion.

For example, the competent Candidate working with infants and toddlers:

☐ Works with parents to identify the strengths and needs of each child.

☐ Develops skills in observing and recording information about children and their families in a nonjudgmental manner for use in planning and carrying out program of daily care.

☐ Maintains up-to-date records concerning the growth, health, behavior, and progress of each child and the group and shares the information with parents and appropriate center personnel.

☐ Considers goals and objectives for each child and for the group as a whole and develops realistic plans responsive to the needs of all.

☐ Implements plans for each child by identifying developmentally and culturally appropriate activities and materials for each day.

☐ Has a clear understanding of her/his responsibilities within the program.

☐ Discusses issues that affect the program with appropriate staff and follows up on their resolution.

☐ Works as a member of a team with others in the classroom and the program, including substitutes, parents, and volunteers.

☐ Supports other staff by offering assistance and supervision when needed.

☐ Makes or obtains materials and equipment appropriate to the developmental needs of the children.

☐ Coordinates program plans (including guidance and discipline techniques) with parents, specialists, and program personnel, when appropriate.

☐ Knows the language resources of each family and uses these in the program.

☐ Works with appropriate staff to choose substitutes carefully, requiring experience with children of the same ages whenever possible.

☐ Orients new or substitute caregivers and volunteers to routines and special needs and abilities of each child.

☐ Implements procedures that help children make a smooth transition from one group to another.

☐ Knows the social service, health, and education resources of the community and uses them when appropriate.

☐ Recognizes possible learning problems, works with parents and specialists to develop plans specific to the needs of each child, and implements recommended treatment by following up on referrals and working with the family to meet goals for the child.

☐ Establishes liaison with community services that respond to family violence, e.g., Parents Anonymous, Child Protective Services, and local shelter programs.

In addition, the competent Candidate working towards a **bilingual specialization**, for example:

☐ Uses knowledge of language development and bilingualism to plan for each child and the group.

☐ Recognizes and helps others recognize the needs of children and families who speak a different language and operate in a different cultural context.

☐ Makes use of available evaluation instruments in the non-English language.

☐ Takes account of families' concerns about such issues as language usage and culturally different styles of relating.

☐ Works with appropriate staff in choosing substitutes who meet the language needs of the children and program whenever possible.

Competency Goal VI

To Maintain a Commitment to Professionalism

13. FUNCTIONAL AREA: PROFESSIONALISM

Candidate makes decisions based on knowledge of early childhood theories and practices, promotes quality in child care services, and takes advantage of opportunities to improve competence, both for personal and professional growth and for the benefit of children and families.

DEVELOPMENTAL CONTEXT:

Professionals working with young children and their families make decisions based on knowledge of early childhood education and family life and demonstrate a commitment towards quality care for young children. The professional caregiver continues to set new goals and take advantage of training or educational experiences that will help her/him to grow more competent. Recognizing that the way they relate to one another directly affects the quality of child care and sets an example for children, adults in a child care setting work to resolve issues and problems among themselves cooperatively and respectfully. They also work together to educate the community at large about the needs of young children. The child care provider should develop relationships with other child care professionals and establish a network for information and support.

For example, the competent Candidate working with infants and toddlers:

- [ ] Enjoys working with young children in a group setting and demonstrates a positive attitude in her/his role.

- [ ] Understands the philosophy of the program and can describe its goals and objectives to others.

- [ ] Continues to gain knowledge of physical, cognitive, language, emotional, and social development as a basis for planning program goals.

- [ ] Keeps all personal information about children and families confidential.

- [ ] Evaluates own performance continually to identify needs for professional growth.

- [ ] Participates in peer evaluation and is able to accept comments and criticism from colleagues, supervisors, and parents in a constructive way.

- [ ] Takes advantage of opportunities for professional and personal development by joining appropriate professional organizations and attending meetings, training courses, and conferences.

- [ ] Keeps informed about child care practices, research, legislation, and other developments in early childhood education.

- [ ] Seeks information relevant to the needs of the children s/he is serving—for example, information on infant development, bilingual development, and handicaps—from professional magazines, community colleges, community services, other caregivers, and community members.

- [ ] Recognizes that caregiver fatigue, low morale, and lack of work satisfaction decrease effectiveness and finds ways to meet her/his own needs and maintain energy and enthusiasm.

- [ ] Works cooperatively with other staff members, accepts supervision, and helps promote a positive atmosphere in the center.

- [ ] Learns about new laws and regulations affecting center care, children, and families.

- [ ] Advocates quality services and rights for children and families.

- [ ] Works with other professionals and parents to develop effective strategies to communicate to decision-makers the needs of children and families.

- [ ] Develops the ability to state needs for additional resources for individual children or some aspect of the program.

- [ ] Recognizes that special skills are necessary for working with children at different ages and developmental stages and seeks appropriate information and training.

- [ ] Is aware that some of the normal developmental characteristics of children (e.g., crying, messiness, dependency, willfulness, negative behavior, curiosity about genital differences, etc.) often make adults uncomfortable. The caregiver can acknowledge these feelings in her/himself, coworkers, and parents while minimizing negative reactions toward children.

- [ ] Seeks information about sexual abuse and child abuse and neglect, keeps up-to-date on laws and policies concerning reporting and treatment of abuse, and learns effective ways of working with affected children and families.

In addition, the competent Candidate working towards a **bilingual specialization**, for example:

- [ ] Demonstrates ability to understand, speak, read, and write in both languages and uses these skills in all aspects of the program.

- [ ] Increases knowledge about bilingual education by reading, attending workshops, and consulting professionals.

- [ ] Maintains and works to increase fluency in her/his second language.

- [ ] Provides opportunities consistently for all children to acquire a second language.

- [ ] Promotes the effective functioning of the bilingual program by attempting to clarify issues relating to bilingualism and multiculturalism.

INDEX